U.S. Agriculture
in a World Context

edited by
D. Gale Johnson
John A. Schnittker

Published for the Atlantic Council
of the United States

The Praeger Special Studies program—
utilizing the most modern and efficient book
production techniques and a selective
worldwide distribution network—makes
available to the academic, government, and
business communities significant, timely
research in U.S. and international economic, social, and political development.

U.S. Agriculture in a World Context

Policies and Approaches for the Next Decade

PRAEGER SPECIAL STUDIES IN INTERNATIONAL ECONOMICS AND DEVELOPMENT

Praeger Publishers New York Washington London

Library of Congress Cataloging in Publication Data

Johnson, David Gale, 1916-
    U.S. agriculture in a world context.

    (Praeger special studies in international economics
and development)
    Includes bibliographical references.
    1. Agriculture and state—United States.   2. Agri-
culture and state.   3. Agriculture—Economic aspects—
1945-   I. Schnittker, John A., joint author.
II. Atlantic Council of the United States.   III. Title.
HD1765 1974.J64   382'.41   74-6732
ISBN 0-275-09450-2

PRAEGER PUBLISHERS
111 Fourth Avenue, New York, N.Y. 10003, U.S.A.
5, Cromwell Place, London SW7 2JL, England

Published in the United States of America in 1974
by Praeger Publishers, Inc.

Food supplies and prices have become a major public policy
question around the world. Consumers are apprehensive about rising
food prices; producers are apprehensive about rising costs of raw
materials, labor, and land, and about their share of the income produced in our economies; governments are apprehensive about rising
costs of farm support programs and about the problem of ensuring
adequate supplies to their populations without excessive inflationary
pressure. And in late 1973, there was a global concern over food
and feed shortages.

Food production and sales are heavily influenced by government policies and programs in each country. All major trading countries, and many of the developing countries, have government policies
for intervention in agricultural markets, technological innovation,
land utilization, incomes of farmers, and other aspects of farming.
These policies are not only aimed at technical and economic objectives,
they are also oriented toward social and political objectives. Among
the social and political considerations that governments often give
heavy weight to are the balance between rural and urban income levels,
the employment opportunities available as alternatives to farming,
the conservation of land and rural environment, the stable supply of
food for national populations including the insuring against shortages
generated in other parts of the world, and the basic political balance
between rural and urban areas.

Problems can arise when the policy objectives of various governments differ significantly, and if the particular actions taken are not
carefully conceived, they will tend to cause trouble for farmers or
food consumers in other countries. For example, governments sometimes get rid of unwanted surpluses generated by domestic subsidies
by applying export subsidies. This, in turn, artificially depresses
prices in other markets in the world, with consequences for production and for farm policies in other countries.

Farm policies developed by governments rarely reflect global
thinking. On the contrary, they are usually based on domestic preoccupations. The conflicts among various national policies have led,
however, to major distortions in production incentives, relative
prices, availabilities, and public as well as private costs. National
agricultural policies are themselves badly in need of rationalization
—but this is true in most countries and not solely or mainly in the
United States. In fact, policies in the European Community and Japan,

the largest agricultural markets besides our own, are even more distortive in meeting world needs.

National policies are now economically inefficient in a number of ways, discouraging, as often as not, the needed adjustments in product mix, land utilization, and labor. For example, while there is clearly a real social problem, the measures chosen often seem to be aimed at the wrong ends. Measures to support prices well above market levels are particularly inefficient instruments for dealing with the income problems of disadvantaged farmers, because the greatest rewards go to the largest producers, who rarely need any assistance.

Because of this, the Atlantic Council of the United States felt that it would be extremely useful to examine U.S. agricultural policies in a world context, with emphasis on what could be done in concert with other nations, perhaps through trade negotiations, and what might be done at home, for our own self-interest, regardless of the policies of others.

The problems we now face internationally have been evolving over many years, and the long-term solutions needed can only be brought about gradually, taking into account social and political realities. The key issues are how to get started moving in a better direction, and how to manage future changes in policies so that this better direction can be maintained.

This study makes important contributions to public discussion in this long-range perspective. It does not attempt to cope with the near-term shortages, but again it should be emphasized that short-term economic problems are usually the symptoms of the balance of long-run strengths and weaknesses of our respective economies.

The outcome of public policy decisions is important. At home, rationalization of our agricultural policies has been going on, but more needs to be done. Internationally, the need for change is much greater. How the United States goes is important to others, because the United States is the world's leading producer and leading exporter —as well as being a very major importer—of agricultural products. The impact of developments in agricultural production and policy in the United States is felt around the world. And how the world market goes is vital to American farmers. To an increasing degree, the economic welfare of U.S. agriculture has become dependent on commercial exports.

Even apart from the unusual agricultural developments of 1972-73, rising incomes and increased demands for livestock products throughout the world are changing the prospects for agricultural production and trade. In such a changing world, the agricultural policies of the United States, other important exporting countries, and importing nations such as Japan and the European Community need to be more responsive than ever before to changing circumstances. There is a problem of balancing world production and world demand, and there is an even more important problem of ensuring that the food available globally can be distributed equitably among the world's population.

Taking these problems into account, the study analyzes U.S. farm policies and the international market situation. It then makes recommendations for domestic policy and for trade negotiations. The options presented are sophisticated, and, especially in the trade field, they represent new thinking and more depth than heretofore made available. One can differ with some of the recommendations on either the domestic or trade policy front, but they are all worth study as an imaginative source of ideas about what we are doing and where we ought to be going. The group that put the report together is a most distinguished group. It includes thoughtful and internationally re-spected economists, government advisers, and representatives of farm interests from at home and abroad. However one comes out on the future of world agriculture and the U.S. role in it, this report is a must in reading.

The Honorable
Harald B. Malmgren
Deputy Special Trade Representative
The White House

PREFACE

Henry H. Fowler

U.S. Agriculture in a World Context: Policies and Approaches for the Next Decade reflects the continuing concern of the Atlantic Council of the United States to provide brief, objective, and timely analyses of issues that are potentially disruptive to relations among the North American and Western European nations and Japan. The discussions of trade in agricultural commodities that are taking place within the context of the broader trade negotiations are highly crucial to these relations.

The present study is the final result of a series of discussions organized by the Atlantic Council in 1972 and 1973 and is made possible by a grant from the Rockefeller Foundation. The several chapters represent the working papers discussed at the meetings, as well as the policy recommendations of the participants. The meetings were co-chaired by D. Gale Johnson and John A. Schnittker, the co-editors of this volume. The Advisory Committee members who participated in the project included Martin Abel, Theodore C. Achilles, Robert Buck, W. Randolph Burgess, Harry B. Caldwell, Robert Frederick, Theodore Geiger, André Herlitska, Timothy Josling, David Kirk, Harald B. Malmgren, Pierre Malvé, Asao Miyawaki, Gene Moos, Kenneth Naden, James G. Patton, Richard J. Wallace, T. K. Warley, Walter Wilcox, and Asher Winegarten, as well as Joseph W. Harned, who acted as project director.

The Atlantic Council wishes to thank the co-chairmen for their able direction and coordination of the study as well as the members of the Advisory Committee for their valuable comments and suggestions. Several written comments and dissents by members of the group are included in the Appendix to Chapter 9. The lack of written dissent by any member of the committee, however, does not necessarily imply agreement on each specific issue. Also, Ambassador Malmgren, Mr. Wilcox, and Mr. Malve contributed to the exercise in an individual capacity. Their signatures should not be construed as implying U.S. government or European community positions or policies, respectively.

In addition, the committee has been assisted from time to time by individuals who have reviewed the several drafts of the document, and we would like to express our thanks for their assistance to Charles F. d'Ansembourg, P. G. H. Barter, Willard Cochrane, Irwin Hedges, Jimmye Hillman, John S. Marsh, Donald Paarlberg, D. H. Priebe, Roger Savary, John Scott, Lauren Soth, and P. Lamartine Yates.

We are most grateful to numerous other individuals and institutions without whose advice and support this study could not have been completed.

It is the Atlantic Council's belief that there is a serious danger, if conditions are not provided for continued expansion of world trade for the benefit of nations generally, that we may face trade conflicts and jeopardize the progress being made in the ongoing monetary discussions and other areas as well. The Atlantic Council has been deeply concerned about the possible damage to Atlantic relations, and those with Japan, that can occur as a result of increasing economic tensions. A key factor in ensuring the future maintenance of peace will be the growth of the economic strength and the cohesion of the countries of Western Europe, North America, and Japan, and agriculture is a key element in the overall picture. While the conclusions reached are those of the respective authors, editors and the Advisory Committee, the Atlantic Council is pleased to present the issues analyzed and discussed in this study for public consideration and debate.

Henry H. Fowler
Chairman
Atlantic Council of the United States

August 1974
Washington, D.C.

CONTENTS

LIST OF TABLES

Mr. Pierre Malvé—Cabinet of the President, European Communities, Brussels

Mr. Asao Miyawaki—president, Central Union of Agricultural Cooperatives of Japan

Mr. Eugene Moos—chairman, East-West Trade Council; former president, National Association of Wheat Growers

Mr. Kenneth Naden—executive vice-president, National Council of Farmer Cooperatives

Mr. James G. Patton—consultant, secretary of agriculture, State of Pennsylvania; former president, Freedom from Hunger Foundation, International Federation of Agricultural Producers, and the National Farmer's Union (United States)

Mr. Richard J. Wallace—director general, Atlantic Council

Prof. T. K. Warley—chairman, Department of Agricultural Economics, University of Guelph, Canada

Mr. Walter Wilcox—senior specialist, Agriculture, Legislative Reference Service; former director, Agricultural Economics, U.S. Department of Agriculture

Mr. Asher Winegarten—deputy director general, National Farmer's Union (United Kingdom)

Project Director:

Mr. Joseph W. Harned—assistant director, Atlantic Council: U.S. representative, the Atlantic Institute (Paris)

Project Officer:

Mrs. Karen C. Taylor—Atlantic Council

U.S. Agriculture
in a World Context

The objectives of this study are to relate U.S. agriculture and the national policies guiding it to the world agricultural system for the coming decade, identify both the principles and objectives upon which greater international accord on agricultural matters can be built, and describe the most urgent tangible steps that can be taken by national governments.

The crucial link between more general trade questions and agricultural production and trade is recognized, but no effort is made in this study to explore that complex question. Farm groups once supported trade liberalization in the hope that U.S. concessions on industrial products would bring concessions from others on agricultural trade. That may still be possible, but our purpose in this study is to examine U.S. agriculture and agricultural policies in a trade context, not to provide a general strategy for trade expansion.

The United States is the world's leading agricultural producer. With only 6 percent of the world's people and 1 percent of the world's agricultural labor force, the United States produces 15 percent of the total value of world food production. She is also the leading exporter of agricultural products, with 16 percent of the value of world agricultural exports in 1972-73, partly on the strength of unusually large grain exports. With 13 percent of world imports, the United States is also a major importer of agricultural products, though a sizable part of those imports consists of tropical products that are not produced in the United States.

Because of this dominant position in agricultural production and exports, the impact of developments in agricultural production and policy in the United States is felt around the world. United States agricultural policies and programs are closely watched and carefully analyzed both in developed and developing countries. They may

1

provide opportunities for some countries to expand their production and exports, or they may be the forerunners of serious production and trade problems for such countries.

Consideration of U.S. agriculture in a world context is thus a difficult and complex undertaking. Agricultural policies in the United States and abroad, the capacity of the United States and her competitors to produce for export, the prospective growth in world food requirements, and the nature of agricultural problems in the developing world must all be considered. These questions involve a wide diversity of views and great uncertainty of outcome. They also involve complex political and economic objectives in the United States and other exporting countries as well as in importing countries.

It is extremely difficult to come to grips with the true direction of agricultural developments in the world. When this study began in 1972, the United States had undertaken a costly round of restraint of grain production, after having encouraged expanded production in 1971 to replenish stocks depleted by the corn blight. Midway in 1972 and in this study, it became apparent that remarkable changes in world crop prospects had occurred. The surplus agricultural production capacity and the farm policies of the United States and other grain and oilseed exporters were suddenly seen in a new light, at least in the short run. The world was reminded once more that plentiful food supplies cannot be taken for granted.

Russian grain production in 1972 was reduced some 20 to 25 million tons below the level of 1971, and a possible 30 million tons below the targets for 1972 in the Ninth Five-Year Plan, with the principal losses in winter wheat. China announced late in 1972 that she had experienced a 10-million-ton (5 percent) shortfall in 1972 grain output, compared with 1971. Scattered crop losses in a number of Asian and African countries, including a sizable decline in the 1972-73 wheat crop in India, added to the world's 1972-73 grain deficit. The resulting demand for grain in world trade in one season removed all the stabilization reserves or surpluses that had been available in the grain-exporting countries (principally the United States and Canada) and brought sharply higher prices for most agricultural commodities by late summer 1972. The 1973 harvests suddenly took on a critical importance. With large reserves no longer available to offset poor crops in 1973-74, only the 1973 harvests stood in the way of record high prices and stringent price rationing of world grain supplies.

The unusual events of 1972, like the 1965-66 drought in South Asia, obscure for the moment the problems that have been the subject of international agricultural policy discussions for nearly 20 years: long-term capacity for surplus production, the tendency of nations to use export subsidies to dump food surpluses, and the continuing need for agricultural price stabilization. These events have brought on a shift from costly and difficult production restraint to substantial expansion of acreage and production in the grain-exporting nations for the 1973 crops. Acreage targets for U.S. feed grains and soybeans have been increased to replenish reserves and meet increasing export demands. Acreage set-aside programs were a minor factor in 1973 U.S. production. Canada and Australia expected to expand their grain areas in 1973 by as much as 15 to 20 percent. The USSR announced incentive plans for 1973 to regain the record level of grain output reached a few years ago, while new investments targets have been set to move the USSR toward the high grain production levels targeted for the late years of the Ninth Five-Year Plan.

The opportunity U.S. and Canadian farmers now have to sell unprecedented quantities of agricultural products to markets that, for the present, pose no visible barriers may also have diverted attention from the long and necessary efforts to improve the conditions of entry for agricultural products into traditional European, Japanese, and other developed country markets. Canada and Australia have cultivated the Soviet and Chinese markets for more than 10 years and paid correspondingly less attention during that period to Europe and Japan. Now that the United States has made large grain and oilseed exports to the Soviet Union, and U.S. agricultural products are again flowing to China, Congress and agricultural interests may tend to look toward these new markets as the best alternative for development in the mid-1970s and may be less single-minded in developing the European and Japanese markets. Widespread expectations that grain imports by Russia and China are likely to continue for some time lend strength to this view.

Even apart from the unusual agricultural developments of 1972 and 1973, rising incomes and increased demands for livestock products throughout the world are changing the prospects for agricultural production and trade. World trade in agricultural products, especially in oilseeds and feed grains, will probably increase, barring crop disasters, between 1970 and 1985, with the United States providing a large share of the increases and with the developing countries that produce groundnut and palm oil also sharing in the expansion. Although the possibility of grain surpluses remains, the growing demand for meat makes this less probable.

In such a changing world, the agricultural policies of the United States, other important exporting countries, and importing nations such as Japan and the European Community (EC) need to be more responsive than ever to changing conditions. Rising uncertainty may be the logical accompaniment of rising expectations in regard to food supplies unless production can be increasingly insulated from the effects of weather or unless the world develops a system that insures the availability of stored reserves large enough to offset the effects of adverse weather.

3

Nations and groups of nations have varying strategies regarding their own agricultural economy in relation to their food needs. Three main groups of nations can be identified in this context.

1. Some nations or groups of nations depend upon their own farmers for 95 to 100 percent of their food requirements, excepting those items not produced in the country or region because of climatic limitations. These nations usually protect and encourage their agricultural sectors through attractive price guarantees and import restrictions so that continued self-sufficiency can be realized. The EC (both before and after its enlargement to nine members), Russia, China, and India are important examples in this group of nations. Well over half the world's population lives in countries that protect agricultural producers to a degree that permits achievement of substantial self-sufficiency. United States policy, including especially the export targets we set for our agricultural products, must relate itself to the farm production intentions of these countries. High U.S. export targets may directly threaten the well-being of heavily protected agricultural groups in some countries and thus will be vigorously opposed.

2. Nations that, for reasons of climate or economy, import a large percentage of their food requirements as a matter of policy and that have tailored the protection provided to their farmers accordingly represent a second group. For 100 years before the 1960s, the United Kingdom relied heavily on food imports. Beginning with 1973, however, her food economy will be closely shielded from the rest of the world. Japan, for the past 10 or 15 years, and a few smaller countries are the best examples of this group. Only a small percentage of the world's population is now represented in the countries that are major agricultural importers by choice, and Japan is the only large nation now on a deliberate, albeit selective, course of increased dependence on food imports.

3. A third group includes nations that produce most of their food requirements except for products not adapted to their own climates and that look to their agricultural sectors as an important source of foreign-exchange earnings. These nations have geared their agricultural development and pricing policies toward export competition, although they, too, retain highly protective policies with respect to certain agricultural sectors. The United States, Canada, Australia, Argentina, and New Zealand are the principal examples here. Mexico and Brazil are recent but somewhat sporadic entrants to this group. Pakistan anticipated becoming a net exporter of grain on the strength of rapid progress in the late 1960s, but has since suffered serious reversals in her agricultural production.

The agricultural objectives of the third group (exporters) are largely in accord with those of nations in the second group, but in direct conflict with countries that aim for self-sufficiency in food. The situation varies widely by commodities. Europe is especially protective of its grain and milk producers in order to limit imports or expand exports, but must rely on oilseed imports because of lack of European sources. Even nations that have elected to import a large and increasing share of their food requirements have usually set limits to their dependence on imports. In some cases, they are unable to shift rapidly to an import strategy for certain agricultural products because of political considerations. Japan's difficulties a few years ago with rice were especially embarrassing since her wheat and coarse grain imports were increasing rapidly while her rice surplus grew. Reconciling the short-term interests of the farmers in countries that lack the natural resources for expanded food production with the long-run consumer interest in low-priced imports is a slow and difficult process.

The most serious conflicts among nations over agricultural and trade policies have arisen in situations where importing (or high-cost) countries have acted to maintain or to achieve a high level of self-sufficiency for key commodities at a time when exporting nations either had come to depend upon their markets or were in a position to meet their past requirements and to expand exports as the market grew. Protection for grain producers in the EC in the 1960s under the Common Agricultural Policy (CAP) worked to the disadvantage of the United States, Canada, and Australia. Grain exports to Europe had been rising until 1966, when the price provisions of the CAP became fully effective. Escalation of U.S. milk price support levels when world dairy product supplies were more than adequate during the past five years and when low-cost producing nations, especially New Zealand and Australia, were in a position to expand exports represents another example.

CHAPTER

2

**U.S. AGRICULTURAL POLICY
IN RELATION TO
WORLD TRADE**
John A. Schnittker

Public policy with respect to stabilization of farm prices and incomes and food budgets in the United States is still in an early stage of development. The long history of heavy protection for its farmers, such as that adopted by France in the nineteenth century, or of explicitly protecting consumers through cheap imports while carefully rationing public expenditures for farm income support or modernization, as was the policy in Britain until recently, is not a part of U.S. history.

The United States is still in an early stage of political development, especially in the Congress. Agrarian interests cling precariously to power in the House of Representatives and are permanently overrepresented in the Senate, with two members from each state by constitutional edict. Thus we are still engaged in deciding how much protection to provide for agriculture and how to provide it. Just 40 years ago President Franklin D. Roosevelt broke free-market tradition and urged the Congress to enact the Agricultural Adjustment Act of 1933. Congress responded by approving within a few weeks an unprecedented farm relief measure. The general economic depression, the agricultural crisis of that era, and the lack of alternatives, coupled with no conviction that federal farm aid would solve problems, were factors behind that swift legislative action. Until 1933 the official policy of both political parties had been to reject all efforts to have the federal government modify the market forces that had periodically generated extremely unstable agricultural prices and low farmer incomes. Bipartisan policy followed the line once laid down by President Calvin Coolidge in the 1920s when he said that the farmers have always been poor and there is nothing we can do about it.

Congress had enacted some farm relief measures in the 1920s to relieve the postwar debt problems of overextended farmers and to provide a degree of protection against depressed world commodity prices, but the latter measures were vetoed by Presidents Harding and Coolidge whenever they were approved by both Houses of Congress. Congress then enacted the Federal Farm Board Act of 1928, designed to keep surplus commodities off the market temporarily, and President Herbert Hoover signed it. The Farm Board was not really a policy, but a badly underfinanced emergency program. The Farm Board rested upon the assumption that depressed agricultural prices and politically sensitive income levels were only temporary dislocations and would shortly right themselves. The government was to hold surplus commodities off the market for a short time, until "normal free-market forces" again came into play. Unfortunately, in the 1920s the "normal free-market forces" that had sustained an expanding and relatively prosperous agriculture throughout the nineteenth century had become price-depressing forces as a result of rapid technological improvements.

Both the Federal Farm Board Act and the Agricultural Adjustment Act of 1933 were directed almost entirely at the immediate income problems of U.S. farmers. Any possible impact of domestic policies on trade in agricultural products was largely ignored. The lack of concern regarding world markets was at first a direct result of the decline in world agricultural trade during the 1930s. United States wheat exports, for example, were only 35 million bushels, or 5 percent of production, in 1932. Three years later U.S. wheat exports reached a long time low of 7 million bushels, or 1 percent of total production. This compared with 50 to 60 percent for 1971 and 1972. Other commodities historically exported by the United States suffered similar declines from earlier levels. Even in the 1940s and 1950s, it was generally expected that after the world had recovered from the economic shock of World War II, the United States would again find a relatively limited demand for its agricultural products in world markets and thus could adopt domestic farm policies without explicit consideration of world markets.

It was not the prospect of expanded international trade, but the embarrassing fact of large and unmanageable surpluses of grains and other agricultural products in the 1950s that again brought world markets to the attention of American farmers and their representatives, including the Congress. These surpluses were owned by the federal government, largely because farm price supports in the postwar years had been maintained near wartime levels, while demand had declined. The renewed interest in world markets did not manifest itself in an effort to price farm products more competitively, or to negotiate for improved trade concessions, but in the Agricultural Trade Development and Assistance Act of 1954, later known as the Food for Peace program. Other exporters of agricultural products looked upon this program as largely a dumping measure, since it involved sales for foreign currency, easy credit terms, and donations, actions that nations less rich than the United States could seldom afford.

The peak years for concessional exports under the Food for Peace program were 1959-60 and 1964-65, when exports under that authority constituted 70 and 77 percent, respectively, of total U.S. wheat exports. By 1970-71 and 1971-72 such exports had declined to 33 and 35 percent, respectively, of total wheat exports by the United States. Wheat was by far the most important commodity exported under PL 480.

While prices of the principal U.S. export crops—wheat, coarse grains, and cotton—were supported at levels substantially above world market levels during the 1950s and early 1960s, exports were possible only through use of cash subsidies, direct government sales from surplus stocks, or donations to needy nations or people.

Export subsidies were paid out of federal funds using several different methods. Fixed unit subsidies were announced in advance of the marketing year in the case of cotton and were generally ineffective as a competitive device whenever other countries had cotton to sell. Daily subsidies were quoted by the Department of Agriculture for wheat at levels judged necessary to make U.S. wheat competitive with offerings of other exporting countries. For corn, periodic bids for subsidy were requested by exporters, to be accepted or rejected on the basis of criteria similar to those used in setting the export subsidy levels for wheat.

In this period of heavy export subsidization, the Commodity Credit Corporation (CCC) of the Department of Agriculture moved ever closer to a position where it was the principal factor in both domestic and export markets for all the major agricultural commodities whose prices were supported. Large annual crop surpluses had to be acquired by the CCC as a part of its statutory price support commitments. In some years, the CCC both acquired large quantities of grain, especially wheat, and delivered sizable amounts into the domestic and export markets in a massive and unnecessary recycling operation.

United States farmers had little direct knowledge or interest in world market values for their crops in this period. United States wheat producers were guaranteed market prices at the farm ranging upward from $2.00 per bushel, while world values averaged some 40 to 70 cents per bushel lower in that period. The difference was accounted for by export subsidies and by sales of wheat out of government stocks directly into export channels. The world was buying U.S. wheat at prices that reflected values of $1.30 to $1.50 per bushel at the farm, but farmers were being told by the level at which U.S.

market prices were supported that their product had greater value in world markets than was actually the case. This situation was largely remedied by the program changes made in the 1960s, but it has not been remedied entirely, as seen by the large export subsidies paid on wheat by the United States in July and August 1972.

Greater contact with world markets, as foreign demand grew late in the 1950s and early in the 1960s, did increase the sensitivity of U.S. policy makers and farm organization representatives to the importance of world trade and to the possibility of export expansion for U.S. agricultural products. Market development and promotional efforts were begun by the Department of Agriculture and cooperating commodity groups to encourage both commercial and concessional sales into markets such as Japan and India, where wheat had not been widely used before. Government-guaranteed credit programs for agricultural exports were also established by law to serve both commercial and concessional outlets.

FARM POLICY CHANGES IN THE 1960s

Most important, however, to the growing adaptation of U.S. agriculture to world markets were changes made in the basic price support programs for major export commodities beginning in 1962. These changes made it possible to end the export subsidy for U.S. feed grains in 1963, to sharply reduce the level of direct export subsidization for wheat beginning in 1964, and to terminate the export subsidy for cotton beginning in 1966. They also provided the means for reduction of surplus commodity carry-overs, a fact that led eventually to the sharp decline in concessional sales and an increasing orientation toward commercial exports of agricultural products.

There was not, however, a particular pattern in the 1960s of development of U.S. price support programs geared more closely to agricultural trade expansion, or toward increased compatability of U.S. farm programs with the established rules of agricultural trade under the General Agreement on Tariffs and Trade (GATT). Rather, the U.S. CCC had found it increasingly difficult to manage the acquisition and storage of farm product surpluses, sales of past surplus acquisitions into domestic and export market channels, and direct subsidization of exports at the same time. By 1961 facilities for storing surpluses, from grains to cotton and butter, were glutted, despite intensive efforts to expand exports. Budgetary expenditures for storage and handling alone reached $1 billion in 1961. The situation was ripe for change.

The peak of economic absurdity in farm programs was reached with the 1961 feed grain program. The average price of corn at U.S.

9

farms was supported by law at $1.20 per bushel. The Department of Agriculture was required to sell surplus, government-owned corn in U.S. markets during the 1961-62 marketing year at prices low enough to keep average farm prices some 15 cents per bushel lower than the guaranteed price support level. This procedure was justified on the grounds that it would deny the benefits of the higher price support guarantee to farmers who were not cooperating in the production adjustment program, while providing such benefits to those farmers who were cooperating. The program accomplished this, but it also required CCC to become the market for a large part of the 1961 and 1962 feed grain crops, while reducing its overall stock of grains substantially at the same time.

The obvious waste in this massive recycling of grain in and out of government ownership led to a series of decisive actions in the Department of Agriculture and in the Agriculture Committees of Congress. Legislation was enacted in 1962 requiring the price support level for corn to be set at approximately world price levels, and directing the CCC to make cash payments to farmers to compensate for the lower guaranteed market price for corn. With U.S. corn no longer priced above world market values, the direct cash subsidy on exports was no longer required to compete with Canadian, Argentine, or South African feed grain offerings. Accordingly, the export subsidy program was terminated in 1963.

The legislative action on feed grains in 1962 was accompanied by similar legislation amending the federal wheat program. For the first time, price support was separated from income support for this important commodity. This was far more than a simple domestic policy change, but carried important trade policy overtones. Under the Agricultural Act of 1962, U.S. wheat prices, beginning with the 1963 crop, were to be supported at levels determined after taking into consideration world wheat prices, the price support levels established for feed grains in the United States, and the relative feeding values of wheat and corn. Farmers were to be compensated for the reduction in market price supports from $2.00 per bushel in 1961 to $1.25 per bushel in 1963, by cash payments on a portion of the crop, financed partly by wheat processors and partly by the federal Treasury.

The linking of U.S. wheat prices to coarse grain prices also made it more difficult for wheat prices in world trade to be maintained by agreement among exporting countries at relatively high levels under the International Wheat Agreement.

Adoption of acreage adjustment programs capable of limiting the production of the principal surplus-prone export crops in the United States also deserves to be mentioned as a significant move in U.S. agricultural policy in the 1960s. After nearly a decade of regular

10

surplus accumulation, and 30 years in which farm production control programs were either a vast game of musical chairs among various commodities or were suspended because of wartime needs, actual requirements during the coming marketing year became the production target under the 1962 Farm Act. Allowances had to be made also for reductions in carry-over stocks, or additions to stocks, in some years.

Creation of production adjustment programs capable of eliminating surpluses was an important factor in reducing the political pressures for exporting U.S. agricultural products under terms so soft that other countries considered them unfair. Farm commodity groups were thus encouraged to shift their interest away from disposal of stored surpluses to the development of commercial markets to be serviced out of annual crops and reserve stocks.

The concept of maintaining adequate reserve supplies of farm products in the United States did not originate in the 1960s, however. Congress had been concerned about reserves in the 1930s, after the extended drought that produced the "Dust Bowl" had seriously depleted agricultural commodity supplies. World War II and widespread food shortages after the war again brought the question of reserve stocks to the attention of Congress and the country. Yet there has never been a settled policy with respect to food reserves. Surpluses accumulated either because of good crops or because ineffective production programs have served as a reserve against droughts or other disasters.

In the 1960s and to the present time, carry-over policy was set by executive determination rather than by legislative action. The secretary of agriculture saw in 1961 that surplus carry-overs of wheat, coarse grains, cotton, and dairy products were so burdensome to the Treasury and to the future of U.S. farm policy that they had to be reduced. The program changes described earlier in this paper were designed to limit production of various crops so that carry-overs could be systematically reduced. Informal determinations were made of supply levels for key crops below which carry-overs would not be reduced. Annual domestic and export requirements, and the degree of production instability affecting the crop, where the principal factors considered. This informal approach remains U.S. policy with respect to commodity reserve stocks.

Later in the 1960s, a number of efforts were made both on the initiative of the secretary of agriculture and of farm organizations to get congressional action on a specific policy, authorizing reserve carry-overs of agricultural commodities and prescribing how they should be managed. This policy was never approved, and there is probably little need for it now. Existing laws and past practice under those laws give the secretary of agriculture wide discretion to acquire

11

and dispose of surpluses of agricultural commodities, but do not require him to dispose of all CCC stocks in any given time period. This makes it possible to maintain adequate reserves on a flexible basis. Since some countries, especially Japan, depend heavily on the United States for stable supplies of agricultural commodities, adequate reserves are an important adjunct to trade policy.

The constructive changes in policies and programs described above for the three major U.S. export crops have not yet been made in federal programs for rice, peanuts, and tobacco. These commodities are also important export products, and they continue to be protected by price support programs which maintain price guarantees above usual world values. Export subsidies have been in operation for these commodities, but exports are not so large that the export subsidies represent either a large burden on the Treasury, or a highly visible target for countries critical of U.S. trade policy.

The level of protection for rice has been quite high in most years. Export subsidies have represented a sizable percentage of the price support level over the past 15 years, except for a brief period in the later 1960s and again in 1973, when a general rice shortage brought world prices above guaranteed levels in the United States.

Tobacco price guarantees have been increased annually for many years by a statutory formula. Yet tobacco has generally been exported in volume with little price resistance. In 1967, however, a fixed subsidy per pound was introduced for flue-cured tobacco, which makes up a large part of U.S. tobacco exports. This subsidy did not result in any tangible increase in tobacco exports and could probably have been terminated at any time without any effect on tobacco exports. The principal effect of the subsidy has been to keep U.S. tobacco prices slightly higher than they would otherwise be. The export subsidy was terminated early in 1973 under general pressure to reduce federal expenditures.

IMPORT COMMODITIES

While policies and programs relating to the principal U.S. agricultural export products were being linked more closely to world markets in the 1960s, there was also a definite trend toward a policy of greater protection for the principal agricultural products for which the United States either has extremely high levels of protection, or which we import in volume. Manufactured dairy products and fresh and frozen beef are the principal items in this category. The volume of imports of these products was limited significantly in the 1960s by administrative and legislative actions. In both cases, however, imports in terms of quantity and value have increased in the past 10 years.

Dairy product imports into the United States have been limited under the provisions of Section 22 of the Agricultural Act of 1938 for many years. This statute authorizes restrictions to prevent the importation of various price-supported commodities in quantities that would tend to render the domestic price support program ineffective. Quotas on specific manufactured dairy products held the volume of imports in the 1950s and early 1960s below one-half of 1 percent of total dairy product requirements in the United States, as measured in milk equivalent.

A severe surplus of milk in the world, both in countries such as New Zealand and Australia which relied heavily upon dairy product exports and in European countries where dairy product exports were largely the by-product of highly supported domestic industries, put the restrictive U.S. policy under severe pressure in the 1960s. As the world dairy product surplus grew and as world butterfat prices declined about 1965, milk production and stored surpluses of dairy products in the United States declined. This took place partly because of technologically induced changes in the structure of U.S. agriculture. Small farmers dropped out, especially in the traditional milk-producing states of Wisconsin, Minnesota, Iowa, and Michigan. Substantial utilization of surplus dairy products in U.S. export programs and domestic feeding programs also contributed to reduced milk supplies. Finally, recovery of beef prices in 1965, after several years of depression, encouraged rapid slaughter of dairy cattle and a shift from milk production to beef on some farms.

By 1966, when world dairy product surpluses were reaching their peak, U.S. surpluses had disappeared. Concern arose in the United States about the possibility of inadequate dairy product supplies and rising consumer prices at a time when a general inflation, based on acceleration of the Vietnam war and the economy, had become troublesome. Pressure from huge world supplies of milk encouraged innovation in dairy product exports. Products previously not in existence were created to take advantage of the loopholes in U.S. dairy product import quotas, which were geared to specific, identified products. Junex, a mixture of butterfat and sugar, was an example of a product designed specifically to evade the U.S. dairy product import quota. Since Junex was not specifically excluded by the U.S. import list, it was allowed to enter the United States until the language of the import quotas could be amended.

Evasions of this type pushed dairy product imports from 760 million pounds milk equivalent in 1961 to 2791 million pounds in 1966, well above the established quota. Strong pressure from organizations representing dairy farmers to tighten quota restrictions, either through administrative action or by amendments to the law, was the inevitable result.

At first these recommendations were not heeded by the secretary of agriculture. In 1966 and 1967, dairy product import quotas were actually further increased for a temporary period while the Tariff Commission conducted an examination of the import quota limitation system for dairy products. Imports peaked at 2908 million pounds milk equivalent in 1967. In the next four years, dairy interest groups repeatedly encouraged the Department of Agriculture and the president to adopt more restrictive limitations on the imports of dairy products, while raising milk price guarantees at the same time. By 1970 dairy product imports had declined to 1874 million pounds milk equivalent, just 1.5 percent of total U.S. requirements for milk products in all forms. This was a slight rollback from 1966-67, but a large increase in percentage terms over 1960-65. Imports will again increase in 1973.

The situation with respect to beef imports is quite different from dairy products, both in terms of policy and effect. Beef prices have never been directly supported by federal programs in the United States, although they tend to be stabilized and supported by federal grain price guarantees. Beef is not readily eligible, therefore, for application of import quotas under Section 22 of the Agricultural Adjustment Act. What finally generated the Beef Import Quota Act of 1964 was the coincidence of rising supplies of beef in the world and large cyclical supplies and low prices in the United States in 1962 and 1963. Economic distress among cattlemen brewed a potential political crisis in 1963 and led Congress to limit beef imports the next year, after a negotiated agreement concluded between the United States and the principal beef exports failed to please U.S. cattle interests.

The Beef Import Act, restrictive as it is, has sometimes been hailed by government spokesmen in the United States as a step forward, or at worst such a mild limitation on the world beef trade that it represents a model for other countries to imitate if they must invoke import quotas on any products. The act has the effect of authorizing importation of about 6 percent of U.S. beef supplies in any year as fresh and frozen product. The percentage eligible to be imported remains constant (assuming foreign suppliers offer the beef in the U.S. market), so the volume of imports may increase as the U.S. demand for beef grows. It is this built-in growth feature that U.S. government representatives have cited in characterizing the beef quota as a relatively unchallengeable aspect of our trade policy. In fact, it is an import quota which is illegal under the GATT. It has kept beef imports lower and U.S. beef prices higher than they would have been. Since the law affords foreign suppliers a U.S. market for a larger tonnage of beef each year, it is recognized by beef exporters as a relatively mild effort to protect domestic producers, and has not been subject to serious official objections.

Wool and sugar represent two additional commodity groups where our domestic price and income programs receive sharp criticism from low-cost exporter-producers in other countries. Both commodities enjoy extremely high levels of protection in the United States. Both are so politically entrenched after many decades of favored treatment that only limited progress can be expected from even the most persuasive case for changes in U.S. policy.

The U.S. Wool Act is another anomaly of U.S. trade policy. By every measure, wool, lamb, and mutton productions have declined in the United States each year for many years, despite the official policy to maintain output. This policy is implemented through federal payments under the Wool Act ranging from a low of $16 million in 1957 to a high of $109 million in 1971. The wool price level guaranteed through these payments has risen from 62 cents to 72 cents per pound since 1961, yet wool production has been about halved in the same period.

In 1971 market prices returned only 19.4 cents per pound to wool producers, while federal payments provided about 53 cents toward the 72-cent guarantee. The absurdity of that situation is readily apparent. Perhaps only a little more time is required until Congress recognizes the futility of such farm policy expenditures, and looks toward a means of bringing the Wool Act to an end, so it does not survive longer than wool production in the United States. Wool-exporting nations have never concerned themselves seriously with the effects of the Wool Act on U.S. imports, since the act was so ineffective in maintaining U.S. production. Exporting countries can depend on an everrising share of the U.S. wool market as our production declines.

Sugar presents a different type of special case. Sugar substitutes have not displaced sugar to any appreciable extent, and sugar consumption continues to increase in nearly every nation, as well as in the United States. Thus the highly protected U.S. sugar market is of intensive interest to low-cost producers around the world. There is little prospect of any change, however, in the level of protection for U.S. producers, or in the shares that domestic and foreign growers have in the U.S. market. The Sugar Act was renewed for five years in 1971 without appreciable changes from the way it has operated for many years. United States sugar price objectives continue to be linked to prices paid by farmers; these prices continue to rise, making the U.S. market more attractive to foreign growers and more inaccesible to them at the same time as U.S. growers respond to attractive prices.

Sugar policy responds to a different set of forces than other U.S. agricultural policies respond to. Hence needed changes in sugar policy will not be developed in this paper.

FARMERS AND TRADE POLICY

Farm organizations in the United States have maintained a deep interest in agricultural trade expansion and in negotiations by the U.S. government directed toward that objective. This is true for organizations representing a broad spectrum of agricultural interests, and those representing narrower commodity interests such as wheat or cotton.

The power of U.S. farm organizations appears to weigh fairly heavily on the side of policy steps that would help to expand trade. This does not arise out of any greater importance for export commodities compared with those commodities imported by the United States. In fact, the beef and dairy sectors are substantially larger than the grain and oilseed sectors combined. Nor does it arise out of any ideological dedication among farmers to freer trade. To U.S. farmers, expanded trade means expanded agricultural exports from the United States. Farmers in the United States know that to sell more abroad we must also buy; to farmers that means larger imports of industrial products. It is seldom admitted that our increased purchases abroad might legitimately include larger amounts of some competitive agricultural products such as dairy products. United States farmers are not unique in this respect. Farm organizations in Western Europe resist imports of agricultural commodities as strenuously and as successfully as American farmers do, despite the sure knowledge that production efficiency is higher and prices lower in many other countries.

When price support guarantees for the major export commodities were to be reduced through legislative action in the early 1960s, U.S. farm organizations did not willingly support the shift, nor were the implications for trade policy ever a significant part of the debate on the farm measures. Farm organization support was obtained only when it was made clear that Treasury payments would maintain and even increase aggregate farmer incomes, offsetting the shift in price guarantees to world trading levels.

The largest U.S. farm organization, the American Farm Bureau Federation, opposed the changes in the price support system strenuously. It did not oppose lower price guarantees in principle, however, but objected to federal payments that were to supplement price support guarantees. The official stance of the Farm Bureau at that time included a gradual phasing out of agricultural price supports and a return to the free market for agricultural products, barring both production restraint and price support. That doctrine was based on the judgment of Farm Bureau that price support guarantees stimulated output and pushed prices down. Without supports, prices would rise, according to the Farm Bureau approach. The Farm Bureau's support

16

for freer trade, however, was never in doubt. Their farm program proposals were, in the traditional sense, more trade oriented than the programs that were adopted in the 1960s, since farm subsidies and production incentives would have been phased out.

The other major farm organizations, operating as a "Farm Coalition," accepted the changed machinery for price and income support only under strong pressure from the executive branch. Congress, responding to the reluctant farm organizations and to farmer constituencies in nearly every congressional district and state, also accepted the program changes without enthusiasm, after having held on to the "high rigid" price support system from the early 1940s through 1961.

If the farm organizations took little part in developing the greater trade orientation represented by changes in the domestic price support programs, they did assume a strong role in U.S. trade legislation and negotiations. Farm groups were among the most powerful supporters of the Trade Expansion Act of 1962; they deserve much credit for passage of that act and for the achievements of the Kennedy Round of negotiations.

The legislative strategy of the farm organizations in 1962 was to bind agricultural products into a general trade negotiation, with the objective of trading U.S. concessions on industrial products for concessions by other nations on agricultural products. It was an article of faith for the farm organizations that trade negotiations under the Trade Expansion Act of 1962 must make a strong attack on the emerging Common Agricultural Policy (CAP) of the European Community (EC).

This tough approach to the EC failed to dislodge the CAP. In retrospect, the U.S. effort was doomed from the start. First, it was badly timed. The CAP was adopted in the early 1960s as the cornerstone of the entire EC. Had it been weakened by a substantial negotiated reduction in the levels of protection provided for European farmers, the EC itself might not have survived as an economic or political entity. Thus, U.S. trade negotiating objectives seemed to threaten not only the CAP but the very existence of the EC.

Faced with contradictory mandates—to create a Community and at the same time to negotiate in the Kennedy Round for expanded trade (which meant expanded imports) in farm products—Europe chose the former. The Kennedy Round floundered and almost failed, both as a result of U.S. objectives and European flexibility.

In the end U.S. negotiators retreated, papering over the fact that agricultural results in the Kennedy Round were extremely limited and that concessions from Europe on agricultural products were barely tangible.

The lessons learned from the 1967 impasse over agricultural trade are directly applicable to the 1970s. United States and European positions remain largely unchanged, with export expansion paramount to most U.S. producers, while strict and even rising protection remains the objective of European farmers and those U.S. producers not involved in export markets.

HARMONIZING ADMINISTRATIVE ACTIONS
BY THE UNITED STATES WITH TRADE NEGOTIATING
OBJECTIVES

In order to consider administrative actions that would, under existing statutes, improve the prospects for long-run trade expansion either through successful negotiations on agricultural products or through increased market demands, one must make certain assumptions regarding the continuity of U.S. policies and programs for the principal agricultural commodities. If we expect an upheaval of the entire U.S. agricultural policy in 1973, the basis for trade negotiations on agriculture would be radically altered.

It is reasonable to assume that the price support and production control programs for grains, cotton, and soybeans will continue throughout the 1970s about the same as in 1973. There is some risk in such an assumption on the eve of major legislative action on U.S. farm policy. Farm programs have become increasingly expensive and are vulnerable to sharpshooting by those who support greater expenditures for other public programs. Yet levels of expenditure under farm programs are very flexible. A wide range of program expenditures can be accommodated within existing program procedures and objectives.

There is a possibility that Congress will begin to limit potentially costly price support and production adjustment programs whose benefits go principally to a few hundred thousand large farmers, virtually bypassing small family farmers. This would be a signal, not that the methods employed in present farm legislation need to be amended radically, but that the programs require amendments so that the benefits are spread more widely among the farmers with substandard incomes. Limiting federal payments to large growers, or limiting overall expenditures for commodity programs as a means of reserving more of the federal budget for nonagricultural programs, may be the prerequisite for continuity in farm programs in the 1970s. These conditions appear more acceptable to Congress and U.S. farm organizations than major new departures in domestic farm programs.

As previously indicated, the essential features of the basic system of price supports, production payments, and production controls established for feed grains and wheat in 1962 and for cotton in 1965 were reductions in price support levels, provision for federal payments to producers to provide income support and incentives to limit plantings, and a degree of flexibility for farmer decision making on cropping patterns. This latter feature arose out of the fact that price support levels for all the grains (except rice) were made comparable on the basis of feeding values. The Agricultural Act of 1970 did not change these principles. Additional flexibility was introduced so that producers could further modify crop production patterns on their farms, but otherwise the programs of the 1960s were substantially continued, and they will probably be continued throughout the 1970s. Farmers like them, and overall income results have been good. This is particularly true for the larger commercial farmers who have received most of the benefits of farm programs, but it is also generally true of smaller farmers who are affected by farm programs. Grain and oilseed trade interests in the United States, for the most part, like current programs better than any available alternatives because CCC manipulation of agricultural markets has been minimized.

Other agencies of the U.S. government also have of some influence on agricultural policy, and they favor pre-1973 programs for their own reasons. The Office of Management and Budget and the Council of Economic Advisers in the executive office of the president know that budgetary restrictions or effective payment limitations could be applied to farm programs more easily under direct payment schemes than under high price support schemes. To the extent they are engaged in agricultural policy determination through their responsibilities for international trade, the Departments of State and Commerce tend to see present programs as more understandable to foreign buyers and less vulnerable to criticism under the GATT on the grounds of excess production, dumping of surpluses, and export subsidies than were programs in effect through the 1950s. These factors help provide further momentum to present programs similar to that which kept the farm programs of the 1940s in operation through the 1950s despite their ineffectiveness. They will help to keep existing farm program procedures largely intact through the 1970s insofar as provisions relating to trade are concerned.

Administrative actions that would contribute to more successful U.S. trade initiatives relate both to export and import commodities. Grains make up the most important group of export commodities. Important administrative actions with implications for trade policy include determination of price support levels, the size and function of federal payments to farmers, and production targets. Administrative decisions with respect to maintenance of reserve carry-over stocks, including procedures established for insulating such stocks from the market and feeding them into the market as circumstances require, also can be important factors in U.S. trade discussions or negotiations.

Price support policy has been closely allied with expansionist international trade policies for the past 10 years. As described earlier, price support levels for grains are required by law to be related to world market values for grains. Historical price support relationships were set aside if not quite forgotten in the 1960s.

For corn, the U.S. price support level has been the principal factor determining the world trading price for coarse grains the past 10 years. Without U.S. programs to limit production and to support and stabilize prices, returns to all grain-exporting countries would have been lower, while importing countries would have faced both price instability and uncertainty regarding future supplies without the maintenance of large stocks by the United States. Action by the United States to continue these programs substantially in their present form would provide assurances of great value to other countries regarding U.S. feed grain policy and minimum world prices. Congressional action raising price support guarantees and setting target prices far above recent average levels would be damaging to the U.S. negotiating position.

Wheat fits the same pattern. Except in periods of short supply such as 1966-67 and 1972-73, U.S. price supports have stabilized world prices, and U.S. export subsidies have been at nominal levels. Only when prices have risen sharply because of increased demand or reduced supplies have substantial export subsidies been introduced by the United States to offset higher domestic prices. United States efforts to keep world wheat prices low in 1972 proved abortive and will not be tried again soon. The manner in which the export subsidy is managed by the United States is, to an important degree, responsible for occasional unusual gyrations in domestic wheat prices. Termination or limitation of the export subsidy on wheat, in the context of continuation of substantially the same administrative framework in effect for the past nine years for wheat, would be an important contribution of domestic policy to trade negotiations. Higher price supports and target prices would have the opposite effect.

The question of administrative or legislative actions to modify the U.S. cotton program raises the issue of the role of federal payments to farmers to subsidize crop production, thus establishing a measurable level of protection for the crop, or taking over a share of world markets in ways considered unfair or irregular by other trading nations. Payments to U.S. cotton growers under present programs are almost entirely a production subsidy. There is no longer even the pretense of production control for cotton, but vigorous efforts to increase production through payments to growers. For any commodity where payments are larger than would be required to limit production to levels required for domestic needs and exports at or near world prices, such payments must be considered as part of the overall level of protection for the commodity.

TABLE 2.1

Functional Distribution of Payments to Farmers, 1968

1968 Program	Payments Serving the Function of Supply Management (Million dollars)	(Percent)	Payments Serving the Function of Income Supplement (Million dollars)	(Percent)
Cotton	276	35	508	65
Feed grains	1221	89	148	11
Wheat	384	51	362	49
Three programs	1881	65	1018	35

Source: U.S. Department of Agriculture.

Several years ago, the U.S. Department of Agriculture provided estimates of the functional distribution of payments to farmers in 1968 under programs for the three major export crops. The "subsidy" or "income supplement" portion of such payments was represented by the extent to which they were larger than would have been required to limit production to market demands. The results are shown in Table 2.1. If similar estimates were available for 1972 or 1973 programs, they would show a similar pattern among the three crops, but in each case the proportion of total payments falling in the "subsidy" category would be higher than in earlier years.

Turning to dairy products, U.S. trade representatives have often been told that reductions in the level of protection for dairy products would represent a major initiative toward agricultural trade liberalization. The United States has the opportunity each year, when setting the price support level for milk, to either introduce a "standstill" on the level of protection or to reduce it. In three of the past five years, however, the U.S. milk price support level (that is, the level of protection) has been increased, and it was again increased by law under legislation considered in 1973.

It would be sensible, so long as dairy products on world markets are cheap and plentiful, to at least stop increasing our milk price guarantees and to import progressively larger percentages of our milk product requirements from countries with low subsidy levels in the dairy sector. Today we import only 1 percent of our total dairy product consumption and 2 percent of our manufactured dairy product consumption while maintaining a level of protection among the highest in the world. We could easily import 10 percent of our dairy food needs in 1980 and still retain a strong fluid milk sector.

What could the United States buy in trade negotiations by making such a move on dairy products? Very little, in my judgment, but we should do it anyway. The European Economic Community (EEC) would not be as grateful as other countries, being a high-cost producer which would not get much of the larger U.S. market. New Zealand and Australia would get most of the expanded U.S. dairy product imports, although Denmark might get a good share. New Zealand has little to offer us in any tradeoff. Australia might respond with some concessions, perhaps on tobacco. United States consumers would gain, and that is worth something, but the chances for reciprocal moves by others to open their markets would be limited.

There is one other area, a rather far-out possibility, where the United States might undertake a major initiative to test the possibility that domestic policy changes would produce reciprocal beneficial moves by other countries. We could terminate, or put strict per bushel limits on, our export subsidies for wheat. Our domestic policies would readily accommodate such a move.

Wheat export subsidies have served for years principally to push domestic wheat prices well above price support levels under certain market conditions and not to increase exports. United States wheat could be priced competitively without daily subsidy quotations by the U.S. Department of Agriculture (USDA). Corn and soybean exports do not seem to suffer from lack of an export subsidy. Those markets respond to the short-run certainty that no subsidy will be offered by adjusting U.S. prices to world values. Wheat prices in the United States, on the other hand, respond to the assurance, under the long-standing export subsidy policy, that if millers in the United States bid prices up while world values are stable, the subsidy will be increased. The subsidy absorbs the difference between U.S. and world prices, and the market need not adjust. The time to undertake such a bold experiment would be when U.S. and world wheat prices are about equal (when subsidies are small).

PURSUING SELF-INTEREST
AS WELL AS NEGOTIATIONS

The political pressures and the rationale for trade restrictive domestic agricultural policies have arisen principally out of the concept certain agricultural pressure groups in various countries have of their own self-interest and that of agricultural producers. The rationale for political actions by governments aimed at limiting the protective impact of agricultural policies, and realizing to a greater degree the benefits of further international division of agricultural labor by consumers (the public), will have to arise out of a political assertion of self-interest by other groups. This is difficult to generate, and it will probably take a long time. Urban and consumer groups are not highly organized in most countries, and making a direct challenge to agricultural policies is seldom high on their agenda. Governments often tend to be more responsive to organizations and traditions that have developed out of the past than to important political groups that are emerging.

If a government is to follow the self-interest of the majority of its citizens in the matter of agricultural price guarantees, budgetary expenditures, food prices, and trade, it must find ways of judging what that interest is. Little definitive study has been devoted to this question so far as agricultural policies are concerned. Yet the author feels confident that there is a broad intuitive judgment among economists and the public that if all the costs and benefits could be weighed, the customary defensive responses by governments to agricultural issues would be seen to have cost more over recent decades and generations than remedial actions would have cost over a similar time span. Farm policy decisions geared to the public interest would not represent a retreat from the long-standing public and treasury commitment to farm people, but a means of compressing the adjustment and income payments into a limited time period while helping farm people and their children to shift into new lines of employment. Decisive agricultural actions of this type have seldom been taken by governments except on a token or pilot basis, because the organizational and power base needed to prepare seriously for the future has seldom been as powerful as the groups organized to preserve the past.

Major trading nations will find themselves on rather different timetables over the next two decades in amending their domestic agricultural policies in a manner that would expand agricultural trade beyond the levels that will prevail under existing policies. This results from the differing stages of economic development and differing balances of political power in various countries. As a result, the time-honored tradition of reciprocity in trade negotiations is not a very useful rationale for altering domestic agricultural policies of major countries, especially when it is applied largely within agricultural sectors, rather than across industry as well. The underlying notion that imports are inherently bad for a country while exports are good and that tariff reductions (or domestic farm policy changes that would have similar effects) by a country benefit other countries most of all is an insidious and self-defeating concept.

Transferred to the idea of altering domestic agricultural policies in ways that would expand trade, the desire on the part of countries for intrasector reciprocity is simply a formula for not improving agricultural policies, even when over the short or long run it is clearly in the public interest to do so.

In the future, the United States (for example) should look at her price support level for milk and the associated quantitative restrictions on dairy product imports, or at her subsidy payments to cotton and wool growers, in terms of her own domestic interests as broadly conceived, and not in terms of what other countries are about to do in such matters. If it is in the public interest to rely more on butter imports than in the past because Americans demand a high price in order to produce enough to go around, we should not wait until Europe has gotten itself into a political position to lower its milk price guarantees or to announce a more favorable grain-meat price ratio to make such a move in respect to U.S. milk prices.

If we are to limit or terminate our export subsidies for wheat while preserving our competitive position in other ways, we should do it because, on balance, it is good policy and because it represents the way we want to spend public money in the years ahead. If other nations will take reciprocal action, so much the better, but we should not hold our breath.

By careful timing, we might use the occasion of such unilateral actions on agricultural policy by one country to encourage other countries to take what would appear to be reciprocal actions, but would be, in fact, actions they were going to take in the interest of their own consumers when the proper occasion arose.

Thus, what would appear to be agricultural negotiations would actually be a series of agricultural orchestrations. Individual countries may want to package domestic agricultural changes made for domestic reasons in the tinsel of an international negotiation. The real impetus for constructive trade-expanding moves on domestic agricultural policies in the 1970s and 1980s will usually be internal.

Various trading countries are in different positions with respect to the internal possibilities for improving agricultural policies in a way that would expand agricultural trade. Japan, despite her continued high level of protection on agricultural products, has for the past 10 years given the world an important example of limiting its agricultural policies in the interest of import expansion without apparent reciprocity on the part of other countries.

Japan embarked, many years ago, on a policy of increasing reliance on agricultural imports. This growing import demand arose partly from limited agricultural resources, and partly from basic changes in the pattern of food consumption associated with higher levels of income. These income patterns seem likely to continue. Japan, with some difficulty, could probably have held the importation of cereals over the past 10 years to lower levels and could have relied more heavily than she has upon food products produced at home. Instead, she went the route of greater reliance on imports. According to a paper by Mr. Michael Tracy, Japanese Agriculture at the Crossroads (Trade Policy Research Center, London), Japan is now becoming reconciled to a situation in which agricultural pursuits by most cultivators will be a subsidiary activity, with income from nonagricultural sources being most important to the farm family.

There is still much room for improvement in the structure of Japanese agriculture and in trade policy. Yet it is generally anticipated that, because of increased demand for livestock products in Japan, her imports of agricultural products will increase rather rapidly over the coming decades, almost without regard to what kind of agricultural policies Japan pursues, or what the rest of the developed countries do.

The EC will one day find itself in a position similar to Japan today. Demands for agricultural products will rise more rapidly than Europe's ability to produce at reasonable prices, even with a rapidly changing agriculture. This will coincide with a rise in urban political power. The time for this is still some distance away. Europe has the technological capacity to increase agricultural production materially in the 1970s, so long as incentives for production are kept high, like today. The potential market for agricultural products in Europe will tantalize but probably disappoint agricultural exporting nations in the 1970s and 1980s, as European governments and the Commission of the European Community find themselves unable to meet the political challenge required to turn increasingly to agricultural imports, while compensating for rapid agricultural change with the gains from food imports. If Treasury ministers were having a strong influence on agricultural expenditures, this might be different, but so far they are not.

The great problem that the rest of the world faces now with respect to Europe is to find the means of helping the EC avoid further increases in the level of agricultural protection as the Community expands in the 1970s. A great deal of momentum has been generated by eight years of increasing levels of protection under the CAP, and by the decisions taken in connection with enlargement of the EC. The political lessons of that period will not be lost on the more sophisticated and better financed farmers of the 1970s, including those in Britain, sharing in the CAP for the first time.

The U.S. role in furthering progress in agricultural trade in the decade ahead can take several forms. Like Europe, the United States is in some danger of falling back into old agricultural policy errors. Some farmers and their representatives still want "cost of production" (including a market return on the capitalized value of land) and "full parity prices." United States producers believe that world trading prices for grains are too low and want to find the means of raising them. Avoiding the error of a new and costly round of producer subsidies on export crops is one contribution the United States can make.

A second contribution is to take some small initiatives toward increased agricultural imports. Dairy products and beef are the best prospects, and a start is being made on both in 1973. But we shall move toward greater imports largely for our own reasons or not at all, and not because Europe will reform the CAP or lower the wheat price, or because Japan has reduced the duty on soybeans.

3

WHERE U.S. AGRICULTURAL
COMPARATIVE ADVANTAGE LIES
D. Gale Johnson

One of the outstanding intellectual discoveries of the classical economists was the principle of comparative advantage as a determinant of the commodities that would be traded among nations if there were no barriers to the trade. The principle is a very simple one; namely, the flow of trade will be determined by differences in comparative costs of the various commodities and services that can be transported. Only if the structure of comparative costs in all nations were identical would there be no trade; any difference in the relative cost structure of different nations would result in the export of commodities with relatively low comparative costs. The principle of comparative advantage also said something else of great importance; namely, differences in absolute costs of production or absolute advantage were of no significance in the determination of trade. Absolute advantage was not relevant for at least two reasons: First, it is not a meaningful concept since it cannot be measured if there is more than one input and, second, even if there were only one scarce input and its productivity differed uniformly from one country to another so that relative costs of various products were everywhere the same, there would be no trade.

The principle of comparative advantage serves as the primary determinant of exports and imports only when there are no departures from competition, both within each nation and in influencing the flow of trade among nations. When there are departures from competition in either situation, the flow of trade will not be what would be determined by the principle of comparative advantage, and some goods may not be imported that would be if comparative advantage were the only criterion at work. And what is often ignored, when goods that are being produced domestically at a comparative disadvantage are not imported or are imported in smaller volume, goods that are produced at a comparative advantage may not be exported at all or exported in a smaller volume.

While the concept of comparative advantage represented a great intellectual achievement, it has not won universal acclaim as an appropriate guide for international and domestic policies that influence trade, production and consumption of farm products, or, for that matter, many other products as well. If there were free trade in all goods and services, including agricultural products, there would be no need for a paper in which an attempt was made to measure comparative advantage in agricultural products. The actual flow of products in international trade would clearly indicate what sectors operated with a comparative advantage in a given region or country. Under free trade, some products might not be produced at all in a given region or country or might be produced in relatively small amounts, compared to consumption, because of what might be called natural protection due to costs of transportation, perishability, or specialized local preferences. But since there is now no free trade but some hope that trade might become freer, it is perhaps not a wholly fruitless enterprise to explore where comparative advantage and disadvantage might lie if circumstances were different.

BALANCES AND IMBALANCES IN WORLD DEMAND AND SUPPLY OF MAJOR FARM PRODUCTS: 1980

While not directly relevant to the estimation of comparative advantage, the prospective trends in the growth of output and consumption of various farm products have an effect upon the possibilities of reducing the barriers to trade in farm products. If the prospects are that with the continuation of present domestic and trade policies that output will increase more than consumption, the decisions of policy makers will almost certainly be affected. While one might expect—perhaps it would be more accurate to say one might hope—that if it were probable that current policies would result in more rapid growth of output than of consumption, as a result policies would be adjusted to bring supply and demand more into balance. Unfortunately, this is not the way things work out in all cases; the policy response may well be to increase restraints on trade in an attempt to avoid adjustment. This is all too often the response when it is possible for one nation or group of nations to impose many of the costs of adjustments upon others.

The Food and Agricultural Organization (FAO) has recently completed a set of worldwide projections of changes in demand, supply, and trade for the main groups of farm products. These projections—which should not be confused with predictions—are for changes over the decade of the 1970s and assume that current farm programs will remain unchanged during the period. As a consequence, it is assumed that relative prices of farm products would remain unchanged in each country. The U.S. Department of Agriculture (USDA) has also undertaken a somewhat similar exercise for a more limited group of commodities. The two sets of projections, however, are not directly comparable since in the USDA projections, supply is equated with demand in 1980, while an end result of the FAO projections is an excess or deficit of supply relative to demand. In the USDA projections, supply and demand were equated in a variety of ways, including adjustments in prices, output limitations, or by aggressive export promotion by the developed countries. Some limited comparisons are possible and are made below. However, the major emphasis is given to a summary of the FAO projections.

A useful summary of the FAO projections is provided in Table 3.1. The outcomes of the projections are shown in terms of projected export availabilities and import requirements summed for individual countries. Obviously, exports cannot exceed imports, or vice versa, for for the world. A discrepancy between the projected export availabilities and import requirements implies that adjustments must occur, either through changes in prices, subsidies, stock accumulation, or governmental restraints upon production or consumption. The projected differences, however, can be used as a rough indicator of the farm commodities that have either a favorable or unfavorable trade outlook if current national farm programs are continued.

On the whole, the projections paint a rather gloomy picture. If present policies are continued and if the other assumptions of the projections turn out to be reasonably close to actual developments, certain international markets for farm products will continue to exhibit considerable disarray with more supply than consumers are willing to purchase at current real prices. According to these projections, significant excess supplies would exist for the grains, fats and oils, oilcakes, tea, cotton, jute, and rubber. Excess demand is projected for beef and veal, mutton and lamb, wine, and, somewhat surprisingly, dairy products. For the grains the projected excess supply would be about 5 percent of projected world production; this might seem to be a small discrepancy, but it should be remembered that less than one-sixth of the world's grain supply moves in international trade.

A reference was made above to the surprising outcome of the projections for milk. Further analysis of the projected excess of import demand of 20 million tons of whole milk equivalent led the authors of the study to conclude that the more probable outcome during the 1970s was a small excess of supply over demand. In the projections as made, it was assumed that the European Economic Community (EEC) would not be enlarged; a special study of the effects of the enlargement indicated that net imports of the 10 countries might decline by 20

TABLE 3.1

Projected World Commodity Imbalances in 1980[a]

| | Export Availabilities | Import Requirements | Imbalances as Share of Trade[b] | |
| | | | Surplus | Deficit |
	(Million tons)		(percent)	
Wheat	55.6	31.1	56	
Coarse grains	95.2	54.0	55	
Rice	11.7	9.2	24	
Milk	23.3	43.3		60
Meat				
Beef and veal	3.8	5.0		26
Mutton and lamb	1.07	1.64		42
Pigmeat	1.56	1.62		4
Poultry meat	0.65	0.72		11
Fish				
Finfish	22.1	29.4		28
Shellfish	0.65	1.17		57
Fats and oils[c]	11.9	9.5	23	
Oilcakes	29.0	26.1	11	
Sugar	21.8	22.2		2
Citrus fruit				
Oranges and tangerines	7.1	6.7	6	
Lemons and limes	1.28	1.29		1
Others	1.08	0.82	27	
Tobacco	0.81	0.85		4
Wine (hectolitres)	34.3	46.4		30
Coffee	4.1	4.1		—
Cocoa	1.64	1.62	1	
Tea	0.88	0.75	15	
Bananas	8.59	7.61	12	
Cotton	3.9	3.3	16	
Wool	1.0	0.9	10	
Jute	2.8	1.8	43	
Hard fibres	0.56	0.56	—	
Rubber	4.1	3.5	16	
Forestry products[d]				
Sawnwood (cubic meters)	22.9	22.2	3	
Industrial roundwood				
(cubic meters)	72.8	65.9	10	
Pulp and paper				
Newsprint and paper	6.3	10.2		48
Pulp	9.4	7.8	19	
Panels (cubic meters)	6.9	6.6	4	

[a]Excluding Asian centrally planned economies.

[b]Imbalances expressed as a percentage of the average of export availabilities and import requirements.

[c]Excluding butter.

[d]The absolute quantities shown under forestry products are considerably smaller than actual gross trade would be because the aggregation based on 11 country groups excludes intragroup trade.

Source: FAO, Agricultural Commodity Projections, 1970-80 (Rome: FAO, 1971), Vol. I, p. 69.

million tons.[1] The other major revision in the projections related to the large projected increase in milk imports by the developing countries. In the original projections, imports by the developing countries were indicated to increase from 5 million tons in 1970 to 19 million tons in 1980 because of the high income elasticities of demand for milk products and the difficulties of expanding local production. However, it was concluded that because of foreign-exchange limitations, imports might actually increase by only a little more than 1 million tons.[2] A further modest revision was made since it was doubted that the United States would increase her imports to more than 1 million tons rather than to the 2 million tons projected on the basis of output and consumption.[3] The total of these adjustments turned a substantial import deficit into a small export surplus.

The USDA projections were made for only the following commodity groups: wheat, rice, coarse grains, oilcake, vegetable oils, cotton, bananas, coffee, tea, and cocoa. The primary purpose of the USDA projections was to analyze the world demand prospects for the agricultural exports of the developing countries, and the commodities selected were determined in terms of those of most concern to these countries.

Rather than attempt a direct comparison between the FAO and USDA projections, a brief summary of the implications of the entire set of USDA projections seems appropriate:[4]

1. Wheat—fair. This prospect is based on a continuation of concessional sales of wheat and increased use of wheat for feed to reduce the downward pressure on prices.
2. Rice—poor. Continued downward pressure on prices is expected.
3. Coarse grains—good. This is based on substantial expansion of imports by Japan and, if there are concessional terms, of feed grain imports by the developing countries. Lower internal grain prices in developed importing areas, particularly in the EEC, could give trade an additional boost. The maintenance of very high internal prices could lead to self-sufficiency in total grains in the EEC, thereby lowering prospects. The difference in the assumptions about grain prices in the EEC would affect trade in coarse grains by 10 million tons or by one-third or one-fourth of total projected imports.
4. Oilcake and oils—fair. Import demand for oilcake would be strong but poor for oil. The favorable demand situation for oilcake depends, in part, upon substitution for high-price grains.
5. Cotton—good. Developed area import demand for textiles will be strong but weak for lint. It is anticipated that developing countries will increase their share of world exports of both textiles and lint, but that cotton demand will grow more slowly than fiber demand generally.
6. Bananas—good.
7. Tropical beverages—fair.

Of the products produced in temperate zones, there is general agreement between the FAO and USDA projections for wheat, rice, cotton lint, and vegetable oil. There are apparent differences for coarse grains and oilcakes. The difference for oilcakes is relatively small—FAO projects an excess supply equal to about 4 percent of the 1980 production—and is due to a quite small difference in projected demand growth. The difference in the projections for coarse grains seems much more striking, but really is not. The USDA projects that world consumption would increase about 14 million tons more than did FAO for the period from 1964-66 to 1980; this is one-third of the FAO export excess of 41 million tons. In its optimism, the USDA projected that the EEC might import 10 million tons of feed grains in 1980, some 6 million tons more than the FAO projection. The remaining differences are due to larger FAO output projections for the developed market economies (10 million tons) and for the developing countries (10 million tons).

But both the FAO and USDA projections must now be modified because of the enlargement of the EEC. The Michigan State study of the effects on trade of enlarging the EEC projected a net import of all grains of less than 2 million tons by the enlarged EEC in 1980.[5] The FAO projections for the same group of countries indicated net grain imports of about 16 million tons.

Implications for Agricultural Adjustment in
Temperate Zone Agriculture

If present national agricultural programs are maintained during the 1970s, except for the changes required by the enlargement of the EEC, international trade in most temperate zone farm products will be even more circumscribed at the end of the decade than at the beginning. The only significant exceptions will be beef and veal, oilcakes, and wine. The demand for wine or wine substitutes may grow even more than projected by the FAO, since its consumption by policy makers in the major exporting countries would almost surely increase substantially because of the problems they would face if the trading world turns out as projected by either FAO or the USDA.

After adjustment for the enlargement of the EEC, the FAO projection indicates an export surplus of about 80 million tons of grain by 1980. Obviously, there cannot be an 80-million-ton surplus of grains accumulated each year, nor is there any possibility that more than a tiny fraction of that amount can be disposed of as food aid. The projected expansion of output underlying the projected export surplus simply cannot occur. With a continuation of present farm and trade policies, the adjustment burden would fall primarily upon North America, Australia, Argentina, Thailand, and South Africa simply because these countries would find no available export outlet for their grain.

32

Another possibility is that farm and trade policies would not remain unchanged in Western Europe and Japan. Given the present level
of per capita income in Japan and the anticipated growth of income over
the decade, a different Japanese food policy could result in a very substantial import level for grains and livestock products. Under free
trade, Japanese imports could reach a level by the end of the decade
that would absorb a very large fraction of the grain export surplus
projected by FAO, either as direct grain imports or indirectly through
imports of livestock products. If Western Europe were also to move
to free trade in agricultural products —and the major exporting nations
were to do so as well—most, if not all, of the projected grain export
surplus would disappear due to increased consumption and reduced
production resulting from lower prices.

Because of the recent large-scale purchases of grain by the
Soviet Union and somewhat increased purchases from Canada by China,
there may be a tendency to assume that adjustments in grain production
can be delayed if not avoided. Such an assumption is likely to be an
erroneous one. A large part of the Soviet grain imports for 1972-73
is a consequence of a disastrous grain crop caused by very adverse
climatic conditions. While it is true that the Soviet Union is having
difficulty in meeting demand for meat products and is likely to import
substantial quantities of feed grains and oilmeals for the next few years,
the quantities that are likely to be involved are small compared to the
potential surplus if present policies are continued. It is difficult to
imagine that the Soviet Union would import more than 10 million tons
of feedstuffs at an annual cost of $500 to $600 million indefinitely. Feed
requirements per unit of livestock output are very high in the Soviet
Union. It would be, in the author's opinion, rather shortsighted to base
long-term plans on resource adjustments on the assumption that the
Soviet Union will make little or no progress in improving feeding effectiveness over the decade. In addition, a significant part of the milk
output in the Soviet Union and Eastern Europe is now used very ineffi-
ciently. According to FAO estimates for 1970, about one-seventh of
all fluid milk is fed to livestock, and a quarter of the remaining skim
milk (or powder) is also fed to livestock. Improvements in the utilization of milk, which would require primarily adjustments in the marketing system and some modification in the seasonal distribution of
milk production, could result in the saving of 10 million tons of feed
units that could be fairly easily transferred to beef production.

GROWTH IN DOMESTIC MARKETS AND SUPPLY OF
U.S. FARM PRODUCTS

A recent projection made by David W. Culver of the USDA indicates that during the 1970s the increase in domestic and export demand,

given the assumptions made, would absorb an 18-percent increase in farm output.[6] While exports are projected to increase by about 30 to 35 percent, this growth is offset in considerable part by the growth of imports. Thus the projected increase in domestic demand is of the order of 17 percent.

The demand for crop products, including feed, was projected to increase by 20 percent. Livestock demand was projected to grow more slowly—about 16 percent. The largest increases in livestock demand were for poultry (nearly 50 percent) and beef cattle (about one-third). Pork demand was projected to increase at approximately the same rate as population (about 15 percent), while the decline in per capita consumption of dairy products would be equal to or slightly greater than the increase in population resulting in a stable or slightly declining aggregate demand. The demand projections included both domestic and foreign markets, but for livestock products the changes indicated are approximately equal to the changes in domestic demand.

Recent developments indicate that some of the assumptions under-lying the demand projections were somewhat optimistic. Population growth of about 15 percent now seems to high; it may be nearer 12 or 13 percent. The enlargement of the EEC means that the export pro-jection of 32 million metric tons of feed grains should be reduced one-third or more—perhaps by as much as one-half. Thus a projection of demand growth for U.S. agriculture during the 1970s, assuming a con-tinuation of current agricultural policies in the industrial countries and some reasonable output expansion in the developing countries, might now be put at not much more than 12 or 13 percent, and more than half of that is likely to come by the middle of the decade. The full impact of the enlargement of the EEC will not be felt until the last couple of years of the decade.

A positive factor in the international market for feed grains that has arisen since the USDA and FAO projections were completed is the projected importation of feed grains by the Soviet Union, a decision that was, in large part, independent of this year's weather. For a discussion of possible developments in trade with the Soviet Union, Eastern Europe, and China, the reader is referred to Chapter 6. At best, it would appear that grain imports by the Soviet Union might off-set the decline in imports due to the enlargement of the EEC. And this may only be true through the middle of the decade.

Output Expansion

There can be no doubt that U.S. agriculture can increase output by the 17 percent projected by the USDA and thus could easily meet the revised smaller-demand projection indicated above with a continuation of the current farm programs. In fact, if the lower-demand projection should turn out to be of the right order of magnitude, there would be great difficulty in restraining output growth to maintain a balance between supply and demand under current farm programs without an increase in costs.

The USDA projections of crop output, given the projected increases in crop yields, result in approximately the same area of cropland harvested in 1980 as in 1970—298 million acres (121 million hectares) in 1980 versus 294 million acres (120 million hectares) in 1970. In 1970 the total cropland used for crops, including summer fallow and crop failure, was 19 million acres below 1960 and 45 million acres below the post-World War II peak reached in 1951.

The USDA projections assumed a continuation of the current acreage diversion programs during the decade and, by implication, the amount of land diverted in 1980 would be very nearly the same as in 1970. Almost all of the projected increase in crop output is due to increased yields; the projected yield increases for the 1970s are somewhat below the actual increase in yields during the 1960s. In effect, these projections indicate that U.S. farm output can increase to meet projected demand increases without utilizing any significant fraction of the currently diverted land. Within the structure of the current farm programs, there is no doubt that a reduction in the diverted area would result in increased output.

How much diverted or set-aside area, as it is now called, would return to crop cultivation if there were no farm programs cannot be predicted at this time. It almost certainly would not be 60 million acres, since this would put land used for crops above the 1951 peak when real farm prices were substantially higher than they are today. It is, the author believes, unlikely that crop area would return to the 1951 peak since the decline in cropland used for crops in several states since 1951 has been substantially greater than the amount of diverted land in those states. The 20 states for which this condition holds had a harvested area of 76 million acres in 1951 and 54 million acres in 1970, while the diverted area in 1970 was only 13 million acres.* Thus the decline in harvested area in those states was 10

---

*There were six additional states in which the decline in harvested area between 1951 and 1969 exceeded the diverted area in 1969 that were not included in the group of states described in the text. These were states (North Dakota, South Dakota, Nebraska, Oklahoma, Wyoming, and Utah) in which summer fallow is important, and the unaccounted-for area may have been due to an increase in summer fallow.

million acres greater than the diverted acreage. It is most unlikely that the area withdrawn from crop use would come back into cultivation at current relative product prices and probable that some significant part of the diverted area would not be used for crops if the current programs were discontinued.

If I were to hazard a guess—and unfortunately it would be nothing more than that at this time—it would be that less than half of the diverted area could return to crop cultivation if the current programs were discontinued. Because of the substantial expansion in the demand for beef, some part of this area might become cultivated or permanent pasture as required for the expansion of beef herds.[7,8] If U.S. farm output could increase by 17 percent in the 1970s with the current farm programs and approximately the same harvested area, with some relaxation of the set aside and continuation of certain other aspects of the farm programs, both crop and livestock output could increase by more than 17 percent.

FACTORS INFLUENCING THE COMPARATIVE ADVANTAGE OF MAJOR U.S. FARM PRODUCTS

Because so many factors can influence the comparative advantage position of a particular product, it is very difficult to make projections concerning changes that may occur in comparative advantage. Comparative advantage is influenced not only by changes in relative costs or supply prices of the whole range of tradable goods, but also by changes in relative costs or supply prices in the "rest of the world." Thus a decline in the cost of feed grains relative to all other tradable goods in the United States would not assure a continuation of a current position of comparative advantage if in the rest of the world the decline in the costs of feed grains relative to all other tradable goods were substantially greater.

In addition, significant departures from competitive situations can mean that the actual flow of products in international trade is not a definitive indication of comparative advantage at a given moment of time. A country can export products for which it does not have a comparative advantage if it subsidizes those products, and similarly, it may import products for which it has a comparative advantage if such products are heavily subsidized by others and it imposes no countervailing import barriers. In the world as it exists, the former case seems much more common than the latter. The farm programs of the industrial countries have created circumstances in which trade flows depart substantially from those that would be determined by comparative advantage.

The Effects of Farm Programs

The current set of U.S. farm programs range from those that exhibit an amazing degree of complexity and ingenuity whose effects upon trade and comparative advantage are difficult to discern to those that are blatantly and decisively protectionistic. In the first group are the cotton, wheat, and feed grain programs, and in the second group, the sugar, peanut, rice, and dairy programs. For reasons to be indicated later, it is not apparent where the tobacco programs and the import restrictions on beef fall.

Two different measures of protection are commonly used. Nominal protection is a measure of the difference between internal or domestic prices and world (export or import) prices, while effective protection is a measure of the difference between value added based on domestic prices. Nominal protection, as defined, does not include direct income payments, though it could be so defined if such payments, were averaged over total output produced. For many purposes the concept of effective protection is the more relevant one, because this measure takes into account inputs purchased from the rest of the economy. Nominal protection may grossly underestimate the magnitude of the inducement to produce a particular product or service when a large fraction of total inputs is acquired from other sectors of the economy or by importation.

Table 3.2 presents a summary of measures of nominal and effective protection for U.S. farm products in 1968 based on the work of Larry J. Wipf. With the exception of sugar, the range in nominal protection is relatively small—from 0.3 percent for cotton to 20.1 percent for tree nuts. However, the range in effective protection is enormous—from a negative effective protection of 19.6 percent for poultry and eggs to a positive rate of 590 percent for sugar. Soybeans and four grain crops (barley, oats, buckwheat, and rye) also had negative rates of protection. (Negative rates of effective protection arise because inputs purchased from the rest of the economy have a higher nominal rate of protection than the product produced.)

Unfortunately, measurement of effective protection does not give us a clear indication of the production, consumption, and trade effects of the major U.S. farm programs. It is true that a great deal of money is transferred from the treasury to the farmers. But because the farmers who participate in the programs are not free to produce as they see fit and may or may not increase their output because of the transfer payments, it is unclear what the effects on output, and thus upon trade, are. Of the three programs, only the wheat program has any effect upon consumption—because of the tax on wheat used for food—but the quantitative consumption effect is small.

There are two recent studies of cotton programs that indicate that these programs have had only a relatively small effect on cotton

TABLE 3.2

Nominal and Effective Rates of Protection for
U.S. Agriculture, 1968
(percent)

Sector or Product	Nominal	Effective
Meat animals	7.5	13.8
Poultry and eggs	0.8	-19.6
Farm dairy products	16.8	48.2
Other livestock products	2.5	3.3
Food grains	8.4	143.5
Wheat	8.6	153.0
Rice	7.3	13.7
Rye	0.0	-16.5
Buckwheat	1.4	-4.3
Feed crops	0.4	8.1
Corn	0.0	20.0
Oats	0.0	-15.8
Barley	0.0	-13.2
Sorghums	0.0	23.5
Cotton	0.3	100.8
Tobacco	17.0	28.2
Oil-bearing crops	11.3	16.4
Soybeans	0.0	-6.7
Peanuts	69.3	204.0
Flaxseed	14.8	26.2
Vegetables	12.4	17.9
Fruits	8.4	9.1
Tree nuts	20.1	25.5
Sugar	195.8	662.2
Livestock and products	8.5	18.9
Other farm products	7.6	32.3

Source: Larry J. Wipf, "Tariffs, Nontariff Distortions, and Effective Protection of U.S. Agriculture," American Journal of Agricultural Economics 53, no. 3 (August 1971): 427-428.

output in recent years. One study—based on a statistical analysis of recent acreages, yields, prices, and the major features of the program—indicates that for recent years cotton output has been determined primarily by expected market prices and not by the other features of the program.[9] A second study, based on programming analysis, indicates that the elasticity of cotton supply is very elastic at the average market price levels of the past few years. With the removal of the cotton program and with no price support or payments, cotton production was projected to decline by about 13 percent compared to the level of production if the 1969 farm programs had continued.[10] The assumed market price was 22 cents per pound. This study also assumed that the wheat and feed grain programs were continued; if these programs were also discontinued, it is probable that there would be a small positive effect on cotton production in those cotton-producing areas where land values are significantly affected by payments under the wheat and feed grain programs. Experience with the cotton program provided under the 1970 Act, under which farmers can grow any desired amount of cotton and allotments can be rather freely leased or sold, in general supports these analyses. Cotton acreage harvested in 1971, when price expectations should have been approximately the same as in 1970, indicated that under the somewhat less restrictive 1971 program, the cotton area harvested increased by only 3 percent. While farmers had to plant 90 percent of their domestic base allotment in order to receive payments in current and future years, the provision for the sale and lease of allotments probably meant that this provision had little effect on output. But it probably had some effect and cotton output would be expected to fall if there were no cotton program, but the decline could well be within the range of 5 to 10 percent.

Thus the effective protection rate of 100 percent exaggerates the output effect of the program. If that rate of effective protection were achieved by a price paid to farmers approximately 60 percent above the price received in 1970, one study indicates that acreage planted to cotton would increase by 75 percent, and the other study indicates an increase in acreage of 35 percent and in yield of 15 percent over the planted area and yields of 1969 or 1970.[11]

Mayer, Heady, and Madsen have projected the output response if all farm programs were eliminated. On the assumption that all long-term adjustments would have been completed by 1970, they found that the combined output of wheat and feed grains would have increased by 9 percent compared to the average output for 1966 and 1967.[12] Measured by acreage diverted, the 1966 program was a relatively tight one, and the 1967 program was relatively freer; the average of the diverted area for the two years was 52 million acres. The average diverted area for 1965-70 was 53.7 million acres. According to their projections, the increase in wheat production would have been substantially greater than the increase in feed grain production even though the effective protection of wheat is much greater than for the feed grains.

It is clear that either measure of protection is relevant as an indicator of the effects of protection upon trade only when the protection is reflected through market prices. Even then, in order to estimate trade effects, we need to know the effects of the higher prices upon production and consumption. These effects depend, in turn, upon the elasticities of supply and demand. A given degree of protection will be much more disruptive of trade when one or the other or both of the elasticities of supply and demand are high than when these elasticities are low.

Impact of Impediments to Trade on World Market Prices of Farm Products

To the author's knowledge, there has not been a published systematic study of how recent world market prices for farm products would differ from those that would prevail under free trade among, say, the members of the Organization for Economic Cooperation and Development (OECD). The author can only report some speculations that are put down in another place.[13]

Of the major temperate zone farm products that move in international trade—wheat, feed grains, oilseeds, meat, and dairy products—only the last two seem to the author to be significant candidates for substantial price changes as a result of free trade. And of the meats, this would probably be true only of beef. While the current relatively low volume of trade in poultry and pork is, to some degree, due to trade restrictions, especially for the former, the elasticities of supply of these two products are so high that free trade would have little effect on export and import prices. But this is not true of beef, and it could be anticipated that the export or import prices of beef would increase significantly under free trade—certainly by one-fourth and perhaps by more.

Dairy products represent the most extreme case with prices of butter and dry skim milk having been significantly depressed by the policies of all exporters, except New Zealand, and by all actual or potential importers, except the United Kingdom (UK). Only a tiny fraction of all dairy production moves in international trade—about 6 percent. Even a very small increase in milk consumption, combined with a small reduction in production in North America and Western Europe, would put great pressure upon the supply potentials of the low-cost producers—New Zealand, Australia, Ireland, and Denmark. Recent experience in the UK market for butter indicates how little supply or demand must change to bring about a substantial increase in price. Under free trade it is most unlikely that international prices for butter would increase by less than 50 percent from the average levels of 1968-70 or perhaps to $1.30-$1.40 per kilogram. Cheese prices would increase by much less, but dry skim milk prices are probably as badly distorted as butter prices and would increase by about as much as butter.

International beef and veal prices have been depressed by one or both of two policies followed in North America, Japan, and Western Europe—subsidies to dairy production and high feed costs. The first unduly expands beef production, and the second restricts consumer demand. Neither policy is of any particular advantage to beef producers and have, in fact, prevented the creation of fed beef operations in many countries. Because of the broad spectrum of beef qualities, it is difficult to know how much international beef prices have been depressed, but it is quite clear that Australian beef has been available at not much more than half the price of comparable quality beef in Western Europe. Beef prices would be higher than they have been in international markets and perhaps substantially higher under free trade or more liberal trade.

Recent wheat prices are probably not far from what would prevail under free trade. Food consumption is not very responsive to prices in the industrial countries, and some exporters have been willing to restrict output and/or to hold stocks to maintain and stabilize the price of wheat to offset the output effects of high prices elsewhere. In the future it is probable that most wheat, excepting only limited quantities of high quality, will sell at feed grain prices. Since it is highly probable that free trade would result in somewhat higher international prices of feed grains than have prevailed in recent years, the price of wheat would remain about what it has been. Feed grain prices would have a tendency to increase because of higher demand for livestock feeding if there were free trade in grains. Because of the fairly high elasticity of supply of feed grains, the price increase might be of the order of 10 percent.

The oilmeals and oilseeds would gain from increased livestock feeding, but would lose the special advantage that has resulted from free entry into the European Community (EC) and relatively low duties into another countries that have high grain prices. Oilmeals at free trade prices have been substituted in substantial amounts for high priced grains. Thus it is a reasonable presumption that soybean prices have been little affected by existing trade barriers.

There are two important products that are produced in both temperate and tropical zones—sugar and cotton. There are few trade barriers adversely affecting cotton, and international prices would be hardly affected by free trade. Sugar is a different story; a very large fraction of the world's output of sugar is highly subsidized.

With free trade, sugar output would decline drastically in Western Europe and North America, and world sugar prices would increase. The amount of the increase would depend upon the elasticity of supply in the low-cost-producing areas, and increase of 25 percent over the level of the late 1960s would be reasonable to expect.

It is not the author's purpose here to argue about the responsibility for the distortions that exist in the international prices for farm products. The author's main point is that, except for dairy products, sugar, and beef, the recent international prices are not far from what it is reasonable to assume they would be under free or more liberal trade. Thus except for beef, sugar, and dairy products, if a country now has a comparative advantage or disadvantage at recent international price levels, it is likely to retain that same position under free trade if the basic demand and supply conditions were to change at their recent trend rates.

Cost and Resource Trends in U.S. Agriculture

During the 1950s total inputs used in agriculture declined by about 3 percent; during the 1960s total inputs increased so that by the end of the decade, inputs were at approximately the same level as two decades earlier. During the 1960s nonpurchased inputs declined by 12 percent, while purchased inputs increased almost a quarter. The long-term decline in farm labor continued, with one-third less labor being used at the end of the decade compared to the beginning. Farm real estate remained unchanged. Fertilizer and liming materials more than doubled, while the nonfarm component of feed seed and livestock increased by more than a quarter.

In terms of cost trends, the largest increases were for hired labor (72 percent during the 1960s) and the price of farm real estate (67 percent during the 1960s), though rents may have lagged slightly behind the increase in land prices. The prices of inputs of nonfarm origin increased about 40 percent during the decade, and, as might be expected, there was substitution of nonfarm inputs for both farm labor and land.

If recent trends in the hired farm wage rate and the value of farm real estate continue, the farm products that economize most in these two inputs probably will improve their comparative advantage position. The price of farm real estate, however, is primarily determined by its net return, while the wage rate is much more strongly influenced by supply conditions—the opportunities for nonfarm employment. Thus, while the trend in wage rates is likely to continue, the trend in land prices will be more strongly influenced by the general level of farm product prices and government subsidies. Prior to 1950 the long-run trend had been for a significantly more rapid rate of increase of farm wages than of land values. The rather similar increases in the two series started in 1950.

Comparative Advantage Position of
Major U.S. Farm Products

As noted earlier, the existence of a substantial degree of protection does not prove that a particular product is being produced at a comparative disadvantage. The appropriate criterion for the determination of comparative advantage when subsidies are paid and output may be influenced by such measures as acreage allotments or set-aside requirements is the direction of change in output level if the various forms of protection were removed and farmers were free to determine the level of output at whatever prices would prevail in the marketplace. Even this is not a complete criterion since the market prices may be distorted by trade restrictions and subsidies.

If the author's speculations about the relationships between recent prices of farm products and those that might prevail under a free or more liberal trade regime have some validity, the distortions in international prices would have a possible effect on comparative advantage only for beef and dairy products. Thus, except for these products, the discussion will be on the basis of current or recent price relationships in international markets.

Feed Grains (Corn, Grain Sorghums, Barley, and Oats)

Corn and grain sorghums account for over 90 percent of total feed grain output in the United States. The comparative advantage position in feed grains is thus determined by corn, primarily, and grain sorghums to a lesser but still important degree.

For the years 1964 through 1970, no more than 45 percent of the planted feed grain area was on farms that participated in the feed grain program. Thus well over half of the feed grain area was planted in response to market prices which, throughout this period, were export prices. (The only export subsidies paid on feed grains during this period were minor amounts—see Table 3.4.) In five out of the seven years, the participating farms diverted a land area approximately equal to the planted area of the feed grains included in the program. The farmers who did not participate in the feed grain program are not a random sample of all feed grain farmers since they opted not to change their farming plans in order to receive payments. In 1969, for example, the feed grain farmer who decided to participate in the program diverted approximately the same amount of land as he planted to feed grains; the payment received for participation (the sum of price support and diversion payments) came to $42 an acre ($104 per hectare). Thus the farmers who did not participate rejected a payment per unit of land that was large fraction (about 40 percent) of the gross value of the anticipated output of the diverted land. Thus we know that over half of feed grain output was produced in response to export prices. In 1971 the fraction of the national corn and grain sorghum area on participating farms increased to 75 percent, but the provisions for participation were significantly less stringent than in 1970 and earlier years. In the previous years, participating farmers could not plant more than 80 percent of their base allotment (with minor exceptions), but in 1971 a participant could plant any area that he desired after he set aside 20 percent of his feed grain base and met his conserving base.

As noted earlier, Meyer, Heady, and Madsen projected that if there were no farm programs, the production of feed grains would increase even though prices declined somewhat. This projection is consistent with the feed grains having a comparative advantage in the absence of program and payments.

Table 3.3 includes data on estimated variable costs per ton of output, farm prices per ton, output per harvested acre, and recent trends in output of the particular crop. These data permit some inferences about the comparative advantage position of feed grains. It is generally, perhaps even universally, accepted that soybeans have a comparative advantage in the United States. The ratio of price per ton to variable costs per ton is higher for soybeans than for corn (2.9 versus 2.2); however, the soybean yield is much lower than the corn yield (0.7 versus 2.0 tons per acre) so that the return over variable costs per acre of land is higher for corn ($56) than for soybean ($44). While these comparisons do not permit one to say definitely that at the margin the profitability of producing corn and soybeans (at 1968-70 prices) are approximately the same, the comparisons are not inconsistent with such a conclusion.[14]

The sharp increase in production of grain sorghums following the development of hybrid sorghums and the doubling of yields, the sensitivity of the area planted to sorghums to changes in the feed grain program, and the relatively high return over variable costs per acre are indications that the production of this product has a comparative advantage. The market price has reflected export prices except for an occasional aberration when some small export subsidies were paid. As indicated in Table 3.2, the effective protection rates for barley and oats were negative in 1968; neither was included in the feed grain program in that year nor in 1967. While oats probably retains its diminishing role in crop rotations because of its complementarity to the

TABLE 3.3

Variable Costs Per Unit of Output, Farm Prices, and Recent Output Trends (United States)

	Variable Costs (1)	Prices Received 1968-70 (2)	(2)/(1) (3)	Yield Per Acre (4)	Recent Output Trend (5)
Corn (ton)	$ 21.60	$ 47.00	2.2	2.00	+
Grain Sorghums (ton)	19.70	41.00	2.1	1.35	S +
Barley (ton)	21.00	41.00	1.95	0.92	S
Oats (ton)	23.00	41.50	1.8	0.76	S -
Soybeans (ton)	32.50	93.00	2.9	0.72	+
Cotton (bale)	75.00	110.00	1.5	1.00	S -
Peanuts (ton)	110.00	295.00	2.7	0.81	+
Tobacco (ton)	837.50	1573.00	1.9	0.90	S
Wheat (ton)	22.80	49.00	2.1	0.76	+
Rice (ton)	49.00	111.00	2.3	2.0	+

Sources: Variable costs estimated by author from Selected U.S. Crop Budgets: Yields, Inputs, and Variable Costs, Economic Research Service, U.S. Department of Agriculture, ERS 457-461. Price, yield, and acreage data from USDA, Agricultural Statistics, 1971.

45

legumes, the ratio of returns over variable costs is not much below that for corn or grain sorghums. Barley acreage has been rather stable in recent years, and its inclusion or exclusion in the feed grain program appears to have little effect on the area planted. Thus it is likely that both barley and oats have a comparative advantage, though not as strong as for either corn or grain sorghums.

Soybeans

There seems little point in belaboring the existence of the current comparative advantage of soybeans. Unless there is more success in increasing yields over the next decade than there has been during the past decade, the price of soybeans will have to increase further to maintain its current position of comparative advantage. From the late 1950s to the late 1960s, the soybean yield increased by only 10 percent compared to 61 percent for the feed grains. Obviously, there were costs involved in increasing feed grain yields, but over the decade the price of feed grains remained stable while output was increasing and the price of soybeans increased by almost one-third. Soybean production increased substantially more than the production of feed grains—nearly doubling compared to a 20-percent increase in feed grain production.

Wheat

As indicated in Table 3.2, the effective protection rate for wheat is very high. In addition, the United States has continued to pay export subsidies most of the time (see Table 3.4) since 1965, though the average rate has been fairly low as these things go. Whether wheat has retained the comparative advantage that it had two decades and more ago turns on whether the continued existence of the wheat program and either fairly high prices or, more recently, substantial payments (see Table 3.4) have induced areas to continue to produce wheat that would not do so in the absence of the program.

The Iowa State study referred to earlier comes to the conclusion that wheat production would increase significantly—in fact, more than feed grain production—if the wheat program and other farm programs were eliminated. This result is consistent with the data on variable costs of producing wheat relative to the recent farm price of wheat given in Table 3.3. The ratio of price to variable cost is the same as for grain sorghums and corn. While the ratio of price to variable costs is substantially lower for wheat than for soybeans, the yield per acre is the same, and wheat is grown on land that has much lower yield potential in alternative crops than is the case for the land devoted to soybeans. When the acreage restraints under the wheat program

46

TABLE 3.4

Feed Grains, Wheat, and Cotton: Prices, Government Payments, and
Export Subsidies Received by Farmers, 1965-71 (United States)

Crop Year	Feed Grains (per ton)			Wheat (per ton)			Cotton (per bale)		
	Price[a]	Government Payments	Export Subsidy	Price	Government Payments	Export Subsidy	Price	Government Payments	Export Subsidy
1965	$45.66	$ 9.70	$1.46	$49.61	$14.66	$17.25	$140.70	$ 4.68	$28.75
1966	48.81	9.05	0.38	59.90	19.02	8.44	104.20	80.73	0.87
1967	40.55	5.42	—[b]	51.08	17.66	2.90	127.50	124.97	—[b]
1968	42.52	8.92	—	45.57	17.41	—[b]	110.75	71.87	—
1969	45.28	10.37	0.83	45.20	21.61	5.50	105.45	82.67	—
1970	52.36	10.45	0.55	48.14	23.35	8.00	112.50	90.36	—
1971	43.50	5.66	—	49.00	19.69	5.13	—	77.94	—

[a]Price for corn only.
[b]— = no subsidy.

are relaxed, the area sown to wheat has increased. It should be noted that when the terms of the wheat program are relaxed, there is also an expectation that wheat prices will be favorable. If it cannot be said that increased plantings of wheat with relaxed program terms implies that farmers would produce more wheat at recent price levels, it can be concluded that farmers will produce more wheat at somewhat higher expected prices.

Thus I would conclude that wheat has retained its comparative advantage in the United States and that substantial quantities of wheat in excess of food, feed, and other domestic uses would be produced if wheat prices were competitive with feed grain prices. During 1968-70 wheat prices were similar to or lower than feed grain prices in many wheat-producing states.

Cotton

Whether or not the United States has a comparative advantage in cotton is apparently quite sensitive to the world price of cotton. If the world price is such as to reflect a U.S. farm price of 20 to 21 cents per pound, the United States would probably export some cotton if there were no cotton program or subsidies. If the U.S. farm price is 18 or 19 cents, domestic production would perhaps equal domestic use; at a farm price much below 18 cents, the United States would probably be a net importer. This is perhaps being more precise than is warranted, but it does appear that the elasticity of cotton supply with respect to price is very high in the neighborhood of recent farm prices (about 22 cents per pound until 1971-72).

A number of major changes have occurred in cotton production in recent years. The mechanization of the cotton harvest has been completed. For this and other reasons, labor requirements per bale of cotton declined by two-thirds from the late 1950s to the late 1960s. The strong uptrend in cotton yields that was evident through the mid-1960s was halted and perhaps turned around when the farm price of cotton was permitted to fall to the export price level in 1966. Other factors besides price may have had some influence, especially increased problems of controlling insects and adverse weather. But the change in the relative output and input prices resulting from the change in price policy appears to have been in part responsible at least for the stabilization of the yield trend.

Tobacco

The tobacco program, involving allotments, marketing quotas, and price supports, has been in continuous operation for almost a quarter of a century. Until 1966, when an export subsidy of 5 cents

48

per pound was instituted, the federal government suffered nominal losses from the tobacco program, and since 1966 the only important loss has been the cost of the export subsidy program. This cost has been about $30 million annually. For the two principal types of tobacco, production is now limited by either acreage-poundage quotas or pound-age quotas. The capitalized value of an acre of tobacco allotment (or its equivalent in terms of pounds) has been variously estimated, and estimates of $2000 to $3000 have been common. The excess of price over variable costs per ton given in Table 3.3 is consistent with values in the range indicated.

The elimination of the export subsidy would reduce the capitalized value of the allotment by about one-third. There is little doubt that the United States could export substantial quantities of tobacco on an un-subsidized basis and that if the tobacco program were eliminated, production would increase quite substantially if world prices did not decline by more than 15 percent as a result of the increased output in the United States.

Sugar

It is not necessary to emphasize the obvious—the absence of comparative advantage for sugar production in the United States. Even with returns to U.S. farmers that are nearly double what international prices probably would be if we imported all or most of our sugar, we produce only a little more than half of our total sugar utilization. The author has found no trends in costs or output that would indicate that the comparative advantage position of the United States is likely to change significantly in the years ahead.

Beef and Dairy Products

It is not possible to consider our comparative advantage position with respect to beef without considering governmental policies, both our own and others, for the protection of dairy products. Nor is the U.S. import and export position on beef independent of the beef price and trade policies of other countries, especially Western Europe and Japan. It is possible that if there were only moderate protection for both dairy products and beef in the industrial countries, the United States would have nil net imports of beef on a value basis. The current international market for beef is a seriously distorted one, and U.S. imports of beef are due largely to the closing of other markets for beef by trade restrictions and the encouragement of beef production resulting from subsidies to dairy production so common among the industrial countries. A major consequence of the domestic farm price policies followed in Western Europe and Japan is a significant reduc-tion of beef consumption.

In Western Europe beef production is primarily a by-product of the dairy sector. In the UK perhaps one-third of the beef is produced outside the dairy industry; in the rest of Western Europe, the fraction is much lower. Thus when domestic and trade policies increase dairy production, these policies simultaneously increase beef production. The same relationship holds in the United States, but the dairy industry is now a relatively unimportant source of our total beef supply.

The author has estimated that a 10-percent reduction of milk production in Western Europe would reduce beef production by 500,000 tons.[15] If the United States produced milk only for fluid purposes plus a 50-percent excess to maintain adequate fluid supplies throughout the year, our production of beef would decline by 500,000 tons. If there were free trade in beef and grains in the EEC, it is probable that EEC prices of beef would decline by one-third. The increase in beef consumption, assuming a price elasticity of demand of -0.6, would be 1.0 million tons. If Japanese consumption of beef had increased at the same rate as their consumption of pork since 1955 (beef consumption in Japan remained approximately constant at 1.1 to 1.2 kilograms per capital between 1955 and 1967), Japanese imports of beef would now exceed 500,000 tons. The total of these projected decreases in production and increases in consumption is 2.5 million tons. This is double the total beef and veal production of Australia and New Zealand and equal to Argentine production in recent years.

If the projected situation were to materialize, prices of beef in international markets would rise significantly. While U.S. imports of lower-quality beef would probably continue and might well increase due to the continued decline in domestic cow beef, it is likely that a substantial export market for fed beef would develop in Western Europe and perhaps also in Japan. Thus on a value basis, we might not be a net importer of beef with free trade or moderate trade restraints on beef, dairy products, and grains.

Any significant move toward determining international trade in beef on the basis of comparative advantage depends upon achieving a greater degree of economic rationality in the domestic and trade programs affecting dairy products in the high-income countries. With the exception of New Zealand, all of the high-income countries of the world interfere with the market prices of dairy products, and even New Zealand is not above a little tinkering in the name of price stabilization. However, New Zealand is the only country with producer returns under $6 per 100 kilograms; three other countries have dairy product prices in the range of $6 to $8 per 100 kilograms—Denmark, Ireland, and Australia. In the general range of $8 to $10, one finds the UK, Austria, France, Belgium, Canada, and the Netherlands; between $10 to $12 are Germany, Italy, Switzerland, and the United States. The data are for 1970; since then the United States has moved to a price in excess of

50

$13. In 1970 both Norway and Japan had producer prices in excess of $12.

Of the total OECD plus Oceania milk production of 200 million tons, only a little more than 10 percent is produced without significant protection. High prices have restricted consumption and increased production in most of the high-income countries. When this happens, it is not surprising that international markets are flooded with highly subsidized exports, and the international prices are largely without meaningful economic implications.

At the present time, the international dairy situation is a chaotic one. The low-cost producers are excluded from markets by all manner of restrictions and must, in turn, face highly subsidized exports. The high-cost producers complain that they must restrict imports and engage in export dumping because almost every other country does so. So long as these attitudes are held, there appears to be little prospect for any improvement in either domestic or international policies.

The sad aspect of the entire international dairy situation is that the magnitude of the quantitative disequilibrium is relatively small. If consumers in the OECD countries had the opportunity of purchasing milk products at international prices, it is likely that present producer prices would be viable in the sense that total output and consumption would be in approximate balance, and the amount of subsidized exports would be greatly reduced, if not eliminated. Furthermore, international prices would rise significantly, and the treasury costs of such a program would be substantially less than is implied by the current differences between producer and world prices in the high-income countries. The substantial increases in butter and cheese prices in 1971 due to lower production in New Zealand indicate how significant even a modest increase in consumption would be in increasing international prices.

Under more liberal trade in beef, the United States would continue to have a comparative disadvantage in certain grades of beef, but might well have a comparative advantage in grain-fed beef and perhaps even a net export of all beef in value terms. Since the U.S. prices of dairy products for manufacturing purposes are now equal to or greater than the average prices received by farmers for all milk in the EEC, it is not possible for international dairy prices to increase to a level that would prevent imports into the United States in the absence of import quotas. Thus the United States now has, and is likely to continue to have, a comparative disadvantage in the production of manufactured dairy products. However, the extent of the disadvantage is much smaller than is implied by current differences between domestic and international prices.

Pork

World pork production is about 90 percent of world beef production and about 35 percent of world meat production. Yet there has been much less international trade in pork than in beef. The reason for the limited trade in pork does not appear to be particularly restrictive trade measures, but is apparently mainly a function of the enormous degree of adaptability of swine to varying conditions and the relative ease with which the resources required for pork production can be brought together almost anywhere in the world. Another consideration is that most people may develop tastes or preferences for locally produced fresh pork and, except for certain specialized items such as ham, are not willing to consume imported pork except at a significant price discount.

The United States is a small net importer of pork, with net imports amounting to about 3 percent of total consumption. Over a half of the imports consists of canned hams. Trade restrictions are small, consisting of import duties that average 3.5 percent.

There is no apparent reason why the U.S. trade position in pork should change in the next few years. A reduction in pork prices in the regions of the world with high grain prices would undoubtedly see an expansion of pork production in those regions. There appears to be very little effective protection of pork production in the EEC, for example.

Poultry

The United States is a small net exporter of poultry meat. Recent levels of exports are about half the peak level reached in 1962. The decline in exports was not the result of a loss in comparative advantage for the United States, but an increase in trade barriers in an important market.

Rice

Based on the size of the export subsidy paid on U.S. rice for the past seven years (1965 through 1971), abolishing the export subsidy would result in a decline in the farm price of rice by about $1.00 per hundredweight or about 20 percent of recent prices. A series of studies carried out by several agricultural experiment stations and the USDA provides results that indicate that if acreage allotments were eliminated, rice production would increase substantially even if the farm price of rice declined by one-third.[16] The projected increase in rice production was approximately 80 percent. At a minimum, it would appear that with reductions in the farm price of rice in the general range of 20 to 25 percent, output would at least not decline if the rice program were discontinued. In recent years rice exports have accounted for approximately half of total disappearance. Thus it appears highly probable that the United States has some comparative advantage in the production of rice.

Peanuts

The peanut program results in farm prices that are nearly double the world price. As indicated in Table 3.3, prices received for peanuts have been 2.7 times the variable costs, and the excess of returns over variable costs has been about $150 per acre. In recent years approximately one-third of the peanut crop has either been crushed for oil and meal or exported. It is highly probable that the United States does not have a comparative advantage in the production of peanuts. A 50-percent reduction in farm price would reduce the return over variable costs to less than $40 per ton of peanuts and about $30 per acre. Competing crops would provide more favorable returns in most peanut-producing areas.

Sheep and Wool

Even though wool was heavily protected during the 1960s, wool production declined by 40 percent during the decade. The decline in sheep numbers and the production of lamb and mutton were approximately the same. In 1971 the incentive price for wool was 72 cents per pound; the price received by farmers was 19.4 cents so that the deficiency payment of 52 cents was more than double the price received. Wool prices have strengthened and are now at or near 30-year highs in international markets; even so, the deficiency payment in 1972 may be two-thirds the farm price. While lamb and mutton are not heavily protected, the protection of meat and wool together is very high. It is clear that sheep and wool are produced with a strong comparative disadvantage.

COST OF U.S. FARM PROGRAMS, 1970-71

In addition to strict considerations of comparative advantage, it is also useful to contemplate the costs of U.S. farm programs to consumers and taxpayers.[17] At the risk of diverging slightly from the main thrust of this chapter, the author has made an estimate of the cost of U.S. farm programs for the 1970-71 production year (Table

3.5).* Before presenting the estimate, the author wishes to note some of the crucial assumptions on which it is based.

Farm programs are defined both more broadly and more narrowly than is usually the case. The author has not included the costs of the food programs—food stamps, school milk and lunches, and direct distribution on the assumption that the primary beneficiaries are consumer and not farmers. The cost of these programs was $2.8 billion in 1970-71. The author has included the net cost of the PL 480 program (Food for Peace) on the assumption that the primary beneficiaries within the United States are farmers.

All form of interferences with international trade in farm products have been considered to be a part of farm programs. If a tariff or an import quota has increased the domestic price of a product, this effect has been included in the cost of farm programs. A very critical assumption has been made; namely, if the interference with international trade were removed, the international market price for the product would not change. This means that the estimate of consumer costs is too high. This is particularly important for those products where trade barriers significantly increase the domestic price and substantially restrict the volume of imports. The two most important instances where consumer costs have been overestimated are sugar and manufactured milk. In most other cases, the effect of the assumption about international prices should be minimal.

Table 3.5 is designed to indicate three types of consumer costs—those associated with higher domestic prices for domestic production consumed or used in the United States, the higher costs of imported products due to restrictions on imports, and the cost of wheat-marketing certificates. The first type of cost is indicated for individual farm products in Section A of the table and the other in Section B. The cost of wheat-marketing certificates is indicated in Section C. Wheat-marketing certificates were required—at $0.75 per bushel—on all wheat used for food.

Section D indicates that the total of excess consumer costs was $4.83 billion, though as indicated above this is an overestimate since in the absence of U.S. farm programs, the international prices of sugar and manufactured milk products would have been higher than they were in 1970-71.

Section E provides estimates of governmental costs of the farm programs, excluding PL 480 indicated separately in Section H. These costs include payments to farmers under the various farm programs

---

*The author wants to express his appreciation to Roger Hitchner, who collected the data and made most of the calculations. The responsibility for the assumptions made is the author's.

TABLE 3.5

Cost to Consumers and Taxpayers of U.S. Farm Programs, 1970-71

Commodity	Domestic Food and Industrial Use (thousand metric tons)	Domestic Price	Import or Export Price ($ per metric ton)	Farm Price	Value of Domestic Use — Import or Export Price ($ millions)
(1)	(2)	(3)	(4)	(5)	(6)
A. Consumer Costs: Domestic Food and Industrial Use of U.S. Farm Production					
Wheat	14,117	49.97	42.64	705	602
Barley	2,613	44.04	37.84	115	99
Corn	9,627	52.36	52.36	504	504
Oats	668	43.12	43.12	29	29
Rice	1,054	112.00	89.50	118	94
Peanuts	718	282.10	147.67	203	106
Tobacco	599	1,604.50	1,494.30	930	866
Sugar (raw)	5,655	182.71	91.35	1,033	515
Cotton (ginned)	1,756	481.80	481.80	846	846
Potatoes	13,193	48.48	48.48	640	640
Vegetable oils (except corn)	3,500	287.95	287.95	1,008	1,008
Beef and veal (l.w.)	18,182	630.00	572.73	11,455	10,414
Pork (l.w.)	9,853	453.84	440.62	4,486	4,355
Poultry (ready to cook)	4,625	449.45	449.45	2,079	2,079
Eggs	3,459	577.94	577.94	1,990	1,990
Sheep (l.w.)	484	517.47	467.70	250	227
Wool (clean basis)	39	1,121.80	908.94	44	36
Milk, mfg.	27,311	105.80	70.31	2,890	1,921
Milk, fluid	23,593	151.13	115.64	3,566	2,728
Total values (A)	—	—	—	(32,891)	(29,059)
B. Additional Costs of Imports					
Beef and veal (prod. net)	587	1,246.20	1,047.00	731	614
Pork (prod. net)	161	1,733.42	1,675.00	278	269
Wool (clean basis)	37	1,420.56	1,060.12	52	39
Tobacco	105	1,614.30	1,323.20	170	140
Sugar (raw)	4,806	182.71	91.14	878	438
Total values (B)				(2,109)	(1,500)
C. Wheat-Marketing Certificates				389	

(continued)

Commodity (1)	Domestic Food and Industrial Use (thousand metric tons) (2)	Domestic Price ($ per metric ton) (3)	Import or Export Price ($ per metric ton) (4)	Value of Domestic Use — Farm Price ($ millions) (5)	Value of Domestic Use — Import or Export Price ($ millions) (6)
D. Excess Consumer Costs				4,830	
				($ million)	
E. Government Costs, 1971-71					
Wheat payments				874.0	
Feed grain payments				1,504.0	
Cotton payments				917.0	
National Wool Act payments				75.0	
Sugar Act payments				86.0	
Conservation payments (avg., 1970 and 1971)				190.0	
Export subsidies and assistance				255.9	
CCC interest cost				544.7	
CCC storage and handling costs				120.9	
CCC transportation costs				61.7	
Total (E)				4,629.2	
Government receipts[a]				814.2	
F. Net cost of E				3,815.0	
G. PL 480—Gross cost			(1,247)		
Gross receipts			(329)		
Net				918	
H. Total of indicated government costs[b]				4,733	
I. Total of consumer and government costs				9,563	

[a]Receipts to treasury—1970-71
Tariff duties (1971) — $189.2
Wheat-marketing certificates — 389.0
Sugar excise tax — 115.1
CCC gains on sales and donations — 120.9
Total — $814.2
[b]Other federal governmental expenditures
Research and extension — $543.0
Soil Conservation Service — 138.0
Total — $681.0
Lending operations are excluded.

NOTES TO TABLE 3.5

Methods of estimation of consumer costs are as follows.

A. Domestic food and industrial use of U.S. production:
   General: Feed and seed use are excluded to avoid double counting of grains used to feed livestock.
   Wheat, barley, corn, oats, and rice: The export price equals the farm market price (exclusive of direct payments) less average export subsidy, if any. Export subsidies were paid on wheat, barley, and rice.
   Peanuts: The export price equals the farm market price less the average cost of CCC disposal of peanuts acquired; peanuts were disposed of by exportation and crushing into oil and meal.
   Tobacco: The export price equals the farm market price less the export subsidy on major types of tobacco (11 cents per kilogram, farm sales weight).
   Sugar: The domestic price is for raw sugar, not the farm price of cane or sugar beets. The price is the New York import price plus tariff and excise tax. The import price is the domestic price minus the sum of tariff, excise tax, and the quota premium.
   Potatoes: Assumed there is no significant protection except that provided by transportation costs.
   Vegetable oils: Corn is excluded because value of corn oil included in value of domestic food and industrial use of corn. Prices are factory prices. Exports were substantial, and no export subsidies were paid except on peanuts, but peanut oil exports were at domestic prices.
   Cotton: No export subsidy was paid, so domestic and export prices were the same.
   Beef and veal: The tariff rate on beef and veal imported averaged 6.4 percent in 1971. The beef imported is competitive with about one-third of the beef produced in the United States. Restraints on beef and veal imports assumed to increase import price of beef and veal by 13 percent. Effect on all beef and veal produced in the United States assumed to increase the price by 10 percent.
   Pork: The average tariff rate on imported pork in 1971 was 3.5 percent, but tariff rate on fresh or frozen pork was 1.9 percent. Most imports consisted of hams. Overall effect on domestic price assumed to be 3 percent.
   Poultry: No evidence that domestic price is above world price.
   Sheep: Same as beef and veal.
   Wool: In 1971 the ad valorem rate of tariff duty on dutiable wool was 34.3 percent, and assumed domestic price exceeded import price by that amount. The import price was derived by dividing domestic price for clean wool by 1343 to reflect quality factors.
   Milk, manufactured: The domestic price is the price received by farmers for manufactured milk. The import price is the Danish producer price for milk plus transportation cost of 5 percent.
   Milk, fluid uses: The domestic price is the farm price for milk used as fluid milk and cream. The import price was determined by holding the absolute margin between the price of milk for fluid use and manufactured use at the 1970-71 level.

B. Additional cost of imports:
   Beef and veal: Assumed quota restrictions increased import price by 13 percent and tariff by 6.4 percent.
   Pork: Average tariff rate of 3.5 percent.
   Wool: More than half of wool enters duty free; the tariff rate on the remainder is 34.3 percent. Wool entering duty free has not been included.
   Tobacco: The average tariff duty on unmanufactured tobacco was 22 percent in 1971.

C. Domestic wheat-marketing certificate:
   About $27.55 per ton on all wheat used for food (14.1 million tons).

57

as well as most of the costs involved in the operation of the Commodity Credit Corporation (CCC). During 1970-71 the CCC had a net gain on its sales and donations; this gain is included under government receipts. Government receipts include the income received from tariff duties, the wheat-marketing certificates, and the sugar excise tax as well as the gains from CCC operations.

The total governmental costs amounted to $4.733 billion. As noted in table footnote b, not all governmental expenditures associated with agriculture were included. In particular, expenditures for research and extension and the Soil Conservation Service were excluded on the grounds that the benefits are shared by the population generally and that farmers receive benefits from these programs primarily in their role as consumers and not as producers.

The total of consumer and government (taxpayer) costs is $9.56 billion for 1970-71. Estimates for other years would give different results, but this estimate is not too far from the mark for the five years ending in 1972.

At the end of the table are notes indicating how the estimates of consumer costs were made. the sources of data have not been given, but inquiries concerning the sources will be answered by the author.

SUMMARY

The United States has distinct comparative advantages in the production of the feed grains, wheat, soybeans, and tobacco and probably in poultry. It is in a marginal position for cotton and pork and perhaps also for beef, especially grain-fed beef. It has a distinct and strong comparative disadvantage in manufactured milk products, though not as serious as is implied by recent differentials between domestic and import prices. In addition, consumer and government costs of current U.S. farm programs are substantial

NOTES

1. FAO, Agricultural Commodity Projections, 1970-1980, Vol. I, p. 123.
2. Ibid., p. 124.
3. Ibid., p. 121.
4. Anthony S. Rojko and Arthur B. Mackie, World Demand Prospects for Agricultural Exports of Less Developed Countries in 1980, Foreign Agricultural Economic Report No. 60, Economic Research Service, U.S. Department of Agriculture, 1970, pp. 50-51.

5. John Ferris et al., The Impact on U.S. Agricultural Trade of the Accession of the United Kingdom, Ireland, and Norway to the European Economic Community, Research Report No. 11, Institute of International Agriculture, Michigan State University, 1971, p. 203.

6. David W. Culver, "A View of Food and Agriculture in 1980," Agricultural Economics Research 22, no. 3 (July 1970): 61-68. In the article projected 1980 output is compared with 1967-69 output levels. The present author has modified the base for comparison to 1969-71 and has called this 1970. Some of the detailed comparisons are from "Statistical Appendix to 'A View of Food and Agriculture in 1980'" (Mimeographed, available from Economic Research Service, USDA).

7. Leo V. Mayer, Earl Heady, and Howard C. Madsen have estimated the acreages of major farm crops (wheat, feed grains, cotton, and soybeans) if there had been no farm programs in 1970. In 1970 the actual harvested acreage of these crops was 197 million acres; the diverted area that year was 57 million acres. If the farm programs had been eliminated in 1969, they estimate that acreages in 1970 would have been 222 million acres (an increase of 25 million acres), but that after time for adjustment the acreage would decline to 207 million acres (an increase of 10 million acres over 1970). A second set of projections was for the effects of long-run cropland retirement programs—one for 50 million acres and one for 60 million acres. Under the 50-million-acre retirement program, the harvest area of the same group of crops was projected to be 192 million, and under the 60-million-acre program, 188 million acres. These projections may be interpreted as indicating that less than half of the currently diverted land would return to cultivation for wheat, feed grains, cotton, and soybeans. (See Farm Programs for the 1970s, CAED Report No. 32, Center for Agricultural and Economic Development, Ames, Iowa, 1968, pp. 31 and 38.)

8. Under the farming conditions in the United States, there has long been a substantial amount of cropland that is neither harvested nor pastured in a given year. In 1950-53 when there were no significant restraints on the area of the major crops (there were allotments in one year—1950—and except for cotton, the allotments were rather large in that year), the acreage of cropland that was neither harvested nor pastured was 67.1 million. In 1959 when 22.5 million acres of land were diverted under the soil bank, the land in this category was 70.9 million, and in 1964 when 55.1 million acres were diverted, the cropland neither harvested nor pastured had increased to 89.8 million acres. More than half of the increase in cropland neither harvested nor pastured between 1950-53 and 1964 was due to an increase in summer fallow (from 23.6 million to 37.0 million acres), and even if some of the summer fallow land returned to annual cultivation, the

effect on net output (yield minus seed) would be quite small. (See Cropland Trends Since World War II, Agricultural Economic Report No. 177, Economic Research Service, USDA, 1970, p. 5, and Agricultural Land Resources, Agriculture Information Bulletin No. 140, Agriculture Research Service, USDA, 1955, pp. 16-18.)

9. G. E. Dudley, J. R. Donald, and R. G. Barlowe, "Yield and Acreage Implications for U.S. Cotton," Cotton Situation CS 247 (August 1970): 9-23. In this study separate analyses were undertaken for yields and planted acreage. In both analyses the price received by farmers lagged one year and had a significant influence upon the dependent variable (yields for acreages). Only one aspect of the programs—the diversion rates required for participation—had an effect on either variable, and this was for 1966-68 and only for acreages. In explaining planted area, the prices of competing crops were used as well as the cotton price. The elasticity of planted acreage with respect to lagged cotton price, holding the prices of substitute crops constant, was about 0.60 for the United States and varied from 0.41 to 1.29 for the four regions. The elasticity of cotton yield to lagged cotton price ranged from 0.45 to 0.64 in the three regions in which it was significantly different from zero. In one region (the Southwest) no relationship could be found between price and yield.

10. P. L. Strickland, W. H. Brown, W. C. McArthur, and W. W. Pawson, Cotton Production and Farm Income Estimates Under Selected Alternative Farm Programs, Agricultural Economic Report No. 212, Economic Research Service, USDA, 1971, esp. p. 18.

11. The estimate of a 75-percent increase in planted cotton acreage resulting from an increase of 60 percent in the farm price of cotton (from 22 to 35 cents per pound) is based on ibid., p. 33. The second set of estimates was derived from the elasticities given in Dudley et al., op. cit., pp. 16 and 20. The weighted yield elasticity for the United States was based on the regional analysis, weighting the significant yield elasticities by the percentage of U.S. planted acreage of cotton in 1969.

12. Mayer, Heady, and Madsen, Farm Programs for the 1970s, p. 31.

13. "World Prices for Agricultural Products: Real or Fictitious?" Chapter 7 in World Agriculture in Disarray (New York: Macmillan, 1973).

14. It may be noted that in Indiana, Iowa, and Illinois—three major soybean- and corn-producing states—the average cash rent per acre of cropland was about $35 in 1969. While the above data are national data and are not strictly accurate for these three states, the return in excess of variable costs and rents would be $9 for soybeans and $19 for corn per acre. Data on farm rents are from R. D. Reinsel and B. Johnson, Farm Tenure and Cash Rents in the United

States, Agricultural Economic Report No. 190, Economic Research Service, USDA, 1970, p. 25.

15. These speculations are included in the author's paper, "Agricultural Price Policies and Effects on Trade: Some Examples from the United States and Western Europe," given at the Fourth Pacific Trade Conference in Ottawa, Canada, November 1971 (Office of Agricultural Economics Research, University of Chicago, paper no. 71:13, revised November 15, 1971).

16. The rather considerable number of studies is summarized by Warren R. Grant and D. S. Moore, Alternative Government Rice Programs: An Economic Evaluation, Agricultural Economic Report No. 187, Economic Research Service, USDA, June 1970. If annual gains from the rice program are capitalized into the value of land or the allotments at 12.5 percent, a reduction in the farm price of rice by $1.00 would result in an annual loss of $45 per acre and a capital loss of $360 per acre.

17. It is rather surprising that there does not exist, at least in published form, a detailed estimate of the total costs of all U.S. farm programs. Two quite approximate estimates have been made and published, one by Charles Schultze and one by the present author. See Charles Schultze, The Distribution of Farm Subsidies (Washington: Brookings Institution, 1971), and D. Gale Johnson, World Agriculture in Disarray (New York: St. Martin's Press, 1973), pp. 48-50.

4

**EUROPEAN
AGRICULTURAL POLICY**
André Herlitska
Pierre Malvé
Asher Winegarten

ORIGINS AND PRINCIPLES OF THE
COMMON AGRICULTURAL POLICY

The gradual process of the coalescing together of national economies to form integrated economic units—of which the European Economic Community (EEC) is the major example in recent years—should be viewed in a historical perspective. The period of strictly regulated international trade that marked the twenties and thirties gradually began to give way, after World War II, to a more liberal trend. Attempts were made to negotiate less restrictive international agreements, and the founding of such bodies as Food and Agricultural Organization (FAO) and Organization for European Economic Cooperation (OEEC)—later to become the Organization for Economic Cooperation and Development (OECD)—introduced a new "social" element. Such considerations as the progressive reduction of barriers to trade became associated with the broader aims of raising standards of nutrition, the promotion of full employment, and the achievement of stable growth.

But it was soon evident that the special nature of agricultural production and its relatively slow response to market forces raised specific problems. The Messina Conference of June 1955 was an earnest determination of the six member states of the European Coal and Steel Community (ECSC) to give new impetus to the movement toward European unity based on economic union. The Treaty of Rome,

---

When this paper was first drafted, the assumption was that the enlarged European Community would include Norway. The omission of Norway, though slightly affecting the statistics, does not alter the thesis. And indeed, the remarkable events of 1973 have supported our original arguments.

which came into force on January 1, 1958, as a concrete expression
of that resolve, laid down two basic principles concerning the agricultural sector:

1. Agriculture was an integral part of the general economy and
an essential element in social life and must not be excluded from the
process of economic integration.

2. The unification of national markets to form a single common
market should be accompanied by the parallel establishment of a
common agricultural policy (CAP) among the member states and a
common organisation of their markets.

The CAP thus became one of the key elements in the process
of integrating the national economies of the member states. Let us
briefly examine these two principles.

1. According to the Europeam Community, in order to obtain
a clear picture of the problems affecting agriculture, the main factor
to bear in mind is the interdependence between agriculture and other
sectors of the economy. On the one hand, the development and modernization of agriculture will clearly benefit the whole Community. On
the other hand, it is necessary for solutions to the more serious
agricultural problems to be devised and to be implemented within the
framework of the Community's general social and economic policy.

Measures taken only within the agricultural sector would have
little impact—or even a distorting effect—on the proper development
of production and the improvement of social structures. It thus becomes necessary to make simultaneous use of the whole range of
economic and social instruments to attain the ultimate aim of the
Treaty of Rome (Article II). This is the promotion throughout the
Community of a balanced development of the various geographical
regions and the different sectors of economic activity. With this aim
in mind and conscious of the fact that farm incomes in the member
states were lower than those of other comparable professional groups,
the Stresa Conference (July 3-12, 1958) stressed the concept of the
parity of incomes.

2. The Community rejects the assumption that the process of
unification of markets in agriculture should be based, as it is in other
economic sectors, simply on the process of tariff and quota disman-
tling. It recommends the establishment of a uniform balanced CAP
based on the organization of markets, including common producer
prices; the improvement of production and marketing structures; a
standardized system of trade with third countries, ensuring a preference
to domestic products on Community markets; and Community financial
responsibility. The liberalization of trade among member states based
merely on trade instruments does not comply with the special requirements of agricultural markets. This is inevitable in view of the variable physical and socioeconomic conditions of production. Moreover,

because of the persistent imbalance of world markets in agricultural produce, the liberalization of Community trade with nonmember states cannot be achieved without adequately protecting EC producers, and, as recent events have shown, consumers against its possible effects. A further point is that in all highly industrialized Western countries, customs duties generally play a secondary role in agricultural support systems. The Kennedy Round of the General Agreement on Tariffs and Trade (GATT) Conference proved this conclusively by emphasizing the need for a new approach to the organization of world markets for agricultural produce.

To achieve stability in the Community market for agricultural products—and this is the basis of a policy which aims at economic and social progress in agriculture—the risks of imbalance, whether external or internal, must be eliminated by giving adequate support to Community agriculture. There are three basic reasons that may be cited to justify such a support.

1. The agricultural policies of the member states are directed more and more toward the twin objectives of increasing incomes and raising the living and working conditions of farmers.

2. In Europe, there is a high density of people per unit of land available for agriculture, and productivity is accordingly related essentially to output per acre rather than to the farm business unit. The two problems that this feature poses are the lack of alternative employment opportunities in the densely populated zones and the restrictions placed by the less heavily peopled countries on large-scale immigration.

3. The confusion prevailing on world agricultural markets in normal times is that prices are much lower on these markets than within the frontiers of the exporting countries, and price formation is affected by surpluses that are invariably placed on commercial markets.

The CAP must also take other essential requirements into consideration. It must aim at adjusting agricultural production to the existing outlets without neglecting the need to promote international trade as well as to encourage specialization in line with the natural conditions prevailing within the Community. The CAP must also guarantee stable and reasonable consumer prices. In this way it will play its part in safeguarding the competitive status of Community industrial production on the world market. Finally, the CAP must ensure the ready availability of supplies.

As far as the aim of specialization is concerned, the first few years' experience has shown that such specialization, as is justified from the economic point of view, can only be achieved insofar as progress is made toward an economic and monetary union among the member states with the harmonization that this implies of monetary, financial, fiscal, and other related policies.

When the mechanics of the CAP were being planned, a fundamental question had to be decided. Should the cost of agricultural support be borne by the consumer through the taxing of imports at the Community frontiers or should it fall upon the taxpayer? The latter formula would enable the domestic market to adjust to the price level of the world market, and deficiency payments to agricultural producers would have to be ensured at the expense of the public purse.

In the early days of the Common Market, the countries of Western Europe were using either system or, in some cases, a composite of both. The deficiency payment system was in use in the United Kingdom (UK). Both before and during the Stresa Conference on agriculture, this system was being considered as a possible basis for the CAP in the EEC. It was eventually rejected, principally because it was considered too expensive and too complex to be applied in a Community of more than 10 million farms.

In its place, a policy of complete trade liberalization was adopted with the removal of all quantitative restrictions, together with a system of flexible protection at the frontier accompanied by market intervention to maintain domestic prices. At a later stage, the deficiency payment system was adopted for a few products such as olive oil, durum wheat, flax, hemp, and rape, that is, for those products that are either restricted to certain regions or for which the Community is not self-sufficient.

The increasingly important part played by the Community in international trade is reflected in the growth rate of its trade since its inception which is higher than the rate of increase of its gross production. The Community has, as a result, been able to make a substantial contribution to the expansion of the world economy.

From 1958 onward, the EEC has been a fast-growing market for U.S. exports as a result of the rapid improvement in the standard of living of its people and the progressive removal of trade barriers. United States exports to the EEC have also been increasing steadily and more rapidly than to the rest of the world, particularly to certain highly developed areas. Acccording to U.S. statistics, between 1960, the year when the European Free Trade Association (EFTA) was set up, and 1971, U.S. exports to EFTA countries increased by 81 percent, while to the rest of the world they increased by 115 percent, and to the EEC countries by 143 percent.

As the establishment of the agricultural Common Market has made it possible progressively to liberalize trade, it has had a motivating effect on international trade as a whole and more particularly on trade with the United States.

The system of border levies, which has replaced the various systems previously used by the member states to control imports, has not hindered the development of trade with third countries. Under such a system, once the maintenance of a predetermined domestic price level is ensured, competition on grounds of quality takes place in a completely free market. (In fact, the degree of protection provided by the levy mechanism is consistent with the level at which prices are being fixed inside the Community.) United States exports of farm produce have largely benefited from this opportunity of competition on the market since in many cases U.S. products are complementary to Community products from the quality point of view (for example, tobacco, canned fruit, vegetables, and so on). Moreover, in many other sectors, since the Community market is free from any quantitative restrictions and as there is little, if any, tariff protection, U.S. exports have taken advantage of the fact that they are complementary to Community production also from the quantity point of view (for example, vegetable fats, feeding cakes, oil seeds, fodder grain, cotton, and so on). Nowadays, over 40 percent of U.S. exports of farm products to the EEC enter the Community duty free, such as the exports of soybean seeds and cake, exports of which to the six amounted to over $800 million in 1972.

To conclude, the CAP has succeeded in making a substantial contribution toward the solution of two kinds of problems which might, at first sight, appear to be irreconcilable. On the one hand, it has contributed to the improvement of the living and working conditions of the rural population in the Community (Article 39 of the treaty), and on the other hand, it has contributed to the development of international trade to the ultimate benefit of all nations (Article 110 of the treaty).

This has been possible because the mechanisms of the CAP, which were intended to stabilize domestic markets, have benefited producers in the EC by bringing about better price and outlet guarantees. As a consequence, it has been possible completely to liberalize the Community market, the largest market in the world for imports of agricultural products and foodstuffs. Encouraged by the abolition of restrictions on the Community market and by its new-found stability, countries with agricultural produce to export have taken full advantage, whenever they could, of any Community outlets available to them.

It is pertinent to note that although exporting countries have sometimes had to bear the uncertainty resulting from the compensatory amounts applied to their exports by the Community, this has been a result of the fluctuations of international market prices rather than Community policy, which is aimed at stabilizing markets.

In fact, this system of compensatory amounts by itself has discouraged sales at excessively low prices, thus contributing toward improving the conditions of competition among countries exporting to the EEC.

EVOLUTION OF THE COMMON
AGRICULTURAL POLICY

Agricultural Production and Trade

Agricultural Output as a Percentage of the
Gross National Product

During the period 1958-70, the proportion of the gross national
product (GNP) identified as "agriculture"(agriculture proper, forestry,
and fisheries) diminished in all member countries. For the six as
a whole, it fell from 10 percent in 1958 to 5.4 percent in 1970. The
percentages for Italy, the Netherlands, and France are above the Community average; in Germany, Belgium, and Luxembourg, they are
below.

In an enlarged Community of 10 nations, the relative place held
by "agriculture"would also have steadily declined. Since, however,
the relative proportion of agriculture is smaller in the applicant countries than in the six member countries of the Community (4.6 percent
in 1967 on average), the relative proportion of agriculture in the GNP
in an enlarged Community of 10 would have been smaller than in the
present Community. It should be noted, however, that the gaps between
the applicant countries are wider than those existing between the member countries. In the UK, for instance, agriculture accounted for only
3.2 percent of the GNP in 1969, whereas in Ireland it still made up
17.8 percent.

In the Community, the increase in the gross value added of the
"agriculture"sector, which varies greatly from nation to nation, is
far below the growth rate of the gross national product of the economy
as a whole (+1.3 percent as against 5.8 percent in 1970 at constant
1963 prices).

Agricultural Manpower in Relation to Total
Working Population

Along with the relative reduction in the contribution of agriculture to the GNP, the agricultural labor force has greatly diminished
in recent years. From 1958 to 1970, agricultural manpower in the
whole Community fell from 16 to 9.5 million workers, that is, an
overall loss of about 6.5 million workers. On a yearly average, the
decrease amounted to around 500,000 people, that is, an average annual
fall of around 3 to 4 percent. The labor force engaged in agriculture,
which accounted for 21.6 percent of the Community's total labor force
in 1958 had fallen to 12.8 percent by 1970.

This general reduction of the agricultural labor force derives from the income level and the living and working conditions, which are relatively unfavorable in agriculture compared with other sectors of the economy. It has also been affected by the significant structural changes that are taking place in agriculture, technical progress, and the development of mechanization which has greatly increased productivity per person employed in farming in the sector. The productivity per person employed in farming has, in fact, been rising by an average of over 7 percent per annum in the Community since 1958, that is, at a higher rate than in industry.

As a rule, this decline in the agricultural labor force has had positive effects on general economic development. The outflow of manpower from agriculture has greatly helped industrial expansion by preventing the problems that arise from a shortage of manpower. Between 1950 and 1965, 46 percent of the nonagricultural jobs that were created in the Community were filled from the decrease in agricultural employment.

However, the massive outflow of people from rural areas—many of them the younger and more active fraction of the population—has affected the age distribution of the population and has prevented some regions from retaining the minimum population required for a normal developing economy. Infrastructures have also been affected, and thus the creation of new productive activities in these regions has been prejudiced in some cases. This raises serious problems.

At present, the agricultural labor force in the four applicant countries accounts for only about 5 percent of the total working population (25.5 percent in Ireland, 10.5 percent in Norway and Denmark, 2.7 percent in the UK). In 1970, in an enlarged Community, the agricultural labor force would have accounted for about 10.5 percent of the total working population.

Capital Investment in Agriculture

At Community level, there is as yet no detailed and systematic statistical data on capital formation and investments at the level of individual farm enterprises. Hence we have to restrict ourselves to a few general observations. The gross formation of fixed capital at current prices in agriculture has greatly increased since the Common Market was set up, from 2099 million units of account in 1958 to 4600 million units of account in 1969. From an OECD survey, it appears that during the period 1957-67 the annual average growth percentage of investments per hectare (hectare = 2.47 acres) in terms of value varied widely between member states from 2.4 percent to 10 percent. Furthermore, investments varied widely in nature. The annual average increase in the value of capital invested in livestock ranged from

2.2 percent to 6.3 percent, that of capital invested in deadstock, from 3.6 percent to 14 percent, and that of capital invested in land, from 2.2 percent to 10.6 percent.

In more recent years, statistical data are available only for Germany and Belgium, but they can be taken as illustrative of the general Community pattern of development.

From the data on Germany, it appears that the total investments (all equipment goods, including current capital, irrespective of owner) per hectare increased by 7.2 percent during the period 1965/66-1970/71. In the same period, working capital per unit of labor increased very rapidly—at the rate of 49 percent during the period under review, giving an average annual increase of about 7 percent.

In Belgium, working capital per unit of labor and per hectare increased by 33 percent and 16 percent, respectively, during the period 1966/69-1970/71. The greatest increases has been in the capital invested in livestock, while the current capital per hectare remained virtually unchanged.

Analysis of Changes in the Principal Commodity Sectors

In the EEC, the annual growth rate in terms of volume averaged 3.2 percent for farm products as a whole for the period between 1959-61 and 1962-63. Since then, the growth rate has tended to increase. Thus from 1963-65 to 1967-69, the various national growth rates of total production were between 3.9 percent and 4.5 percent per annum. This range exceeds the average rate of increase of demand for agricultural products, which is only a little above 2.5 percent a year.

However, the expansion of agricultural production has involved additional investment and an increased demand for industrial inputs. Agriculture has thus provided an increasingly important outlet for industry. In 1966, more than 40 percent of the value of Community agricultural production was used for purchases in other sectors. In agriculture, intermediate consumption, with an average annual increase of 8 percent, has increased more rapidly than production.

The same trend is also discernible in the four applicant countries. Whereas final agricultural production has expanded more in the UK than in the Community (particularly in cereals), there has been little expansion in Denmark and hardly any in the case of Norway. The growth of final agricultural production is mainly due to the considerable increase in yields in agriculture.

A significant characteristic of agriculture in the Community is the predominance of animal production over crops. In the present Community, animal production accounts for 57 percent (18 percent milk) of total final agricultural production as against 42 percent for crops.

It is worthy of note, however, that in Italy the proportion of crops
(61 percent) is well above the Community average, and the proportion
of animal production (38 percent) is as clearly below the Community
average. The trend is for this predominance of animal production
over crop production to become more pronounced.

While total production was at index 124.9 in 1970 (1963 = 100),
total crop production was at 122.7 and animal production at 126.7,
that is, an annual increase of 3.5 percent for animal production and
3.3 percent for crops. In an enlarged Community of 10 nations, the
trend toward animal production will be even more marked as the applicant countries are clearly moving in this direction. In a Community
of 10, the ratio of animal crop production would have been 60:40 in
1970.

Trend of Agricultural Imports and Exports

The setting up of the Common Market has had a considerable
impact on world trade. The figures of intra- and extra-Community
foreign trade show that the EEC is both the major customer and the
main supplier in the world.

In 1970 the Community's imports from third countries amounted
to $45,600 million or 18.7 percent of world imports against 17.1 percent
in 1958. Exports to third countries amounted to $45,200 million in
1970, 19.2 percent of world exports against 17.8 percent in 1958. The
Community's foreign trade expanded by 183 percent from 1958 to
1970.

In 1970 trade within the Community amounted to $43,000 million,
that is, a rise of 530 percent over 1958. Hence intra-Community trade
increased more rapidly than extra-Community trade. While in 1957
it accounted for only 29.6 percent of overall trade, in 1970 it accounted
for 48.4 percent.

If we add the value of extra-Community trade to that of intra-
Community trade, we can see that in 1970 the EEC was responsible
for 30.3 percent of world imports and 31.7 percent of exports. With
nearly one-third of world trade, the Community has reached a position
never so far achieved in international trade. Trade alone accounts
for 18 percent of the Community's GNP (40 percent in Benelux, 12
percent in France). Between 1958 and 1970, the average annual increase of Community trade was about 12 percent (total increase 1958/
70: 286 for imports and 288 for exports). In these 13 years, EEC
participation in world trade increased by 2.5 percent on a yearly
average, while U.S. participation declined by 0.5 percent on a yearly
average.

The expansion of foreign trade has, however, been accompanied
by a change in the pattern of trade implying a considerable increase

in the proportion of manufactured goods and a much slower increase in the proportion of foodstuffs. Between 1958 and 1970, as far as extra-Community trade was concerned, the proportion of foodstuffs in imports fell from 25 percent to 16.5 percent and in exports from 9.6 percent to 6.8 percent. The same holds true in respect of intra-Community trade, where the proportion of foodstuffs dropped from 33 percent to 22.5 percent between 1958 and 1970.

Intra-Community trade in farm products has increased more than sixfold since 1958 to a total of $6500 million in 1970 and nearly $7800 million in 1971. Imports of farm products from third countries have almost doubled to reach $12,500 million in 1970 and over $13,000 million in 1971, while exports to third countries have increased from $1900 million in 1958 to $3600 million in 1970 and $4100 million in 1971. It is interesting to note that imports of products subject to EEC regulations increased more than those that are not subject to regulations. From 1969 to 1970, the increases were 17 percent (33 percent in the case of the United States) and 4 percent, respectively. While in 1958 all Community member countries (except Benelux) were selling more farm products outside than within the Community, since 1967 the process has been reversed.

Though the Community's general trade balance shows only a slight deficit, the balance of its agricultural trade is in heavy deficit ($8900 million in 1970). Purchases of tropical products from developing countries (coffee, tea, peanuts, cotton, jute, bananas, and so on) account for some 60 percent of this deficit, and 20 percent results from trade with the United States (mainly maize and soya).

It should be emphasized, however, that the Community's agricultural balance with the four applicant countries shows a surplus as the UK's imports from the Community largely offset Ireland and Denmark's exports (credit balance of $301.9 million in 1970). Most significant is the increase in fodder imports into the EEC; in eight years, fodder imports have more than doubled. They equal 30-million-ton cereal equivalents, or the output of about 25 million acres. The increase in fodder imports into the member states between 1958/59 and and 1966/67 corresponds to an "import" of nearly 12.35 million acres more than in 1958.

In 1970 the Community's major exports were cereals ($638 million), fruit and vegetables ($815 million), wine and other beverages ($503 million), dairy products ($499 million), meat ($304 million), and sugar ($141 million).

The European Community is the main outlet for U.S. exports of farm products. In 1964, the year before the CAP came into effect, U.S. exports of farm products to the EEC amounted to $1227 million. In 1971 they amounted to $1747 million. In the past seven years, U.S. exports of farm products to the Community have increased by

42 percent compared with an increase of only 26 percent to the rest of the world. The percentage of U.S. exports of farm products that the Community has absorbed since it was set up has been comparatively steady, with an increase in 1971. In 1958, the EEC accounted for 21.3 percent of the whole U.S. export market for farm products; in 1964 it was 21.7 percent, and in 1971, 24.5 percent.

The Community's exports of farm products to the United States are considerably lower. In 1958 they amounted to $205 million, and in 1971 to nearly $423 million. With imports amounting to $1747 million in 1971, the Community's trade for farm products with the United States showed a deficit of $1324 million.

It may be noted that of all EEC imports of agricultural products, $10,343 million in 1968, imports from developing countries accounted for $4637 million. These import figures have since grown to reach $5229 million in 1969, $5562 million in 1970, and $5510 million in 1972. The Community is the major exporter of agricultural products from the rest of the world and especially from developing countries. The EEC alone absorb more than 1/4 of the total agricultural export of these countries.

The four applicant countries, which have been traditionally in favor of a free trade policy, have traded with the world. The result is that their sources of supply and their exports are more diversified than the Community's. They will further reinforce the essential role to be played by the enlarged Community in world trade. In farm products, two countries show a deficiency (the UK and Norway); two countries which are net exporters (Denmark and Ireland) rely upon the products of stock breeding for 90 percent and 80 percent, respectively, of their receipts. In 1970 the deficiency in foodstuffs in the UK, which had to be met by imports, amounted to $3800 million. Although Denmark and Ireland were in credit, the agricultural trade balance of the four applicant countries taken together showed a deficit of some $2700 million in 1970.

Changes in Community Reliance on Internal Products to Meet Needs, Commodity by Commodity

The Community's overall agricultural self-sufficiency rate, which was estimated to be 85 percent before World War II, went up to 87 percent in 1954/55 and to 89.2 percent in 1958. At present, this rate exceeds 90 percent. But within this figure, there is a large range of variations from product to product. In the case of cereals, for instance, the Community of six had a deficiency in durum wheat and a surplus of soft wheat. Although it was about self-sufficient in barley, it had a considerable deficiency in other feed grains, partic- ularly maize, and also in vegetable oils and fats. Where livestock products are concerned, the six were tending toward self-sufficiency with the exception of beef.

The main agricultural products of the Community of six may be grouped as follows:

- products in which the EEC was a net exporter in 1968/69, 1969/70, and 1970/71: soft wheat (102 percent), sugar (106 percent with the French overseas territories), butter (104 percent), cheese (102 percent), milk powder (148 percent), and concentrated milk (154 percent);
- products in which the EEC was more or less self-sufficient in 1968/69, 1969/70, and 1970/71: fresh vegetables, pigmeat, poultry meat, eggs, whole milk, and skim milk;
- products for which the EEC's self-sufficiency rate is subject to cyclical variations around 100 percent: rye (104 percent in 1968/69 and 94 percent in 1970/71), barley (91 percent in 1970/71 and 107 percent in 1968/69), rice, excluding broken rice (91 percent in 1968/69 and 134 percent in 1970/71), wine (95 percent in 1968/69 and 104 percent in 1970/71);
- products of which the EEC was a net importer in 1968/69, 1969/70, and 1970/71: durum wheat (74 percent), oats (88 percent), maize (66 percent), "other cereals," particularly millet and sorghum (16 percent), fresh fruit (88 percent), citrus fruits (52 percent), fish (89 percent in 1969/70), vegetable oils and fats (40 percent in 1969/70), fats from slaughtering (81 percent in 1969/70), and beef (88 percent).

The four applicant countries as a whole have considerable deficiency in crop production and surpluses in animal production, particularly in animal processed products based on cereals. Hence in 1969/70 the self-sufficiency rate in a Community of 10 nations would have been as follows: cereals, 85 percent; sugar, 84 percent; fats, 40 percent; pigmeat, 110 percent; beef, 94 percent; poultry meat, 102 percent; eggs, 101 percent; butter, 90 percent; cheese, 98 percent; vegetables, 97 percent; fruit, 81 percent.

Thus the self-sufficiency rate of the 10 would be higher more particularly for the animal processed products based on cereals. The self-sufficiency rate of the 10 taken as a whole, exceeded 85 percent in 1969/70. This slight discrepancy with regard to the present Community's self-sufficiency rate results from the fact that of the four applicant countries, two are small countries with surpluses (Denmark and Ireland) and one (the UK) is a large importing country.

Income Position of Agriculture

Production has increased. Techniques have been improving steadily, and the agricultural labor force has diminished. The structure of agriculture, too, has been improved. During the period 1962-67, the number of farms in the Community decreased by 2.5 percent a year; in the next three years, the numbers fell by 4 percent a year. As a result, the average farm size increased by 3.6 percent a year, from 27 acres in 1958 to 32 acres in 1970. But although labor productivity in agriculture has risen, it must be acknowledged that farm incomes remain lower than in other sectors of activity and that the trend is for them to fall even further.

From a macroeconomic point of view, the ratio between agriculture's contribution to the GNP and the proportion of the working population engaged in farming, which was already well below one-half of that in other sectors of activity in 1960 (0.46), had fallen to 0.43 by 1970. Disregarding production and looking now at the gross added value at factor cost (income), we see that in agriculture the ratio is lower by one-half than in other sectors: 0.47 in 1970. It should, however, be noted that these ratios vary greatly among the member states of the Community.

From a microeconomic point of view, it is more difficult to approach the problem of disparity between incomes in agriculture and in other sectors. Data are sometimes lacking, and, more often than not, the available material is not homogeneous. Another difficulty is that income positions in agriculture vary widely according to the region and the sector of production.

Broadly speaking, farm incomes are on average from 10 to 45 percent below the level of incomes in other sectors of activity. In Germany in 1959/60, the difference amounted to 27 percent. It increased to 34 percent in 1966/67. In 1968/69 and 1969/70, the figure fell only to increase again to 40 percent in 1970/71. It stood at about 38 percent in 1971/72. In Belgium there was a disparity of 32 percent in 1959/60. It decreased to 18 percent in 1966/67, then increased but has now again decreased to about 12 percent.

One of the causes of the occasional rise in this figure is to be found in the terms of trade, that is, in the ratio between the indices of prices received and those of prices paid by farmers for their inputs. In recent years, this ratio has been steadily declining, to the detriment of agriculture. In Germany the ratio decreased from 97.1 in 1968 to 88.3 in 1970; in France, from 97.9 to 96.4; in Italy, from 99.3 in 1969 to 96.5 in 1970; and in Belgium from 92.7 to 90.5 in 1971.

Since there are disparities both between incomes in agriculture and those in other economic sectors and internally between the different agricultural sectors, and since, moreover, the problem is increasing despite the CAP, there are evidently grounds for adopting measures to improve the CAP if an attempt is to be made to close these gaps.

Search for Additional Solutions

Since agriculture is an integral part of the general economy and an essential element in the Community's social life, it is necessary, if the problems affecting this sector are to be solved, for the other Community policies to advance swiftly. With a view to the eventual economic and monetary union, progress is especially important in the development of the Community's labor policy within the framework of a regional development policy and in the EEC social policy. Any progress made in these other sectors will, in fact, greatly assist the "reform of agriculture" program which is designed to act as a base for the development of Community agriculture in the seventies.

A regional development policy at Community level is essential to promote the economic welfare of the many regions that are still developing—they are usually predominantly agricultural regions. Even as late as 1970, about 12.5 percent of the working population of the Community was engaged in agriculture. But in some developing regions, the proportion was as high as 50 percent. In most cases, therefore, the modernization of Community agriculture must proceed together with a dynamic labor policy within the framework of a regional development policy.

However, some regions have to face the problem of retaining a minimum working population in the interests of ecological balance. This is particularly true in the case of hill and mountain areas. In high uplands, no economic sector other than agriculture can retain and make use of natural resources. Such specific measures as are adoped must, therefore, compensate for the natural handicaps prevailing in those areas (for example, permanent income aids). It should be emphasized at this point that the Community is still at the stage of preparing plans for intervention, while at national level some aids are already partially operative.

If the Community's economic growth is to be smooth (Article 2 of the Treaty of Rome) and if it is to meet the requirements of society, it must be backed by a social policy at Community level. In the farming sector, the social policy should give priority to the following aims:

1. to facilitate the changes affecting farming and farmers resulting from the integration of the member states' economies and technological progress, particularly through measures intended to offer farmers:
- an alternative livelihood;
- a general and vocational training on a permanent basis;

2. to help bring about parity in incomes and in working and living conditions between agriculture and other socioprofessional sectors, in particular by means of:

- an income policy which, through a better distribution of available resources, would contribute to leveling out the disparities between sectors and regions;
- the harmonization of social legislation in the farming sector with that in other sectors of activity, irrespective of the extent to which the farmer can contribute.

In point of fact, in 1970, farms in the Community averaged 31.4 acres; farms between 2.5 and 12.3 acres accounted for 46.3 percent of the total number but contributed no more than 9.2 percent of the agriculture acreage in use. Consequently, the modernization of Community agriculture, with its double aim of improving the competitive quality of Community agriculture on the world market and of increasing the profitability of European farms, implies the solution of problems that are predominantly social.

In view of the fact that farms are scattered over the Community, a policy aimed at strengthening the economic and contractual position of farmers remains a major requirement for EEC agriculture, since the coordination process, which is taking place in the processing industries and the distribution trade, tends to increase such inequalities as already exist between producers and buyers of primary farm products.

This aim of strengthening the economic and contractual position of farmers will have to be achieved by developing forms of association and by an increased participation of farmers themselves in the added values arising from processing and marketing farm products. In this context, the setting up of producer groups and the development of cooperatives are basic steps. The development of contractual forms between groups of farmers and buyers in industry and trade will ensure better prices and marketing guarantees for farmers and a more regular supply for the purchasers.

Thus we have a situation where on the one hand, the terms of trade between agriculture and other economic sectors have steadily deteriorated, and on the other, the per capita income of farmers has not shared to the same extent as that of other sectors in the Community's economic growth. It, therefore, becomes apparent that price policy for farm products plays a basic role in that it represents an essential component of farm incomes. The policy of market organization plays an equally important part, as an effective instrument in ensuring price stability.

There is a growing tendency within the EEC to base price policy on objective criteria calculated to cover rises in production costs—which are generally rapid during periods of inflation—and to ensure a fair return on capital and reasonable remuneration for labor. But price policies must also help to influence production so that the best possible balance between supply and demand may be achieved through the correct ratio of prices to each other.

The organization of markets must be extended to all agricultural products including those with only a regional economic importance (for example, potatoes, mutton, lamb, and wool). It must be improved in some sectors (for example, fruit and vegetables, wine, eggs, and poultry) in order to ensure equal market stability guarantees to all Community producers. And it should perhaps be modified in certain other sectors, such as fodder grains, to improve price ratios in livestock production, particularly in the meat sector.

The inability of price and marketing policies alone to resolve the problem of fair incomes for producers whose farms are below the structural par or are in areas with difficult environmental conditions means that there is a need for additional measures, such as an incomes support policy. Two approaches to such a policy are now under review in the EEC:

1. It might be introduced as a temporary measure to be phased out gradually, within the context of the present CAP, in order to correct the income position of those who are

- either in process of modernizing their enterprises and as a result will eventually be in a position to achieve income parity with other sectors on the basis of a rational price policy only after completing several stages of development (temporary support to be phased out progressively);
- or prepared to give up farming, but have not yet reached the required age to be eligible for the farm retirement allowance provided by the Community (temporary, but not decreasing, support).

2. It might exist alongside the CAP as a permanent measure to compensate farmers for the natural handicaps prevailing in some regions and for the services that they render for the maintenance of the landscape (particularly in hill and mountain areas).

Agriculture and Society

The system of supporting agriculture essentially through consumer prices may involve some conflict of interest with manufacturing industry, the trade unions, and the processors and distributors of food.

On the part of industry, the main fear is that the CAP, by engendering a greater degree of self-sufficiency, could disturb trade relations between the Community and third countries and lead to retaliation by the latter against Community exports. The principal concern of the trade unions is the alleged effect of the CAP on the cost of food. Increases in food prices are a key element in demands for higher wages. Food processors and distributors may dislike having to pay more for their essential raw materials and switching their imports to Community sources of supply.

It should be said, however, that in Europe it is becoming increasingly clear that the impact of a given rise in the price of food at the farm gate has only a minimal impact on the cost of living. The Services of the Commission have estimated that a 1-percent rise in the farm gate price results only in a 0.07- to 0.12-percent rise in the cost of living. It is also in the interests of the food industry to have continuity of supply of their raw materials at reasonably stable prices.

The interrelationship between these elements in society and agriculture accounts for the advisory role given to them in the various institutions set up by the Community concerned with the formulation and administration of the CAP. The feeling among agriculturalists is that only too frequently these groups may have the predominant say. There is little quid pro quo as agriculture seems incapable of being able to bring its own influence to bear on industrial and social policy. It is fair, for example, to claim that whereas the pressure of nonagricultural interests were successful for some three years in the late 1960s in keeping agricultural prices frozen, agriculture had no success whatsoever in its own endeavors to keep down the costs of the items that it needed for production.

In the UK, the central organizations concerned with industry and commerce have increasingly shown awareness of the vital role of British agriculture in the national economy. The national farm organizations have established close links with those for industry and commerce, providing full opportunity for frequent exchanges on problems of common interest. Industry and commerce have accepted that agricultural expansion is necessary to enable the UK to achieve equilibrium in its balance of payments. The farmers are equally aware of the interest of our exporting industries in a general expansion of overseas trade. Industry is now aware that the advocacy of oversimplified policies of trade liberalization cannot resolve the problem of ensuring production and market stability in agriculture and a narrowing of the income gap. British industrial opinion is becoming increasingly aware of the fact that any solution of the problems that arise from the existence throughout the world of uncoordinated national support policies will have to be found in the direction of specific international commodity arrangements or agreements along the lines that the International Federation of Agricultural Producers and other bodies have been adovcating for many years.

In the enlarged Community, the risk of a direct conflict between agricultural organizations and other groups in society over the evolution of the CAP can only be avoided if a much better understanding is encouraged to emerge about, on the one hand, the consumer's need for food at reasonable and stable prices and, on the other, the problems and difficulties concerning European agriculture. Too often slogans such as "cheap food" are mistaken for policies and are

advocated regardless of the economic and social impact that they would
have on farmers and workers in agriculture.

THE FUTURE OF THE COMMON
AGRICULTURAL POLICY

Fundamental Principles

The purpose of an agricultural policy for any country or region
is to serve the needs of the consumers of that area in ways that are
consistent with the economic and social welfare of those who are
engaged in producing the food and fiber required and with the social
and environmental needs of the country or region. If the policy is
completely inward looking, one which, for example, disregards international economic relations, it will fail in its objective. A policy that
is based solely on the principle of comparative costs and is neglectful
of social, environmental, and other factors is also unsatisfactory. It
is thus important to achieve an acceptable balance between all the
factors—economic, social, political, and strategic—which must be
basic to any agricultural policy.

The main contention of the critics of the existing CAP is that
despite its complex and somewhat cumbersome apparatus of support,
it has failed to achieve a sufficient improvement in the standard of
living of the agricultural community. The critics argue that in agriculture, the CAP has also had the undesirable effect of widening the earnings gap between those who farm larger and structurally more viable
businesses and the smaller family farmers who still constitute the
majority. It is alleged that existing prices, while resulting in abnor-
mally high net incomes for the relatively small number of large farm
businesses, fail to provide an adequate return for the vast majority
of small farmers. As price policy has failed, something else must
be tried; the cure, they say, is to be found in moving the emphasis
away from price policy toward structural reform, regional policy,
and selective aids to income. The substitution of a more discriminatory
approach in place of general support would, it is claimed, assist those
farmers who are most in need of help while not really prejudicing the
position of those whose circumstances are, in any event, more favorable.

The claim that under the present policy a relatively small
number of farms make excessive profits may appear to be conclusive
when absolute levels of profit are quoted and comparisons made with
profits on smaller units. Two points are, however, generally overlooked. First, the argument that price policy has been determined

in the Community and in the acceding countries by reference to the unit costs of the least efficient producers is far from the truth. If this were true, not only would contentment reign among European farmers, none of whom would then be required to leave the land, but also profits on the bigger farms would be excessive in relation to the capital employed. Secondly, it is quite wrong to disregard the enormous increase in the capital requirements of large farm businesses endeavoring to use the most up-to-date techniques and equipment and to develop better marketing. The modernization and improvement of farm buildings, improvements to the land, and the financing of regular inputs have transformed the scale of capital needs and the problem of sources of finance. This capital has to be paid for and serviced. During the middle 1960s, when the British government, in a period of severe inflation of farm costs, failed adequately to adjust prices, it was noticeable that the main outcry came, not so much from small producers but from the medium-sized and larger farms, especially arable and mixed farms where, on the basis of substituting more capital for falling manpower, the best progress in productivity had been achieved during the previous decade. During the period of price standstill in the Community, the same situation applied, the burden on the bigger farms in the Netherlands and Germany evoking particular criticism. Today in the six countries, the larger fruit-growing farms are experiencing more difficulty than smaller farms.

Unlike manufacturing industry which raises the bulk of its risk capital in the money market, agriculture has to rely primarily on its own resources for capital for further development. These are often inadequate and have to be supplemented by borrowings from credit institutions and by state aids. On smaller farms, returns are low and represent in the main payment for the farm family's own labor effort—the capital at risk is generally not very great. On larger farm businesses, however, where the capital involvement is considerable, the yield still tends to be less than normally to be found in manufacturing industry. Lower prices would widen this gap and aggravate the financing problem of those farms responsible for a high proportion of output. As manpower in agriculture continues to decline in the years ahead, the sources and methods of capitalizing the agricultural industry in Europe and North America will need to be examined with even greater care than in the past.

Under Article 39 of the Treaty of Rome, one of the objectives of the CAP is an increase in agricultural productivity. The evidence given earlier in this chapter shows that the productivity of European agriculture has undoubtedly increased during the last decade. Whether this was boosted by the CAP or would have occurred anyway could be debated at length. What is surely clear is that the impetus given to agricultural production and trade within the six countries undoubtedly helped to produce an atmosphere conducive to the development of productivity—not only in agriculture but also in other sectors of the economy.

The development of the CAP was foreseen not only as a way of enabling farmers and workers to raise their living standards but also to stabilize markets, guarantee regular supplies, and ensure reasonable prices in supplies to consumers. Clearly, the CAP has had only limited success in achieving these aims. For some commodities, for example, cereals, sugar beet, and milk products, the CAP in operation has provided some market stability. The operation of threshold prices and variable levies coupled with market intervention must, at any rate in the short term, stabilize market prices. For other commodities, especially the intensively produced livestock products, such as eggs, poultry meat, and pigmeat, no serious attempt has as yet been made by the Community to introduce regulations which would result in either price or market stability. The external protection afforded through variable levies, sluice gate prices and, in pigmeat, internally through support buying, is of little relevance in the case of products for which the existing six meet virtually the whole of their needs. In the case of fruit and vegetables and wine, the CAP has also failed to bring about stability either for producers or consumers; this explains why attempts are now being made to change the existing regulations.

To guarantee regular supplies is a much more difficult objective. Though the interdependence of the modern world is taken almost for granted, there is no country that is prepared to pursue a laissez-faire policy in agriculture. A high level of domestic production is regarded everywhere as giving some protection to consumers against the inevitable vicissitudes of production and trade outside the country's borders and a guarantee to them that under certain conditions they will not be held to ransom by overseas suppliers. Food and the cost of living are among the most highly sensitive political issues in any community. The degree of reliance on indigenous food production was high in most of the six countries before they came together; over the 1960s the ratio of Community production to total needs has, in fact, increased only marginally, from just under 90 percent in 1958 to just over 90 percent today. Of the candidate countries, the UK, as the world's largest single importer of food, has traditionally been in a more vulnerable position. Even today, despite the fact that the volume of domestic agriculture has more than doubled over the past three decades, British farmers and growers supply only 52 percent of the consumers' total food needs; of the products that can be grown economically in Britain, the share is 66 percent, well below the level in the six countries. An outbreak of foot and mouth disease, bad crops in Europe, North America, and elsewhere, a dock strike—and the vulnerability of the British consumer is immediately exposed, not to

say that of the animals dependent on imported feed grains and protein.
Having said this, the Europe of the enlarged Community will still
require to import a substantial part of its food needs from other countries, and its agricultural policy will continue to recognize this factor.
The need to ensure regular supplies must underlie both the internal
and external aspects of agricultural policy.

It is not easy to disentangle the CAP's role in ensuring reasonable
prices in supplies to consumers. In Europe, retail prices for some
foods are certainly high by comparison with what they are in North
America, but this is certainly not true of all foods. In the UK where,
since the repeal of the Corn Laws in 1846, the traditional policy has
been one of cheap food, there is naturally public concern about the
higher prices which will have to be paid as a result of adopting the
CAP, though the impact, it should be observed, is being spread over
a five-year transitional period. However, it is relevant to observe
that in the past year the large increases in market prices of cereals,
meat, and other foods have been due primarily to world developments
and not to the introduction of the CAP.

In Europe as in North America, though with a time lag, three
tendencies are clearly discernible. The first is that consumer expenditure on food as a proportion of total personal expenditure at the retail
level is falling. This is, of course, a reflection of the considerable
rate of economic growth, especially in the six countries, during the
1960s. Secondly, the farmer is obtaining a decreasing share of every
dollar which the consumer spends on food. In the Federal Republic
of Germany, the ratio fell from 54 percent in 1960 to 51 percent in
1968; during the same period in the United States, the figure remained
at 39 percent.[1] Thirdly, within this smaller share, the element contributed by purchased farm inputs is increasing and that determined
by value added on the farm is diminishing. The FAO study sets out
the changes typical of any industrial country. Twenty years ago, the
value added on the farms of such a country represented 55 percent
of the total retail value. By 1965 this had fallen to 35 percent, and
by 1980 or soon after it will almost certainly have fallen to around
20 percent, a situation already reached in the United States. Purchased inputs, which represented 10 percent of retail value in 1950,
had reached 15 percent in 1965 and could be as high as 20 percent in
1980.

All this underlines how difficult it is to establish a close relationship between farm price policy and food prices at the retail level.
While the determination of prices at the farm can take account of the
cost of farm inputs and can clearly affect the input prices of food
processors and distributors, it is also evident that the impact of
processing, distribution, and advertising costs on retail prices is of
growing importance on both sides of the Atlantic. Any criticism of

the CAP for its impact on consumer prices must accordingly be qual-
ified in the light of the consumers' quite natural desire to see more
preparation and sophistication in the preparation of food for the table.

There cannot be any absolute judgment on the level of Community food prices. Prices for some commodities, notably grains,
which looked high only a little while ago, now look reasonable as world
prices, themselves affected by domestic support policies, respond to
these longer-term developments. There is also a tendency to disregard
the effects of inflation. During the 1960s, farm prices have lagged
well behind the rise in the general level of prices. This means that
in real terms farm prices have, in fact, risen very little or in some
countries have actually fallen.

It is next necessary to consider whether there are likely to be
any changes in either the basic principles or the fundamental mechanisms of the CAP. Our view is that these will not be negotiable.
Membership in the Community has always postulated the obligation
to accept the CAP. However, while the principles are undoubtedly
sacrosanct, this is not necessarily true of either certain mechanisms
by which the policy is applied or the degree of support fixed in accordance with it. The methods by which the CAP is implemented can change
and evolve over time to meet the changing circumstances—internal
and external—of an enlarged Community

On the internal side, possible changes can be grouped under
four headings:
1. price policy;
2. structural and social policy;
3. policies from farms in especially handicapped areas;
4. selective income aids.
Externally, stimulus to change will stem from the need to establish
a new modus vivendi in international agricultural trade between the
enlarged Community and the rest of the world.

Criticisms of price policy have focused in the main on three
aspects: the general level of prices, commodity price relativities,
and impact on trade with third countries. Producers have been critical
of the Community's reluctance to allow of more than very modest
increases from prices which, by non-Community standards, are already
considered to be too high. Yet in the EEC as elsewhere, the real
value of prices has been eroded by general inflation; in many countries,
rises in factor costs have more than absorbed any benefit to income
accruing from increasing productivity.

There is next the criticism that the relationship between commodity prices is inappropriate to the real needs of the Community.
It has been evident for a long time that the wheat price, while tending
with other factors to make Europe self-sufficient in soft wheat, did
little to improve the income of small farms. The related prices for

coarse grains coupled with the absence of protection for grain substitutes, have tended to limit the use of grain for animal feed and the
development of more intensive production of the conversion products.
In part, this stemmed from the fear that low grain prices would mean
the disappearance of the traditional farmer and an upsurge in factory-
type production of broilers, eggs, pigmeat, and even beef. There are
signs, however, that in this respect attitudes are beginning to change
as an increasing number of farmers themselves switch over to large-
scale livestock production. Britain's entry into the EEC may, in this
respect, be an important catalyst. Britain's output of meat, poultry,
eggs, and dairy products has been established on the basis of allowing
home-produced feed grains, including wheat, and protein to compete
fairly liberally with imported grain and protein. Some 70 percent of
the UK's production of cereals is, in fact, utilized for animal feed.
Although British farmers today produce some 3 out of every 4 tons
of the total concentrated feeds required by the country's livestock
population, annual imports of grain for animal feed still amount to
some 3 to 4 million tons; imports of other feeds total about 2 million
tons. In the six countries imports of animal feed, despite increasing
domestic production, have more than doubled during the past eight
years and amount to 30 million tons (cereals equivalent). Imports of
grain substitutes, which are included in this figure, are considerable
and amounted in 1970 to some 4 1/2 million metric tons. Yet between
the six and the UK, the vital difference is in price; a measure of this
gap can be gleaned from the trading compensatory amounts for cereals
(wheat, 18.76 pounds per ton; barley, 17.92 pounds per ton; maize,
15.63 pounds per ton) agreed in July 1972 as part of the mechanism
by which the applicant countries will, from February 1, 1973, begin
the task of aligning their market prices to those of the Community.
At the time of writing, the gap between market prices in the six and
the UK had narrowed considerably as a result of the general rise in
world prices in recent months. The latter have indeed in some cases
risen above the Community threshold prices. It should be possible
to consider two types of price adjustment: first, to give greater encouragement to feed grains than to grains for human consumption;
secondly, to give greater emphasis to the prices of livestock products,
including special incentive arrangements, relative to those for cereals.

In Europe, because of relatively high cereal prices, the tendency
has been for manufacturers of feed compounds in some countries to
reduce the cereal content of animal rations and to introduce such
substitutes as cassava, manioc, and tapioca. Moreover, because of
the binding of duty-free entry under General Agreement on Tariffs
and Trade (GATT), the use of soya in cattle rations has grown considerably. This has been of great benefit to U.S. agriculture in the
1960s, a considerable offset to any restriction of outlets on the

cereals front. Exports of soybeans by the United States to the ten rose from 1.9 million tons in 1960/62 to an average of 4 1/2 million tons in 1970 and 1971. It can be argued that European grain growers would not have lost these outlets to competing materials had grain prices during that period been somewhat lower relative to those for livestock products.

It is highly unlikely that in the 1970s it will prove feasible for the enlarged Community to adopt a deficiency payments system on the UK model. Britain, in accepting the CAP, has accepted the levy system. Indeed, in political and farm organization circles in the UK, the deficiency payments system has been under severe criticism in recent years on account of the constraints it imposed on agricultural expansion and for its failure to achieve a more satisfactory level of farm incomes.

Objections in Europe to the concept of deficiency payments as a method of price support for some commodities are, however, less vehement than they were a decade ago. The suggestion that the system might be applied in Europe has been opposed primarily for two reasons: first, because it was felt that with Community production at a high level of self-sufficiency, support by Treasuries was politically more vulnerable than if it were subsumed in the prices paid by consumers; secondly, because of the great difficulty of administering the system for many millions of farmers. On the first point, the fact is that if allowance is made for existing national aids, a part of existing agricultural support costs in the six is already funded out of national Exchequer contributions; the income from levies and customs tariffs falls short of the present budgetary needs of the CAP quite apart from the national aid. The real political argument is more concerned with the issue of total resource use in agriculture than with the method of support. On the second point, it has to be acknowledged that under present circumstances, despite the substantial decline in the number of farmers in the six during the last decade, the administrative difficulties of introducing a deficiency payments system would still be formidable. Yet the possibilities for the future should not be disregarded; it may be possible to extend the system to other products.

The reform of agriculture proposed in the Mansholt Plan is based upon the concept of "a total recasting of agricultural policy." Since 1970 the Mansholt Plan has, in fact, been substantially revised; it no longer provides, for example, for reducing the area of farmland by reforestation and is generally conceived on much more modest lines. Essentially it is to be implemented by the provision of Community funds to promote the modernization of farms, to help outgoers from farming, and to improve production and marketing techniques through producer groups. Although it is true that Mansholt was originally looking for a shift in emphasis from price support to structural reform, it is untrue to imply that this would have meant a departure from the basic concepts of the CAP.

In "A Future for European Agriculture,"[2] proposals were set out for switching the emphasis on support policy from price to selective income aids. Those favoring this method believe that it is possible to divorce support payments from the product itself and to relate these essentially to the needs of the farmer. They are primarily envisaged as payments for the least-favored farmers whose problems would thus be dealt with on the basis of social rather than economic criteria. By this route, the way would be open, it is claimed, to the establishment of an agricultural price policy based upon economic criteria. In practice, however, it is extremely doubtful whether it would be feasible to achieve a separation of the economic and social elements in price policy. Moreover, the idea that payments not directly related to the commodity have little or no effect on its production is not borne out by recent experience in the United States. In any event, most farmers would be reluctant to switch from a price system to one of social welfare handouts.

Permanent income support measures could, however, have a role to play in certain circumstances. They could be of real value where, for social or environmental reasons, the country or region might wish to retain the appearance of the countryside and its general well-being. Another obvious example is provided by the need to maintain farms in hill and mountain regions where special aids are required to overcome the disadvantages of natural handicaps, but direct income aids may also be applicable in semiurban or "greenbelt" areas where only farms of modest size may be feasible.

We believe that much of the criticism made of general price support policy could be overcome if prior to the determination of prices of the basic commodities, the enlarged Community were to institute an annual review of the economic state of agriculture modeled on the existing British procedures. The annual review in the UK establishes a basis not only for reviewing the financial condition of the industry as a whole (changes in farm incomes, costs of production, and so on) and of its different sectors, but also for taking account of other major factors that are held to be relevant in the process of price determination. The principal ones are the trends of production and consumption, commodity by commodity; imports and exports of food; world price trends; the trend of agricultural productivity; existing resource use and claims by agriculture for additional resources; the capital needs of agriculture.

The review is thus an annual monitoring of agriculture in all its aspects. It provides the opportunity for effect to be given to necessary changes in agricultural policy, bearing in mind the varying production cycles for different commodities. Above all, it provides the opportunity for prices to be based, to some extent, on objective economic criteria, not leaving them to the mercy of purely political considerations.

It is also possible, as British experience has shown, to have an annual review operating within the compass of a longer-term agricultural policy. The knowledge that there is this annual appraisal of agriculture's circumstances helps to sustain producer confidence at a time when, in the light of the growing capital demands postulated by modern agricultural technology, it becomes increasingly important to assure producers an element of stability in their expected returns, which must be at a level sufficient to cover an appropriate yield on their capital. Unless this is so, funds for further investment will be lacking, the rate of improvement in productivity will inevitably be slowed down, and agriculture's claim on resources will be weakened. Experience in the UK has shown that the stability afforded by the system of annual reviews and guaranteed prices has had a distinctly beneficial effect on productivity—whether measured in terms of added value per man or as output per unit of all inputs used, agriculture's record compares most favorably with that of other sectors.

The agreement concluded between the UK and the six countries during the preentry negotiations, envisaging the institution of an effective and meaningful annual review, could well be the basis for a reshaping of the modalities of the existing CAP, notably in the field of price policy.

Production and Trade Prospects

Trade between the EEC and the United States in
Agricultural Products

There is little evidence to justify singling out the CAP as a major reason for the decline in the relative importance of agricultural products in the U.S. export total. In fact, the proportion of U.S. exports of food and live animals accounted for by the EEC countries was slightly higher in the years 1968/71 than in 1960/62 (21 percent as against 19 percent), while the EEC share of all U.S. agricultural exports showed only a fractional decline over the period.

United States exports of feed grains, corn and barley, to the six were 5.1 million tons in 1970, 5.7 millions tons in 1971, and 6.8 million tons in 1972 as compared with only 3.2 million tons in 1960/62. The volume of wheat exports has fluctuated from year to year, but a considerable trade has been maintained in high-protein varieties.

The slump in U.S. poultry meat exports to the six has been one of the most, if not the most, widely quoted examples of the deleterious effect of the CAP on international trade. Although the application of import levies has had a major effect on the EEC poultry situation, it is likely that the rapid development of the European broiler industries would, in any case, have reduced the opportunities available to U.S. exporters. There have also been certain health preoccupations on the part of European consumers.

United States exports to the EEC of nonvariable levy commodities have generally shown an upward trend since the inception of the CAP. The composition of these exports, however, has changed considerably. The overall rise has, in fact, occurred in spite of a marked fall in cotton exports—a fall due to factors such as the decline in U.S. cotton production and the increased use in Europe of man-made fibers, rather than to the CAP.

The outstanding expansion in U.S. exports to the six has been in soybeans and their products, trade in the beans alone being currently in the region of 4 million tons against the 1960/62 average of barely 1 1/2 million tons.

In addition, it may be argued that U.S. exports have been increased indirectly by the formation of the EEC itself. Certainly overall demand for feeding stuffs in the Community has been increased by the rise in demand for livestock products which accompanied rising income levels and, if it is accepted that the formation of the Community has aided economic growth, then it would seem also to have been of benefit to U.S. exporters of soybeans.

Whereas U.S. exports of all agricultural products to the six rose by some 38 percent in the 1960s, the value of exports to the UK in 1970 was a little less than it was in 1960/62. Exports to the Irish Republic, Denmark, and Norway rose by some 29 percent, but the total value of trade is rather small. Britain's traditional dependence on food imports for an important part of her needs has handicapped her attempts in the postwar world to achieve a faster rate of economic growth. It is, therefore, not surprising that against the background of the UK's selective expansion program in the 1960s, a policy designed essentially to save imports and thereby help the balance of payments, there should have been little buoyancy in her agricultural trade with the United States.

It cannot be denied that in consequence of enlargement and the application of the principle of Community preference, the demand for the key temperate zone products by the ten is likely to be met increasingly from production within the area and that there is likely to be some net contraction in imports. This situation arises principally from the trade-diverting effects following the entry of the UK.

By joining the EEC, the UK has undertaken to accept the terms of the CAP, subject only to the various derogations and arrangements made during the preentry talks. Although there has been considerable debate about the extent of the impact, membership and adherence to the CAP must mean some rise in the UK's bill for imported food. This will occur both because imports from third countries will be subject to levies, the proceeds of which have to be transferred to the Community fund, and also because higher prices will be paid for food imports from inside the Community.

However, estimates of the impact of the CAP on UK food prices and the balance of payments have been outdated by the transformation during the past year or so in the world commodity situation. Soaring increases in prices of wheat and feed grains, soybeans and meals, sugar, meat, and other products have already had an impact on the British economy that far outweighs the effects of the CAP. It has been estimated that in the year since mid-1972, of the 15 percent rise in food prices in the UK, only 1 percent is attributable to the effects of the CAP.

Though there is a five-year transitional period, the arrangements are designed to ensure that the principle of Community preference is applied in full at the outset, that is, from February 1, 1973. The actual burden on the UK's balance of payments was expected to be small to begin with, but would rise during the transitional period.

So there will be two principal factors at work: Community preference which inevitably must entail some switch in Britain's imports from nonmember to member countries, leading to an increase in their production, and an added incentive to British agriculture to increase its own production in order to reduce the net cost to the balance of payments.

While special arrangements have been made to deal with the special problem of New Zealand dairy products, the treaty provides only for transitional safeguards (Protocol No. 16) for other third countries. There is the assurance that there will be no sudden cutoff of trade. However, for grains, sugar, milk products, meat and poultry, and fruit, some shift will occur as between the enlarged Community and the major nonmember supplying countries in the volume and pattern of trade.

In regard to trade between the enlarged Community and developing countries, the principal items in the agricultural field relate to sugar and to oilseeds. For the developing countries of the Commonwealth, an arrangement will be made to follow the termination at the end of 1974 of the existing Commonwealth Sugar Agreement. For oilseeds, much will depend upon the agreements reached between the enlarged Community and the territories associated with it through trade and other agreements. In this respect, it should be observed that the UK will be expected to phase out the existing tariffs on certain oilseeds and oil cakes that have hitherto been maintained in order to grant a measure a Commonwealth preference. The United States is likely to gain in this regard as the 10-percent duty on imports of soybeans into the UK will eventually disappear. The successive devaluations of the U.S. dollar will also help to boost certain exports.

In light of all these possible developments, it is impossible to be too specific as to how the production and trading pattern of the late 1970s will eventually emerge. There are three aspects meriting further study. First, there is the potential development of trade between the United States and the central planning countries. The new understandings between the United States, China, and the USSR could lead to a substantial development of exports of agricultural products from the United States to these countries on a permanent basis. Canadian experience has shown that the long-term contracts negotiated with China and Russia have been repeated several times. Political detente should be the precursor of trade expansion. On the basis of the three-year deal negotiated between the United States and the USSR in 1972 and arrangements made subsequently, prospects for the development of trade should be favorable. Domestic prices for wheat in the United States have already risen sharply during the past year.

Secondly, there is the prospect of an expansion of trade between Japan and other southeast Asian countries, on the one hand, and the food-exporting countries in the Pacific zone, on the other. During the last 10 years, significant progress has been made by New Zealand and Australia in expanding their exports of livestock and dairy products to Japan. Japan has become a most important outlet for U.S. agricultural products, notably for such commodities as cereals and lard. If Japan succeeds in making her own agreement with People's Republic of China, there is likely to be a considerable stimulus given to further economic development in Japan, which should be accompanied by further liberalization in her food import arrangements. There are also strong possibilities of trade with other areas in southeast Asia, notably with Indonesia and Malaysia.

Thirdly, greater attention will have to be given in the future to the possibility of extending trade among the developing countries themselves. There has been a tendency on the part of the developing countries to look to the developed countries for outlets for commodities in which they themselves are deficient. It is really questionable for a country like Pakistan to become an exporter of cereals when large sectors of her own population are suffering from malnutrition and undernourishment and she lacks the necessary food reserves to meet periodical emergencies and disasters. The formation of regional groupings among developing countries could be an important stimulus to trade in this regard and an incentive to the better use of agricultural resources within these areas. These countries will however, continue to need aid on a substantial scale. The role that food aid played and can continue to play under such schemes as the World Food Program must be properly assessed and encouraged.

It would accordingly be quite wrong, in setting the scene for the 1973 trade negotiations, for the countries of the North Atlantic area to take what could be regarded as essentially an inward-looking perspective. If the developments, which have been broadly depicted above, are disregarded or even ignored, the negotiations will be largely conditioned by fears of narrowing trade outlets which, in the event, are unlikely to be realized. If, however, full account is taken of the wider possibilities mentioned here, there will be a better chance of negotiating arrangements for agriculture, which will assist toward an orderly expansion of world trade in the 1970s.

Need for a New Approach to Agricultural Trade Policy

It has been fashionable to regard agricultural protectionism as the main obstacle toward further attempts to liberalize world trade. Before the Kennedy Round, the U.S. government made it clear that it would seek significant concessions in the agricultural sector as a condition of any further liberalization of trade in manufactured products. In the event the fairly limited results of the Kennedy Round in agriculture did not prevent the United States from undertaking obligations covering manufactured products, some of which incidentally remain to be fulfilled. It is perhaps easier to understand the pressure for agricultural concessions from countries like Australia and New Zealand, where agriculture constitutes a higher proportion of both the gross domestic product and of external trade than it does in the case of the United States whose manufacturing apparatus is the largest and often the most advanced in the world.

The impression has been allowed to develop that countries give much more protection to their agriculture than they do to their manufacturing industries. While it is true that, under successive rounds of GATT negotiations since World War II, the level of tariffs on industrial products has been brought down and a large number of quotas have been eliminated, it is extremely difficult, if not impossible, to assess the protection afforded to industry in most developed countries through other arrangements. How, for example, does one assess the real protection afforded by the emergence of near monopolies and their extension across borders in the form of multinational corporations? How does one assess the considerable support from public funds given to manufacturing industry? What about the preferences shown to local industries by public authorities? There are many arrangements that perhaps attract less publicity than the well-known American selling price system. In fairness and in view of the mounting volume of criticism of agricultural protectionism, these facts should be mentioned.

From the European standpoint, there is another feature that must be brought into the open. Numerous criticisms have been directed by government and other authorities against the protectionist policies of European agriculture and more specifically against the protective aspects of the CAP. These criticisms rose to a crescendo after the measures taken by President Nixon on August 16, 1971. There has been virtually what amounts to an organized campaign against European agriculture accompanied by threats of massive retaliation, which would be directed against the manufacturing exports of Europe to the United States if nothing were done to reduce the extent of agricultural protectionism. Yet the fact remains that the expansion in U.S. agriculture during recent decades would hardly have taken place had it not been for the support policies begun by the United States in the era of depression after World War I and continued with variations ever since. According to Mr. Don Paarlberg, the level of protection for agriculture, both direct and indirect, in the United States was recently calculated to be on the order of $9500 million. American farmers are helped not only by such schemes as market intervention undertaken through the Commodity Credit Corporation (CCC) for certain basic commodities, but also by strict control of imports for certain key commodities, "voluntary" arrangements negotiated with exporting countries for the regulation of their exports to the United States, marketing orders, and by many other devices. What in Europe would be termed national aids for the improvement and modernization of holdings and for the improvement of the infrastructure of rural areas has been characteristic of the U.S. scene for many years.

Under the new Farm Bill, signed albeit reluctantly by President Nixon in August 1973, the United States will operate during the next four years what is tantamount to a deficiency payments system for key crops coupled with loan supports and import controls. If world prices remain high, the cost to the U.S. taxpayer will fall from existing levels but should prices fall, the cost could of course be considerable.

Against this background it is really difficult for Europeans to accept that agricultural protectionism is the primary reason for the present balance of payments difficulties of the United States. It is perfectly possible for Europeans to understand why, for U.S. farming and trading interests, the opportunity to develop markets overseas is a matter of some importance. It is not, however, easy to accept the thesis that the CAP and protectionist policies pursued by other countries were the primary cause of the United States having to take roundabout steps to devalue the dollar and to sever the link with gold. The causes of the U.S. financial crisis are much more deep seated and nonagricultural in origin.

The joint U.S.-EEC announcement of February 4, 1972, contained essentially a declaration of intent to start a new multilateral round of world trade negotiations in 1973. Its main provisions are:

1. a review of international economic relations, including measures "which impede or distort agricultural, raw material, and industrial trade";

2. an agreement to initiate and actively support multilateral and comprehensive negotiations in the framework of GATT beginning in 1973;

3. a statement by the Community that ". . . in appropriate cases the conclusion of international commodity agreements is also one of the means to achieve these aims"(that is, of trade liberalization and improvements in living standards);

4. a statement by the United States that such agreements do not offer a useful approach to the achievement of these aims;

5. the negotiations to be conducted "on the basis of mutual advantage and mutual commitment with overall reciprocity and shall cover agricultural as well as industrial trade";

6. an agreement to initiate and support in 1972 an analysis and evaluation in the GATT "of alternative techniques and modalities for multilateral negotiation of long-term problems affecting all elements of world trade."

On February 28, 1972, the British government made a statement welcoming this agreement, indicated that it had been fully consulted during the course of the discussions and that it would support the objective of initiating negotiations in 1973 within the framework of GATT for the further liberalization of world trade, covering agricultural as well as industrial trade.

It will be recalled that during the Kennedy Round, the Community— at a time when the CAP was still in its first phases—adopted a positive reaction. The Community proposed to all of its trading partners to make commitments on the content of national agricultural policies in the framework of international commodity agreements. These proposals included:

Consolidation of the margin of support (montant de soutien), i.e., the difference between the level of agricultural prices on the internal market and the level of prices operative on the world market. Negotiation of a minimum price that should be respected in international trade. This price would be fixed at a level which would assure farmers of a certain level of income. The existence of such an international reference price would help to avoid low price wars. As the Community would have to respect this minimum price, it would clearly limit the amount of Community export subsidies or restitutions, a factor which would be of considerable importance for other exporting countries trading in third markets.

A commitment on a self-sufficiency ratio, i.e., on a rapport between production and consumption, constituting an indirect step toward the better adaptation of supply to demand. If the self-sufficiency ratio were exceeded, there would be an agreement whereby the country responsible would refrain from offering the surplus commodities on the commercial market and instead take all necessary corrective measures.

A multilateral food aid program including diversification cooperation among donor countries.

The U.S., British, and other governments rejected the main elements in the Community's proposal at that time. There are three main reasons why the proposal failed to command general support. First, other countries drew attention to the technical difficulties of establishing the margin of support, commodity by commodity, in a situation in which most countries used indirect as well as direct methods of supporting their agricultural producers. Secondly, the Community was criticized for having put forward a proposal for consolidating the existing degree of protection and of refusing to make any reductions. Thirdly, the Community insisted that in the event of inflation and further increases in agricultural costs, countries would have to be permitted to raise their farm prices in order to restore the level of support in real terms. This was alleged to provide too many loopholes for the effective operation of the scheme.

Only in the case of the International Grains Agreement did one or two or the ideas contained in the montant de soutien approach yield fruit. The Grains Agreement negotiated in 1967 provided not only for an agreement on price ranges, but also for the direction of stocks of wheat into food aid. This commitment was to expire on June 30, 1971, but its value disappeared in 1970. The concept was, however, partially reborne early in 1972 in the bilateral agreement between the United States and the six countries to remove a limited amount of surplus wheat from the market.

Proposed Basis for Agricultural Cooperation

If any solution to the world agricultural problem is to stand any reasonable chance of acceptance in the forthcoming world trade negotiations, it must respect a number of principles. First, the solution must not be biased in favor of any particular group of countries. Secondly it must provide reciprocal benefits as well as reciprocal obligations. Thirdly, nations and regional groupings must retain their freedom to determine their agricultural policies subject to constraints which are freely undertaken in accordance with international agreements. Fourthly, these constraints must be such as are likely to be respected by national executives and legislatures. Fifthly, the solution must have regard to the interests of developing as well as to those of developed countries. Sixthly, while recognizing that consumers desire to buy their food as cheaply as possible, the policy must have regard to the basic need of producers for a fair return for their efforts and capital investment. Finally, granted that resource adjustment in agriculture is a relatively slow process and that there are inelasticities on the part of both supply and demand, the solution must recognize that the laws of economics and, in particular, the principle of comparative advantage, do not work smoothly in agriculture.

In order to have any chance of acceptance, a scheme must endeavor to fulfill the following aspirations for exporting countries:

- It must provide them with some assurance of access in their traditional markets.
- It must provide some safeguard for their exports against competitive dumping in third markets.
- It must give them some knowledge of the future potential for their exports, thereby enabling them to adapt their domestic production policies to the prospective total of domestic and export demand.

For importing countries, any acceptable scheme must:

- put an end to full-blooded competition at arbitrarily low and totally uneconomic prices, resulting in great difficulties for domestic producers and national exchequers;
- enable such countries to determine farm prices at a level that takes proper account of the income and other needs of their producers;
- have regard to the fact that accumulation of stocks may lead the national or regional authorities concerned to bring in measures of limitation;
- place limits on the extent of export restitutions.

To be acceptable to developing countries, the scheme must also fulfill certain criteria. First, to the extent that such countries wish to increase their earnings for primary commodities, it must provide an element of stability in the prices at which these commodities are traded across frontiers. Secondly, the developing countries must have some assurance from the industrial countries that their policies will ensure a degree of access for their products. Thirdly, developing countries still dependent upon imports of food will require assurances that such imports do not disturb their own efforts to increase their agricultural production.

The plan set out below is designed initially to be applied, according to the particular circumstances of the commodity to a limited number of temperate zone products. Some of these would naturally be of direct interest also to the developong countries. The commodities for which agreements are contemplated are grains, dairy products, certain oilseeds, sugar, and meat, though for the present this commodity is not a priority sector. The principles of this arrangement could, however, be extended to include agricultural products of the tropical zone.

The Plan

An international reference price would be agreed for ordinary commercial transactions for, say, a three-year period. This price would be for an appropriate grade or quality of the product at a base point or a series of base points.

The price would be fixed somewhere between the lowest existing export price in a main exporting country and the highest producer price, also in an important producing area. For example, in the case of wheat, the price could be fixed somewhere between the U.S. price and the producer price in the EEC. In order to narrow the debate as to where the price should be fixed, it should be agreed in advance of the negotiation that the point should lie in the range of one-third to two-thirds of the existing gap between the highest and lowest prices.

In assessing the level of existing prices, account would be taken of any direct grants or subsidies which could be measurably attributed to the commodity. Grants of a general or structural character would not, however, be taken into account. A second tier lower international reference price would be determined to apply to noncommercial transactions. Entitlement to supplies at this price would be governed by strict rules.

Within the limits of the criteria set out below, the agricultural support policies for participating countries or areas would still be determined by the governments and/or authorities responsible for these countries and areas. However, the reconciliation between these policies and the needs of the international community would be sought by adhering to the following criteria:

- Each contracting nation or region would be free to vary the level of its price guarantees or other commodity commitment to allow for changes in the level of farm incomes in the area as a whole and, in the particular commodity sector, changes in production costs and other relevant factors.
- Exporting countries would undertake to sell their product abroad at not less than the agreed international reference prices for commercial transactions (subject to the fifth criterion below).
- Self-sufficient countries or areas, and net importing countries which occasionally produce more than their domestic needs, would also agree to abide by the international reference price for their exports on world markets.

- A generalized undertaking would be given by all countries participating in the agreement to pursue trading policies which will, as far as possible, assure an orderly expansion of trade within the boundaries set by the agreed international reference prices.
- The lower tier reference price would apply to purchases by developing countries that undertake to observe the conditions of participation in the scheme. Such countries would, for example, have to accept supervision by the appropriate international commodity council to ensure that such purchases were not being made for resale on the world market at the higher reference commercial price. Care would also have to be taken that the developing country did not use lower-priced imports to substitute for its own home production, which would then be reexported at the higher commercial price. The financing of noncommercial transactions would be a matter primarily for the international lending or aid agencies concerned (World Food Program, special loans or grants).
- In order to respect the international reference prices, participating countries would agree to hold additional stocks as, and when this became, necessary (see below).

Where bodies do not already exist for commodities for which agreements on this pattern are contemplated, it is suggested that in anticipation of the world trade negotiations scheduled to commence in 1973, an intergovernmental commodity council should be established consisting of representatives of all countries whose production of that commodity is of any international significance. To assist in the expeditions working of agreements due to be negotiated, it is suggested that government delegates should be assisted by advisers drawn from producer, processing, and trading organizations.

Although agreements would in principle be negotiated for three-year periods, participating governments, through the medium of the international commodity council, would undertake an annual review of the operation of each arrangement, arising out of which they should be free to make any variations in reference prices should the need have arisen as a result of production and trade developments in the course of the preceding year.

The commodity council would keep the market situation under constant surveillance during the year. In the event of any actual or foreseen disturbance to the market, it would be open to any government to ask for a special session of the council, a request which would normally be granted on an affirmative response from an agreed minimum number of governments, though in exceptional circumstances the council could be convened at the request of only one government.

It is imperative that all the main importing countries and areas of the world should participate in these agreements. If the international reference price is to be respected, all major exporting and importing areas must accept the degree of discipline involved. Now that trade relations between the United States, the USSR, and other central planning countries are on the threshold of major development, it should be possible to involve these countries in any world agreements. It is also of particular importance that Japan, likely also to be a major food-importing area in the years ahead, should play a part in these agreements. The Japanese market for food has been developing in the postwar period and is of growing importance for agricultural exporting countries in the South Pacific as well as for the United States itself.

The establishment of an international reference price would, from a technical point of view, ease the position of importers in the Community who are often critical of the frequency with which changes are made in the variable levies. An international reference price, which was properly respected, would clearly reduce the need for frequent changes in the levies. Indeed, it might be possible to institute a system which would be nearer to a fixed levy scheme, the levies being subject to change in the event of the failure by certain countries to respect the international prices. Levies would, however, be reduced when world prices exceeded the international reference price. What is said here about levies would also apply to export restitutions.

One of the key commodity sectors for any negotiations on the pattern envisaged in this note is that of dairy products. It will be recalled that in the preentry negotiations between the UK and the six leading to the Treaty of Accession, an agreement was reached to seek a permanent solution of the problem of New Zealand dairy products through the medium of an international commodity agreement. In this respect, the model agreement for dairy products drawn up by the nongovernmental International Dairy Committee should be of considerable assistance to governments if and when they begin to negotiate for an agreement in this sector.

In Europe, the view is strongly held that the butter problem cannot be resolved in isolation and that it will also be necessary to tackle the question of alternative fats from vegetable oils. The production of oilseeds constitutes an important element in the farming pattern of developing countries, whose interest in market stability and access has recently been reechoed at the United Nations Conference on Trade and Development (UNCTAD) Santiago meeting. These countries compete with richer agricultural economies like the United States in seeking to find markets for such products as soybeans. The plain fact is that in Europe, the price of butter is the most important factor governing the milk producer's return for his product. (This is not so in the UK, where the basis of the milk producer's return until now has been the price determined by the government for liquid milk.) An attempt should be made to achieve a satisfactory price relationship between butter and alternative fats. What cannot work in the long run is a managed market for butter operating alongside a completely free system for vegetable oils.

Stocks

We do not believe that the main agricultural trading nations of the world are ready to accept the principle of direct international supervision of their national agricultural support policies. There is, however, an increasing awareness of the fact that something more must be done than in the past to ensure that national policies, or policies for regional groupings such as the EEC, should have greater regard than in the past to world production and trade considerations. There has to be an indirect and acceptable way by which national support policies are atuned and adjusted to these factors.

In the plan outlined above, the main discipline is imposed by the required adherence to the international reference price system and, coupled with this, a policy on stocks. In our view, the participating countries must be agreed that when prices fall or threaten to fall to the international reference price (for commercial transactions), governments will intervene in the market by acquiring stocks.

The World Bank, in accordance with Resolution No. 54 adopted at the recent UNCTAD Conference in Santiago, could in some cases help to finance such stocks through the appropriate international commodity council in the context of price stabilization schemes, which could be of particular help to developing countries and enable them to participate in the arrangements. The international council will first decide the global quantity that, in their view, must be taken off the market to ensure an element of judgment as well as of commodity expertise. However, the knowledge that action is being taken to support the market should have a beneficial effect.

To ensure the smooth functioning of the arrangement, the basis for the shares of participating countries in any stockholding operation must be agreed beforehand. Perhaps the most effective formula from the disciplinary viewpoint would be one which measured the obligation by reference to the degree to which the current production of the commodity in the participating country or regional grouping exceeded the output in an agreed base period. Those countries that had increased their production most since the base period would thus be required to make the biggest contribution to the stockholding operation at times when world market prices were at or near the reference level.

When world prices rose, the stock previously acquired would gradually be released, if possible, at prices that at least covered the costs, including interests charges, of acquiring the stock. Postwar experiences have shown that although surpluses for some key commodities may be sustained and held for two or three years, the onset of bad harvests sooner or later, and the development of new markets, can result in a rapid change in the supply and price position. This is indeed the position in which we now find ourselves for several key products.

However, if excess stocks were accumulated over a long period as a result of the support policy pursued by a country or regional grouping, the authorities would be obliged, largely for budgetary reasons, to consider modifications to their support policies. Not only would there be the costs of acquiring and holding stocks, but there would also be the problem of storage capacity. It should be permissible under the international arrangement to try to dispose of any surplus stocks on the domestic market, at prices not less than the international reference prices, to selected groups. The changes in the national support regime would take the form either of altering the relationship between prices of associated commodities, for example, by encouraging the production of feed grains in lieu of bread grains or of introducing measures to regulate production and/or marketing.

In some countries, measures are already in being to limit production. In the United States, for example, acreage allotments and marketing quotas have operated for a number of products. Countries that already operate methods of supply control may continue to pursue these in the hope that they would, when prices fell, be able to limit their obligation toward the cost of the stockholding operation. Those countries that, for policy reasons, prefer to use price adjustments as the main method of influencing supply would be free to do so, provided they fulfilled their obligations through the stock adjustment policy.

There is much to be said for the idea of establishing an international selling office to which excess stocks that could not be disposed of on the world market at above the international commercial reference price would be declared. It would be possible to use this agency not only for commercial sales, but also for sales at the lower reference price to developing countries. The agency would be financed by appropriately determined contributions by the countries declaring the stocks. The advantages of this proposal are first, that it would ensure respect for the world reference price in a specific manner, secondly, that it would ensure more effective discipline in the disposal of stocks acquired as a result of the fall of the world market level, and thirdly, that it would obviate the risk that prospective buyers, by delaying their purchases, might hope to play one exporting country off against another, in the hope that, notwithstanding the international undertaking, some exporters would eventually sell below the reference price level.

Commodity agreements of the traditional type have had only limited success in the postwar era. If any new and comprehensive arrangements are to be successfully negotiated for agriculture as part of the world trade negotiations, concepts will have to be developed and horizons expanded. Many of the elements in the scheme outlined in this paper are hardly novel. They have been the subject of international debate for years. Perhaps, the time has now come to bring them together in a cohesive plan and to seek to build from these principles a number of arrangements covering the key commodities directly of interest to producers on both sides of the Atlantic.

POSTSCRIPT

Since this chapter was completed, there have been three main developments relevant to our examination of European agricultural policy, and in particular to the proposals which we advanced for "new style" international commodity arrangements as a means of reconciling the agricultural trading interests of the United States and other exporting countries with those of Europe and other importing or self-sufficient areas.

First, there occurred in 1973 an almost unparalleled explosion in world prices of food and raw materials. Between the beginning and the end of the year, commodity prices rose by about 60 percent. Wheat, feed grains, sugar, vegetable fats and oils all showed remarkable advances during the year. The terms of trade were altered drastically in favor of countries exporting these products.

In the European Community, the effect was to identify the importance and relevance of the common agricultural policy in stabilizing supplies. Almost overnight, Community producer prices for several commodities, which had been above the world level, were overtaken. This is perhaps best illustrated in the case of wheat: the Community target price for the 1973 crop at £56.47 per ton (January 1974) may be contrasted with the Minneapolis spot quotation (January 1974) of £83.28 per ton. To safeguard the interests of consumers the Community instituted levies on exports equivalent roughly to the difference between the world price and the EEC target price. These have had the effect of keeping down consumer prices within the Community. They have also prevented producers from earning higher returns from the world market. Indeed, in some areas of the EEC, producer returns have fallen below even the target price.

Except in the three applicant countries, and particularly in the United Kingdom where prices for cereals rose in one year to full Community levels and beyond, the CAP has effectively moderated the impact domestically of the rise in world prices and has provided an assurance of supply in circumstances when reliance on third countries would have entailed much higher prices to consumers and a big increase in the value of imports.

There is, secondly, the impact on European agriculture—indeed on world agriculture—of the energy crisis. In Western Europe, the prices of fuel and oil have quadrupled during the last six months. The direct and indirect ramifications on European farm costs have been substantial, especially on supplies and prices of such essential inputs as fertilizers. In the next few years, the energy situation will inevitably limit the capacity of agriculture in both industrialized and developing countries to expand in accordance with the development of world demand. The problem of access is likely to become less relevant in this situation: the need to guarantee continuity of supplies will become even more pertinent than it is now. With a huge balance of payments deficit on account of oil in prospect, all industralized countries will be more than ever watchful of the need to take steps to safeguard their food supplies.

The third factor is the deterioration in the Atlantic Community's political relationships and structure. Between the United States and Europe, political differences have unfortunately become more acute. What effect these are likely to have upon future trading relationships between Europe and the United States cannot as yet be foreseen. The Trade Bill is making very slow progress through Congress.

We remain convinced that despite these vicissitudes, the chances of a satisfactory resolution of the agricultural problem in the multilateral trade negotiation will depend essentially upon governments' willingness to accept the basic approach outlined in our chapter. Indeed we are convinced that in governmental circles on both sides of the Atlantic, as well as in other countries (Japan, India etc.), the principles to which we attach importance are beginning to take root. The world needs a growing supply of agricultural products to meet the expanding needs of the developing countries and to avert the threat of starvation which is currently challenging us. The production of food as well as energy will have to be brought within a new international framework of principles and rules to insure a more orderly development of world trade in the interests of producers and consumers.

NOTES

1. "Agricultural Adjustment in Developed Countries," FAO Paper ERC 72/3, June 1972, for Eighth FAO Regional Conference for Europe.

2. "A Future for European Agriculture," Atlantic Papers 70/4 (Paris: Atlantic Institute for International Affairs, 1970).

5

**CANADA, AUSTRALIA,
AND NEW ZEALAND
IN INTERNATIONAL
AGRICULTURAL TRADE**
T. K. Warley

The three countries that are the concern of this paper are all highly developed urban-industrial societies. Nonetheless, the agricultural and food system (farming, ancillary supply and service industries, and food processing and distribution) is still of substantial importance in their economies. Primary agriculture alone represents 4, 10, and 16 percent of gross domestic product of Canada, Australia, and New Zealand, respectively. Furthermore, for the same three countries, exports of temperate agricultural products account for one-third, one-half, and over 90 percent of gross farm income and for 10, 50, and 80 percent of total merchandise exports. Tables 5.1-5.4 provide an overview of the imports of each country in world trade in temperate zone products, of the commodity component of their agricultural exports, and of the principle markets they serve.

All three countries possess farming, food, and ancillary industries, which are technologically advanced and favorably structured. Hence they are, with exceptions to be noted later, efficient low-cost producers of the major temperate zone products. The maintenance and expansion of their position as world food and fiber producers are therefore not unimportant in terms of the more efficient utilization of world agricultural resources.

To the countries themselves, sustaining and enhancing their farm exports are important for three reasons. First, fuller utilization of their agricultural capacity is potentially a productive use of their national resources and a direct source of economic growth. Second, despite rapid growth in their exports of manufactures and minerals,

---

The assistance of T. G. MacAulay and W. J. Steel in preparing background material for this paper is gratefully acknowledged.

TABLE 5.1

Commodity Exports as Proportion of Total World Trade
(quantity basis)

	Canada[a]	Australia[b]	New Zealand[b]
	(percent)	(percent)	(percent)
Beef and veal	—	15.4	8.1
Mutton and lamb	—	19.5	64.9
Butter	—	10.5	25.3
Cheese	2.3	4.2	11.5
Wheat and wheat flour	18.2	12.4	—
Barley	18.1	5.1	—
Cane sugar	—	8.2	—
Wool	—	47.0	19.5
Tobacco	2.5	—	—

[a]Average of three years ending December 1970.
[b]Average of three years ending June 1970.

Source: FAO Trade Yearbook 1971, vol. 24.

agricultural exports are a decisive element in their balance of payments accounts. Typically, the surplus on agricultural trade constitutes a large proportion of their overall surplus on merchandise trade and helps minimize their customary current account deficits. Thirdly, with generally slow rates of growth in domestic consumption and a reluctance to embrace policies that transfer income from the nonfarm sector, growth in export earnings is the prime source of increased income and improved returns for resources in farming and is their main hope for sustaining the economic and social viability of particular regions and communities.

In these regards, Canada, Australia, and New Zealand are in much the same situation as is the United States. That is to say, these countries find themselves facing the same obstacles frustrating their ambitions: pursuing broadly similar global economic objectives; adopting comparable strategies, policies, and programs in respect to restructuring and diversifying their agricultural industries; and pursuing agricultural trade development along similar lines.

Each country has, of course, its peculiar circumstances, constraints, and opportunities, and attaches unique weights to different markets, commodities, and alternative approaches to international agricultural trade problem resolution. Further, each of the four countries has a rivalrous relationship with the others insofar as they wish to sell the others increased volumes of foods and fibers—an ambition which is frequently frustrated by their respective farm and trade policies—and compete in the same foreign markets for sales of a narrow range of the same or substitute temperate zone products. Nonetheless, the communalities of their broad goals and concerns constitute the dominant characteristic of their relationship.

Thus, in the broadest terms, each favors an open multilateral trading system, as well as stability and absence of distortions in the supportive international monetary system. All have a common interest in ensuring that the trade negotiations scheduled to begin in 1973 maintain the momentum of postwar trade liberalization, make a significant impact on nontariff barriers, minimize trade distortions

TABLE 5.2

Commodity Exports as Proportion of Production
(quantity basis)

	Canada[a]	Australia[b]	New Zealand[c]
	(percent)	(percent)	(percent)
Beef and veal	—	46	39
Mutton	—	43	57
Lamb	—	17	93
Butter	—	44	80
Cheese	20	45	90
Wheat and wheat flour	64	78	—
Barley	18	21	—
Sugar	—	69	—
Wool	—	94	89
Tobacco	22	—	—

[a]Average of three years ending December 1970.
[b]Average of three years ending June 1971.
[c]Average of three years ending June 1970.

Sources: FAO Production and Trade Yearbook; Bureau of Agricultural Economics, "The Australian Farm Situation 1971-72," Quarterly Review of Agricultural Economics 25, no. 1 (January 1972); New Zealand Department of Statistics, Official Yearbook 1971.

associated with the formation and enlargement of the EEC and the development of the Community's preferential trade arrangements, result in the normalization of commercial relationships with the centrally planned countries, and make provision for expanded trade opportunities for the developing countries. More especially, all share an interest in the inclusion of agriculture in trade negotiations in such a manner as to contain the protectionist tendencies in domestic agricultural policies, to halt and if possible reverse the erosion of the net agricultural import requirements of Western Europe, to mitigate the consequences of enlargement of the European Economic Community (EEC) and to still further accelerate the pace of liberalization of access to the Japanese market. Each supports the amplification of the General Agreement on Tariffs and Trade's (GATT) rules and procedures so as to encompass the trade-distorting effects of domestic farm programs and associated agricultural trade practices, and there is a common interest in working toward international trade arrangements for farm products that result in greater stability in international commodity markets and enhanced assurance about conditions of access for farm exports to importing countries.

This broad communality of goals between Canada, Australia, and New Zealand, on the one hand, and the United States, on the other, in reshaping the international economic system in the 1970s is important. But there is also value in sharpening the focus on the circumstances, ambitions, and actions of each country. Particular interest lies in an examination for each country of present patterns of agricultural trade and the threats to them, of the scope for diversification of production and markets and the policies being pursued to bring these about, and in the identification of specific areas of complementarity and conflict with the United States.

CANADA

Agricultural Trade

Canada is a major net exporter of agricultural products. Foreign sales of farm and food products currently exceed $2 billion per year. During the 1960s the average surplus on agricultural trade was almost equal to the average surplus on merchandise trade. Exports of farm products accounted for an average of 15 percent of all exports in the decade of the 1960s, falling to 10 to 11 percent in recent years.

Canada is also a large importer of farm products. Agricultural imports have shown steady growth and were valued at $1.3 billions in 1971. About half of these comprise noncompetitive products.

Products of this type face few trade barriers. The major exception is sugar, where a high rate of effective protection is given to the small sugar beet industry. Additionally, as in most countries, tariff rates on agricultural imports escalate with the degree of processing or fabrication, thus giving substantial protection to domestic processing industries.

The United States is the principal supplier of competitive agricultural imports. Fruits, vegetables, oilseeds, and oilseed products are the major products concerned. Trade barriers for these products are modest. Imports of lamb, mutton, and beef originate mainly in Oceania. The low tariffs on these products were suspended in early 1973. The major impediments to imports of temperate zone products into Canada are licensing and other arrangements for dairy products, wheat, barley, and oats. In practice, there are no significant imports of these products.

Exports of agricultural products have shown an upward trend but have been extremely erratic. Exports of wheat are becoming progressively less dominant; even so, they accounted for over 40 percent of all agricultural exports in 1971 (See Table 5.3). Fluctuations in wheat sales have been the main cause of instability in the total value of farm exports, and variations in sales to the centrally planned economies have been the principal source of this instability. Exports of feed grains (primarily barley) and of rapeseed and rapeseed products have been climbing rapidly. Exports of live animals, meats, fruits, vegetables, and tobacco are also important in terms of value.

Historically, Canada's export trade has been strongly orientated to the United States and the Atlantic (See Table 5.4). The United States and Western Europe are still Canada's largest markets and will remain so for some time. However, lately rising sales of wheat to the centrally planned countries and of wheat, barley, oilseeds, and pork to Japan have resulted in significant diversification of markets.

Although one of the world's major exporters of temperature zone products, it is only in wheat that Canada's share of world trade is sufficiently large to make her a dominant supplier (See Table 5.1). Her share of world wheat and flour exports has generally lain between 20 and 25 percent, but fell as low as 16 percent in 1969. By contrast, even with rapid growth in exports of barley and rapeseed, globally Canada is still a minor supplier of feed grains, oilseeds, and oilseed products. The same situation pertains with less buoyant commodities such as tobacco, meats, fruits, vegetables, and dairy products.

Trade Problems

The major externally generated problem that Canada faces in her agricultural trade is that which is common to other exporters of

TABLE 5.3

Contribution of Selected Commodities to the Value of
Agricultural Exports, 1967-68 to 1970-71

Product		Canada	Australia	New Zealand
		(percent)	(percent)	(percent)
Wool	1967-68	—	42	22
	1968-69	—	46	25
	1969-70	—	39	23
	1970-71	—	28	n.a.
Wheat and wheat flour	1967-68	53	20	—
	1968-69	43	15	—
	1969-70	44	17	—
	1970-71	45	22	—
Dairy products	1967-68	2	5	22[a]
	1968-69	3	5	19[a]
	1969-70	3	5	17[a]
	1970-71	3	5	n.a.
Meats	1967-68	5[c]	14	34[b]
	1968-69	6[c]	14	36[b]
	1969-70	6[c]	18	40[b]
	1970-71	5[c]	19	n.a.
Sugar	1967-68	—	5	—
	1968-69	—	7	—
	1969-70	—	6	—
	1970-71	—	7	—
Oilseeds and oilseed products	1967-68	8	—	—
	1968-69	10	—	—
	1969-70	11	—	—
	1970-71	13	—	—
Tobacco	1967-68	4	—	—
	1968-69	5	—	—
	1969-70	3	—	—
	1970-71	3	—	—
All others	1967-68	28[d]	14	21
	1968-69	33[d]	14	19
	1969-70	33[d]	15	20
	1970-71	31[d]	20	n.a.

[a]Dairy products in New Zealand were subdivided into butter 16, 14, and 12 percent and cheese 7, 5, and 5 percent for the years 1967-68, 1968-69, and 1969-70.

[b]For meat exports from New Zealand, the following breakdown was available:

	1967-68	1968-69	1969-70
Lamb	18	18	}20
Mutton	3	2	
Beef and veal	12	13	17
Others	3	2	3

[c]In most years meat imports balance exports.

[d]Barley exports were a major part of the remainder, forming the following percentages for each of the years: 3, 3, 8, 10 percent.

Note: n.a. means not available.

Sources: Canada Department of Agriculture, Canada's Trade in Agricultural Products: 1970 and 1971; Bureau of Agricultural Economics, Quarterly Review of Agricultural Economics (various issues); New Zealand Department of Statistics, Official Yearbook 1971.

TABLE 5.4

Agricultural Exports by Principal Countries of Destination,
1967-68 to 1970-71

		Canada[a]	Australia	New Zealand
		(percent)	(percent)	(percent)
United Kingdom	1967-68	19	15	43
	1968-69	21	14	39
	1969-70	16	15	36
	1970-71	15	15	n.a.
United States	1967-68	20	16[b]	17
	1968-69	24	18[b]	17
	1969-70	21	19[b]	15
	1970-71	17	18[b]	n.a.
EEC	1967-68	11	16	10
	1968-69	12	18	12
	1969-70	14	16	11
	1970-71	17	13	n.a.
Japan	1967-68	12	20	8
	1968-69	12	22	7
	1969-70	11	21	10
	1970-71	12	20	n.a.
Communist countries	1967-68	17[c]	10	—
	1968-69	10[c]	8	—
	1969-70	13[c]	10	—
	1970-71	15[c]	8	—
Australia	1967-68	—	—	—7
	1968-69	—	—	8
	1969-70	—	—	8
Canada	1967-68	—	—	1
	1968-69	—	—	2
	1969-70	—	—	4
Other countries	1967-68	20	23	13
	1968-69	20	20	15
	1969-70	26	20	16
	1970-71	25	27	n.a.
Total value of	1967-68	1395	1839	820
agricultural	1968-69	1211	1878	989
exports ($million)[d]	1969-70	1685	2116	1087
	1970-71	1984	2114	n.a.

[a]Data for Canada are on a calendar year basis with data shown as 1967-68 for the 1968 calendar year.
[b]Figures include Canada.
[c]Figures for USSR and China only.
[d]Currencies are those of the countries concerned.

Note: —means figures included in totals for other countries; n.a. means not available.

Sources: Canada Department of Agriculture, Canada's Trade in Agricultural Products: 1970 and 1971; Bureau of Agricultural Economics, "The Australian Farm Situation: 1971-72," Quarterly Review of Agricultural Economics 25, no. 1 (January 1972); New Zealand Department of Statistics, Official Yearbook 1971.

temperate zone agricultural products—the agricultural protectionism of importing regions and the failure to mitigate its magnitude or consequences in the GATT. The principal focus of this concern is the support policies practised by West European countries, especially by the members of the EEC. Japan's slow pace of liberalization of her agricultural trade has also hampered Canada's trade expansion. However, this is viewed as a transient problem, since the food supply and balance of payments circumstances of Japan seem bound to compel her to expand her temperate zone agricultural imports at a brisk pace in future years, and Canada is well placed to share in the growth of this market.

The same comforting prospect does not pertain for Western Europe. The Common Agricultural Policy (CAP) of the nine countries is viewed from Ottawa in much the same way as from Washington. Canada, like the United States, regards the CAP as holding agricultural exports far below their potential and would like to see it changed in much the same ways. These include a shift away from product price supports and toward direct support of farmers' incomes, a corresponding lowering of target and threshold prices and levies, lower prices to farmer-users for feed grains and to consumers of livestock products so that the demand for feed grains and protein feeds was greater, restraint on the use of export subsidies (for example, for wheat and barley), a more ambitious structural reform program, and expanded willingness and capacity for managing supplies, and a halt to the further erosion of the most-favored-nation principle through the spread of preferential trading arrangements (the latter affect Canadian sales of (tobacco).

Canadian agriculture has also faced the prospect of the enlargement of the EEC with foreboding. Enlargement will adversely affect Canadian exports in four ways: by the encouragement to production given by the generally higher prices accorded producers in the new member countries, by the further reduction in net import requirements through demand contraction resulting from higher consumer prices, by the disruption of other foreign markets attributable to supplies diverted from Europe, and by the change in conditions of access to the United Kingdom (UK) market. This latter point has two dimensions: the reversal of preferences in favor of member and associated states and the loss of preferences viz-a-viz other residual suppliers, notably the United States. The likelihood is that some 90 percent of Canada's present agricultural exports to the UK will be adversely affected to some degree by the latter country's adoption of the CAP. Commodities most affected include wheat, barley, cheddar cheese, tobacco, and apples. Hence Canada is as anxious to engage the EEC of nine countries in discussion of agricultural trade issues in the current trade negotiations as is the United States.

Another major externally generated problem faced by Canada is instability in agricultural export earnings, particularly from sales of wheat. These have been mainly attributable to fluctuations in purchases by the socialist countries. Variations in wheat sales have a profound and direct destabilizing effect on the economy of the prairie provinces, and beyond that on the stability of the national grain-livestock complex.

Past failures in Canadian farm and trade policies have also contributed in no small measure to problems in her agricultural export trade. Until recently, there was a propensity to retain for too long export dependence on an undynamic commodity (wheat) in undynamic (European) markets, and a corresponding sluggishness in diversifying production and exports into commodities and markets with better opportunities. The Canadian Wheat Board's quota, pricing, and grading systems compounded the external market problems faced by wheat. Until the prairie grain situation reached the point of crisis in the late 1960s, there was little evidence of systematic thought by government and industry leaders about Canadian agriculture's potential trade contribution and needs, or of an attempt to devise and implement coherent policies that would permit to it move purposefully in the direction of a desirable future. Happily, there is new evidence of firm leadership, a broad concensus on purpose, and the makings of coherence in and between agricultural and farm trade policies.

Agricultural and Trade Policies

Because of Canadian agriculture's dependence on export sales based on low-cost production and efficient international merchandizing, agricultural policy in Canada has not been characterized by a high degree of government intervention or extensive income transfer programs. In the main, policy has emphasized the promotion of bio-physical efficiency, resource development, improved domestic marketing, international market development, and income stabilization through such measures as crop insurance and modest stop-loss price guarantees. Governments at both federal and provincial levels have traditionally been wary of measures that involved significant direct expenditures on agriculture.

The major departures from this "hands-off" posture have been for grains and milk. Prairie grains producers have benefitted from a variety of income-enhancing programs including publicly subsidized transportation and storage and discriminatory high prices to domestic consumers of wheat and nonprairie users of prairie feed grains. Imports of wheat, barley, and oats are excluded by licensing, though in practice it is unlikely that this has significantly distorted trade. Milk producers have been allowed to differentiate the market for fluid and manufacturing uses. Manufacturing milk producers have received substantial direct payments, virtually absolute protection from competing imports of dairy products, and large subsidies have been paid on exports of the skim milk powder surplus associated with a position of self-sufficiency in butterfat.

The traumas associated with huge prairie wheat surpluses in the late 1960s, low prices and instabilities in the livestock sector, and the threatened deterioration in the European market for grains and other products have recently forced a prolonged and searching reexamination of Canadian agricultural policies and farm trade goals and opportunities. The broad result has been an explicit reaffirmation and intensification of the thrust of previously implicit policy. It is not the avowed intent of the federal government to foster a commercial agricultural industry that is market and development orientated, internationally competitive, and economically viable without sustained transfer payments, and to achieve this goal within this generation.

Government has, however, accepted an enhanced role in indicative planning, in facilitating changes in the product mix of agriculture, in promoting market development and diversification, in fostering supply management, and in providing enhanced stability.

The agricultural industry is to be encouraged to secure additional revenue and improved returns by exploiting market opportunities for products with favorable demand prospects in which Canada is, or can become, a low-cost supplier. Where possible, value will be added domestically by exporting semiprocessed and final products rather than raw products. Subsidies and other assistance programs will be used (to a greater extent than hitherto if necessary), but will be regarded as transitional measures to accelerate the pace and ameliorate the disruptions of necessary changes.

A variety of specific programs have been introduced or redirected to accomplish these broad ends. Notable examples include the following. A real attempt is being made to restructure the economy of the prairies. The Lower Inventory for Tomorrow (LIFT) program reduced inventories and production of wheat and encouraged production of feed grains, oilseeds, and livestock. Initial prices and guaranteed minimum delivery quotas for prairie grains are being used in a more purposeful way to ensure the availability of required quantities of salable grains. Changes in the quota delivery and wheat-grading systems, reform of grain handling and transportation, the provision of long-term credit to grain-importing countries, and a more flexible and aggressive pricing policy on the part of the Canadian Wheat Board are all designed to make Canadian grains more competitive in world markets. A joint federal-provincial adjustment assistance program, the Small Farm

Development Scheme, is designed to enhance the long-run competitiveness of the industry by accelerating the rates of departure of surplus labor and of the disappearance of nonviable holdings.

More generally, the federal government is exercising leadership in a total market development program. This embraces international commercial diplomacy to improve conditions of access to foreign markets; the enhancement of efficiency in production, handling, processing, and distribution systems; market promotion and development through market research, product development, trade fairs, and missions; and more aggressive and agile international merchandizing of Canadian farm products. Under a scheme labeled "Project 75" (involving federal and provincial governments, farm organizations, and agribusiness groups), an attempt is being made to adopt an integrated systems approach to the development and harmonization of the total assistance given to Canadian agriculture with a view to promoting its market orientation and competitive efficiency in an international setting and to ensuring that it maximizes its market opportunities.

Potentially all commodities are affected by this developmental thrust. However, particular emphasis is being given to bread wheats (sales of which are still huge), barley, rapeseed and its derivative oil and meal, beef, calves and feeder cattle, and pork. A great diversity of other raw and processed products offers opportunities for expanded sales and these are not being neglected, but the above are those that have the greatest potential for significantly affecting the future level of earnings from agricultural exports.

Similarly, there is no propensity to concentrate sales expansion efforts and aspirations on a narrow range of markets. Thus the possibilities for meeting future growth in consumption in Canada, or of successful import substitution, are given equal weight with the expansion of sales in foreign markets. However, expanded sales will be sought mainly in the United States (pork, beef, and possibly feeder cattle), Western Europe (feed grains, oilseeds and their products), Japan (wheat, barely, oilseeds and protein meals, beef, breeding stock and pork), and the socialist countries (wheat, barley, rapeseed and meal, breeding stock and tobacco). A host of individually small but cumulatively significant commercial markets in developing countries are also being cultivated.

Export Availabilities

Numerous attempts have been made both to project and to forecast the likely future size of Canada's export sales of agricultural products. No two studies agree, which is not surprising given the different assumptions that must be made about necessary and likely

113

developments in both the domestic sector and in potential foreign markets. Summaries of recent projections are contained in Table 5.5 and 5.6

The most decisive factor influencing agricultural production patterns and commodity export availability is the future demand for grains by the socialist countries. Buoyed by Soviet and Chinese purchases, total grain sales in both 1971-72 and 1972-73 are likely to reach almost 1 billion bushels. There is little doubt that this volume of sales could be sustained in the future if demand were to persist. Ample productive capacity exists, and the storage and transportation system has been significantly improved. However, even with less buoyant world grain markets, Canada will be reluctant to sell less than 700 to 800 million bushels of grains per year over the next few years, with the relative proportions of wheat and barley being readily changed. Rapeseed exports could well be 75 to 100 million bushels a year. Additionally, there is a real prospect that exports of pork to Japan and the United States will be substantially increased. On the other hand, the expanding domestic demand for beef and important restraints on the supply of calves will together probably mean that Canada will remain a net importer of manufacturing grades of Oceania beef (and mutton) and will not be able to export significant amounts of prime beef or large numbers of calves and feeder cattle to the United States.

AUSTRALIA

Agricultural Trade

Although the value of farm exports has been rising and stood in 1972-73 at $3.8 billion (U.S. dollars), the proportion of exports of rural origin has declined over the 1960s largely as a result of the rapid rise in the exports of minerals, ores, and manufactures. Even so, agricultural products provide just under one-half of total export income.

Historically, exports were strongly oriented toward supplying the West European market, the connection with Britain being reinforced by the Ottawa Agreements and a variety of bilateral trade arrangements entered into during World War II and the postwar years. However, the combined effects of increasing self-sufficiency in the West European market, recurring periods of low prices for wheat, dairy products and wool, the rapid development of the Japanese market for food imports, shortages of grains in the socialist countries and of meats in North America have together wrought important changes in the geographic pattern and commodity composition of Australia's farm trade and

TABLE 5.5

Summary of Projections of Canada's Agricultural
Exports, 1975 and 1980

Study	Wheat	Coarse Grains	Oats	Barley	Corn	Beef		Pork
						Animals	Meat	
		(million bushels)				thousand head	million lbs	million lbs
CDA, 1980	625	43.5	10	25				
Task Force 1980	364	105	5	100	-10[a]	500	100	50
Bjarnason 1980	720	56						
ERS, 1980	437	(1.1)[b]						
Hudson, 1975	362			125				
Huff, 1975	260[c]							

[a]Minus indicates imports.
[b]Million metric tons.
[c]Midpoint of the projection range.

Source: E. Missiaen and A. L. Coffing, "Canada: Growth Potential of the Grain and Livestock Sectors," Foreign Agricultural Economics Report No. 77, ERS, USDA, June 1972, Table 46, p. 100. The sources of the various projections are identified in this study.

TABLE 5.6

USDA Projections of Area, Yield, Production, Domestic
Disappearance, and Implied Export Availability for
Selected Agricultural Commodities under Two
Alternative Grain Price Levels
(Canada, 1975)

Category	Wheat	Barley	Oats	Corn	Beef	Pork
	(million acres)			(thousand head)		
Area and livestock numbers:						
1967-69 average	28.2	8.8	7.5	0.9	3310	9039
Alternative A[a]	24.5	11.6	5.9	1.5	3881	9767
Alternative B[b]	22.1	11.6	5.9	1.3	3881	10465
Yield:[c]	(bushels per acre)			(carcass wt.)		
1967-69 average	22.8	36.0	45.8	81.3	543	129
Alternative A	27.6	45.4	49.4	94.5	565	129
Alternative B	24.7	37.8	47.2	80.2	565	129
Production:	(million bushels)			(million lbs)		
1967-69 average	642	317	346	76	1798	1166
Alternative A	676	527	291	142	2193	1260
Alternative B	546	439	279	104	2193	1350
Domestic disappearance:						
1967-69 average	168	242	331	108	1795	1102
Alternative A[d]	186	338	289	157	2282	1246
Alternative B[e]	186	367	279	157	2282	1246
Export availability:						
1967-69 average	474	75	15	(32)[g]	2	64
Alternative A[f]	490	189	2	(15)	(89)	14
Alternative B	-360	72	0	(53)	(89)	104

[a]Assumes that 1967-69 average price levels will prevail through 1975.

[b]Assumes 1975 grain price levels are 15 percent below recent levels, while recent
livestock prices are maintained.

[c]Crop yields under Alternative A are based on a modified 1960-70 yield trend.
Under Alternative B, the 1966-70 average yield was used. Carcass weight for beef is
a modified 1955-69 trend, while for pork the 1967-69 average is used.

[d]Projections for wheat were taken from an Organization for Economic Cooperation
and Development (OECD) study and from a Canadian Department of Agriculture (CDA)
study for meat. Projections for coarse grains were made by extension of the 1960-69
trend.

[e]Projections for wheat, corn, and meat are taken from domestic disappearance
projections under Alternative A. Barley and oats projections are based on domestic
disappearance projections under Alternative A, with adjustments made for the shortfall
in oats production and increased feed requirements due to increased pork production.

[f]Figures given represent export availability, not actual exports or imports.

[g]Numbers in parentheses indicate net imports.

Source: Missiaen and Coffing, op. cit., Table 48, p. 104

associated changes in production. There has been a turning away in trade from the West European market toward the countries of the Pacific Rim, particularly Japan and the United States, which each now account for around 20 percent of agricultural export sales. Wool has lost its dominant position in the composition of exports, falling from 60 percent to less than 30 percent over the 1960s. Exports of meats, particularly beef and veal, have been significantly expanded, rising from 10 to 20 percent in the same period (See Table 5.3). Export proceeds from wheat and sugar have been unstable, but have made gains.

Trade Problems

The major agricultural trade problems faced by Australia are the same as those described for Canada and shared by all exporters of farm products, agricultural protectionism, and instability in world commodity markets.

The general adverse effects of the EEC's agricultural policy on exports to Europe and on competitive conditions in third markets need no elaboration, except to note that they affect all Australia's farm exports except wool. The enlargement of the Community to include Britain and the extension of preferential arrangements are expected to have particularly adverse effects on exports of wheat, dairy products, apples and pears, dried and canned fruits, and sugar. The future of exports of beef to Europe seems secure.

Particular concern attaches to future prospects in Europe for dairy products, sugar, and grains. Unlike New Zealand, no special arrangements have been made to cushion the effects on Australia's exports to Britain of dairy products on Britain's adoption of the CAP and termination of the import quotas, which have previously assured access for butter and cheese. In 1970-71 Britain took 60 and 30 percent of Australia's butter and cheese exports, respectively. Eventual total loss of this market is anticipated. While some success has been achieved and further prospects exist for finding alternative markets—particularly for cheese in Japan and for butter oil in Southeast Asian countries—competition for the residual world markets will be intense, not least with New Zealand. A contraction of the size of the dairy industry will likely be necessary. For sugar, the immediate problem is the loss of a large part of the market in Britain of around 400,000 tons (335,000 tons being at the negotiated price quota under the Commonwealth Sugar Agreement) to European and to Commonwealth and other low-income suppliers having preferential trade arrangements for sugar with the enlarged Community. In the absence of a bigger quota for sales to the United States, maintaining the present size of the Australian sugar industry would be dependent on securing an enlarged quota under the revised International Sugar Agreement and success in finding satisfactory markets for these quota supplies in such countries as Canada, Japan, and a number of minor markets around the Pacific Rim (for example, New Zealand, Singapore, Malaysia, and Kong Kong). The agricultural policy of the enlarged Community is viewed as adding still further to the problems of the Australian grain sector. Net import requirements for wheat in Europe are likely to fall, thereby intensifying the need to seek alternative markets, restrict wheat supplies, and diversify crop production into feed grains and oilseeds. The extent to which this situation will be alleviated in the future by continuation of the present strong demand for grains by the centrally planned economies is unclear.

Another major area of concern relates to future market opportunities in the United States. The latter country's dairy and sugar quotas presently prevent Australia from providing a larger proportion of U.S. domestic consumption. The U.S. tariff on the types of wool that Australia supplies and the compensatory tariff on woolen garments are significant trade impediments. The U.S. Meat Import Law of 1964 and the associated voluntary restraints arrangements have not been so restrictive as to prevent the United States from becoming Australia's largest customer for meat. Nonetheless, permanent liberalization of access to this market would provide a remunerative outlet for the increased supplies of beef that are in prospect and would help restore buoyancy to the sheep industry.

Agricultural and Trade Policies

As becoming to a low-cost exporter of farm products with, historically, a favorable rate of return to resources engaged in agriculture, government support for agriculture in Australia has generally been modest by international standards and extended only reluctantly, and on an ad hoc basis, to deal with particular situations. Much of the assistance involving direct expenditure has been for subsidies on inputs (fertilizer, fuel, and tractors), resources development (transportation, land and irrigation development), contributions to market promotion, and research and extension. Producers' incomes have also been supplemented by direct government payments under various commodity stabilization schemes, including wheat, wool, and dairy products. Moreover, indirect assistance of unknown proportions has been provided by such means as import licensing, charging higher prices to domestic than foreign consumers (wheat, dairy products, sugar, rice, eggs, and dried fruit), mixing regulations for tobacco, and stringent plant and animal health regulations. As in Canada, the most heavily subsidized commodity group is dairy producers. Assistance to the dairy industry has been accorded by the "home consumption price scheme" import licensing, control over the production and prohibition of importation of oleomargarine, and the subsidized export of butter, cheese, and processed milk.

Faced with shifts in external market demands and low and unstable prices for wheat, wool, dairy products, and other commodities, the Commonwealth and state governments have recently been compelled to adopt a rather higher profile in respect of intervention in the agricultural industry. This has taken various forms. First, a real attempt is being made to diversify markets. Market development efforts have been intensified and embrace such measures as bilateral trade agreements, improved credit facilities, and increased market promotion expenditures. Second, emphasis is being given to changing the commodity composition of output. Producers have been encouraged to substitute feed grains and oilseeds (barley, sorghum, sun flowers, and rape) for wheat, and the output of beef is being rapidly expanded. Third, production is being tailored to available markets by active supply management programs. These include delivery quotas for wheat, limiting guaranteed prices to a specified quantity of dairy products, regulation of sugar as well as rice and egg production, and a tree-pull program for deciduous fruits. Finally, two (as yet very modest) schemes for adjustment assistance have been introduced in recent years. One is aimed specifically at marginal dairy farms. The other is a general reconstruction scheme, but in practice is likely to have most attraction for producers on wheat-sheep farms.

Export Availabilities

The results of various attempts to project future Australian production and trade are summarized in Tables 5.7 and 5.8.

Australia has a vast capacity for producing wheat. This is clearly borne out by the projections, each of which suggests an upward trend in export availabilities, unless, as indicated by the U.S. Department of Agriculture (USDA) study, quotas and prices decline to such an extent as to induce substitution of barley and sorghum. The future supply of Australian wheat is very dependent upon demand in the socialist countries.

Coarse grains are one of the more dynamic of a set of products, the future of which will depend very much on what happens in wheat policy. The USDA projections indicate this and show the large expansion in barley and sorghum production that is possible. Exports of coarse grains have been growing rapidly, with 50 million bushels of barley and 19 million bushels of grain sorghum being shipped in 1970-71.

TABLE 5.7

Export Projections for Selected Australian Grains
and Livestock Products
(Selected Studies and Years)

Item	Unit	Actual 1970	Gruen 1975	Gruen 1980	OECD 1975	OECD 1985	FAO 1980
Wheat	million bushels	286	397	478	336	384	404
Oats	million bushels	12	16	19			
Barley	million bushels	28	25	28			
Corn	million bushels	0					
Sorghum	million bushels	2					
Beef and veal	thousand ton	500	449	496	592	827	446
Mutton	thousand ton	230	123	125	313	408	868
Lamb	thousand ton	47	-27	-50			
Wool	million lbs	1929	1950	2020			
Sugar	thousand ton	1546			1814	1793	2443

Source: R. E. Friend et al., "Australia: Growth Potential of the Grain and Livestock Sectors," Foreign Agricultural Economics Report No. 80, ERS, USDA, May 1972, Table 19, p. 75.

The projections for beef and veal are somewhat conflicting when actual trade trends are taken into account. The United States is the major outlet for Australian beef and should continue to take increasing quantities. For lamb and mutton, each of the projections indicates an upward trend in export availabilities, although by varying amounts. Any expanded levels of exports of mutton are likely to be in the smaller and less remunerative markets. For lamb, the major export outlets are the UK, the United States, and Canada. The lamb industry is basically orientated to the home market, but the demand for lamb is being cultivated in North America and Western Europe, and steady, if unspectacular, growth is anticipated.

The outlook for wool is uncertain. Demand will likely increase in Eastern Europe and the USSR, and recovery in total sales is expected from recent low levels as the economies of the United States, France, and Japan expand. However, the longer-term outlook would seem to be one of gradual reduction in world and Australian wool production.

One of the few major agricultural products that is expected to experience significant long-term downward trends in exports is dairy

TABLE 5.8

USDA Projections of Australian Production and Export of
Agricultural Commodities

Item	Wheat	Oats	Barley	Corn	Sorghum	Beef and Veal	Mutton	Lamb	Wool
	(million bushels)a					(million lbs)			
Production average: 1966-68	492	81	57	7	13	1988.1	844	584.6	1.83
Assumptions, 1975									
No. 1b	504	88	67	9	15	2699.2	1097.6	683.2	2.07
No. 2c	459	80	61	8	14	2714.9	1129.0	703.4	2.13
No. 3d	375	99	142	10	54	2098.0	1097.6	728.0	2.07
Export availability average: 1966-68	338	23	19	0.6	3.9	940.8	349.4	47.0	1.75
Assumptions, 1975									
No. 1b	395	25	17	1.8	4.0	1368.6	582.4	11.2	1.99
No. 2c	350	16	11	0.8	2.4	1384.3	613.8	31.4	2.05
No. 3d	265	35	92	3.5	43.0	1689.0	609.3	22.4	1.99

aBushel weights in pounds are: wheat, 60; oats, 40; barley, 50; corn, 56; sorghum, 60.
bContinuation of average 1966-68 prices and an elastic export demand.
cSame as Assumption 1 but with a 15 percent decline in grain prices.
dContinuation of wheat quotas and selected price adjustments.

Source: R. E. Friend, "Australia: Agriculture in Transition," Foreign Agriculture X, no. 13 (March 27, 1972).

products. With Britain's entry into the EEC and the abolition of guaranteed access to the UK market, there is a rather dismal longer-term prospect for dairying in Australia.

Projections for sugar suffer from similar problems to those of dairy products in that a major component of Australia's export of sugar will be affected by entry of the UK into the EEC. Much will depend on the outcome of negotiations in 1973 for revision of the International Sugar Agreement. If there are no reasonable means of dealing with the problem of the excess availability in Australia after the end of the Commonwealth Sugar Agreement in 1974, then some degree of market disruption would seem inevitable.

NEW ZEALAND

Agricultural Trade

The strength of the New Zealand economy is her comparative advantage in pastoral farming. Her efficiency in the production of grass, and hence in the products of ruminant animals, milk, beef and veal, lamb and wool, is unsurpassed. Exports of minerals, forestry products, and manufactures have been growing rapidly; even so, exports of pastoral products still represent four-fifths of total merchandize exports.

Historically, the New Zealand economy has been closely linked to that of the UK. This dependence was reinforced by the Ottawa Agreements, by wartime and postwar bulk purchase and trade agreements, and by the fact that Britain was the world's largest importer of dairy products and lamb as well as a large importer of mutton, beef, and wool. This dependence has lessened considerably over recent years as the British connection has proved increasingly inadequate and as New Zealand has orientated her economic relationships more toward countries around the Pacific Rim. But trade with Britain still accounts for about one-third of two-way trade, and Britain still provides an outlet for approximately 90, 80, and 85 percent of New Zealand's exports of butter, cheese, and lamb, respectively. In 1970 shipments of these three products represented 70 percent of all exports to Britain and 24 percent of total exports. Exports of mutton, beef, and wool are shipped to a much wider range of markets, 80, 90, and 80 percent, respectively, of these products going to markets other than Britain. Japan is the major market for mutton, taking some two-thirds of total shipments in 1971, and the United States has recently taken around 60 percent of exports of beef and veal. Wool, which faces few trade barriers—even in the United States where tariffs are not levied on the coarse grades of carpet-type wools produced in New Zealand—is shipped to a very wide range of markets.

Trade Problems

In the immediate past, New Zealand's commercial diplomacy has been focused sharply on minimizing the disruption of her agricultural trade arising from Britain's applying the Community's CAP. The prime concern has been to secure an agreement for dairy products. The Luxembourg Agreement provides guaranteed access to the British market for specified quantities of butter and cheese. These quantities will be reduced by regular steps over the five years ending in 1977, but in that year New Zealand will have access for 80 percent of her present contractual entitlement for butter and 20 percent of her entitlement for cheese. Additionally, New Zealand is guaranteed a price level representing the average price obtained in the British market for the four years 1969-72. This arrangement will not obviate the need for market diversification and stabilization arrangements. Hence the further assurances providing that the EEC will not frustrate New Zealand's attempts to develop alternative markets and will promote the conclusion of a world agreement on dairy products are also important features of the Luxembourg accord.

With rising demand and a sustained deficit in beef supplies in Western Europe, the adoption by the UK of the tariffs and market regulations for beef and veal is not likely to have much impact on total shipments to Europe. Nor is the adoption of the 20-percent tariff on lamb and mutton likely to have too severe an effect on shipments to Britain in view of the rising prices of competitive meats. However, it is important to New Zealand (and Australia) that the EEC not adopt a restrictive market regulation for sheep meats in the future.

Trade problems with other countries center mainly on the United States, Canada, and Japan. Discontent has focused on the various restrictive import quotas for beef and veal, mutton, and dairy products. The U.S. tariffs on apparel wools and scoured wool are also of some concern. Maintenance of New Zealand's share of permitted imports of beef, veal, and mutton into the United States, continued free access to the Canadian market for meats, continued growth in demand for manufacturing grades of beef and mutton in North America, and further liberalization of the Japanese quota for beef (mutton is already unrestricted) all combine to suggest that New Zealand can anticipate steady growth in her meat exports to these countries. No such prospect is presently envisioned for dairy product exports to North America, but Japan is likely to take increased shipments, particularly of cheese.

Agricultural and Trade Policies

A far-reaching system of import licensing has been in force in New Zealand for many years. Licensing has extended to most agricultural products and has conferred an unknown degree of support on the farm sector. Recently, the decision has been taken to replace most import licensing with tariffs over a five-year period, but many products will remain under import monopoly control. Animal and plant health regulations are significant trade barriers. There are mixing regulations for tobacco and a controlled price system for wheat. These latter measures do not appear to be particularly protectionist; a higher proportion of local tobaccos is used rather than the minimum requirement, and the local price of wheat has seldom risen above the delivered cost of imports. However, with a population, albeit wealthy, of less than 3 million, New Zealand is such a small market for farm products that her less-than-immaculate behavior evokes cynicism rather than concern in world councils. Most other elements of her domestic agricultural policy are unexceptional, and government expenditure on all forms of assistance is less than U.S. $100 million a year. The major program is the operation of commodity stabilization funds for dairy products, meats, and wool. These smooth out fluctuations in receipts arising from volatile world markets and offer minimum floor prices. They are expected to be financially self-supporting over a period, but may have access to cheap credit in adverse periods. Otherwise, assistance to the industry comprises mainly input subsidies on fertilizers and pesticides, taxation advantages, and disaster relief.

Commercial policy has consisted in the main of attempts to secure agricultural trade liberalization in GATT, of the cultivation of bilateral trade agreements with Britain, Australia, and other countries, of support for international stabilization arrangements for whole and skim milk powder, and of a very active policy of product and market diversification. In the latter regard, expanding exports of beef and mutton to the United States, Canada, and Japan have been the most successful venture, and there has also been considerable success in shipping dairy products other than butter and cheese (mainly skim milk powder) to markets other than Britain, and especially to Japan and Latin America. The North American market for lamb is being actively developed. However, overall, and for dairy products and lamb especially, New Zealand has achieved less success and has fewer opportunities in market and product diversification than has either Canada or Australia.

Export Availabilities

The future export potential of New Zealand is particularly difficult to evaluate because of the uncertainty that attaches to market
opportunities for dairy products, the dominant trade item. The future
of dairy exports has an important influence on the supply of beef.
Stagnation of the former would accelerate the rate of expansion of beef
production from specialized herds and, more importantly, the pace
at which beef was produced from the dairy herd by breeding to beef-
type bulls and retaining calves. Estimates suggest that export supplies
of beef and veal could rise from the 175,000 tons of 1969-70 to perhaps
250,000 tons in 1975 and 350,000 tons by 1985. Hence New Zealand
will continue to be concerned about the conditions of access for beef
and veal to the U.S. market. The same holds for exports of mutton.
Lamb exports are dependent on the successful cultivation of demand
in high-income markets, the relative prices of lamb and other meats,
and the future price of wool, but export supply availability is also
likely to increase. Dairy exports are problematical. The capacity to
increase production is great, but in the absence of improved access
to Western Europe and North America, the extent to which Japan and
the socialist countries meet future consumption growth by imports
will be decisive.

It may finally be noted that indicative planning for the New Zealand economy continues to lay great stress on the expansion of exports
of agricultural, and particularly pastoral, products. As Table 5.9
shows, it is hoped to increase exports of pastoral products by 27 percent in the next decade, representing a similar proportion of the growth
in total export receipts.

OVERVIEW

It will be seen from the foregoing review that the relationships
between Canada, Australia, and New Zealand, and the United States
are complex. The three former countries share with the United States
a primary concern with minimizing the trade reduction and deflection
effects of Western Europe's agricultural policies; all wish to see
continuation of the recently rapid liberalization of the conditions of
access to the Japanese market and greater willingness on the part of
that country to import livestock products and processed foods; all
look to normalization and expansion of trade with the socialist countries
to replace markets lost elsewhere and to provide opportunities for
releasing their very considerable productive capacity.

All three countries are experiencing underlying shifts in supply
and demand conditions for their major export commodities and changes

TABLE 5.9

Export Targets Adopted by the New Zealand National Development
Conference, March 1972*

$NZ

Sector	1972-73	1975-76	1978-79	1981-82	Increase for Full Target Period	Share of Target Increase in Export Receipts
Agriculture-pastoral	974	1046	1149	1241	267	24.4
Horticultural	40	48	56	65	25	2.2
Total agriculture	1014	1094	1205	1307	293	26.8
Forestry	83	144	171	192	109	10.0
Minerals	5	15	20	25	20	1.8
Fisheries	14	18	27	36	22	2.1
Other manufacturing	140	186	247	329	189	17.2
Travel (tourism)	39	56	81	109	70	6.3
Others (mainly services)	113	147	189	215	102	9.2
Total	2422	2754	3145	3519	1097	100.0

*In constant 1969-70 prices.

in the terms of their access to the West European market. Hence all three have been forced to make real efforts to bring about changes in the commodity composition of output and exports and to pursue active market diversification programs. Thus Canada is emphasizing feed grains, oilseeds, beef, and pork relative to wheat. Australia similarly needs to switch emphasis from wheat, wool, dairy products, and sugar to feed grains, oilseeds, and meats. New Zealand faces better market prospects for meats than for dairy products and wool. All are looking to Japan, the socialist countries, and the North American market for increased sales of the products in which they have a comparative advantage and face more favorable market prospects.

And therein lies the source of a number of conflicts with the United States. The United States, impelled by the imperatives of her own balance of payments and farm income situations, is pinning its hopes for farm product export expansion on the same commodities (particularly feed grains and oilseeds) and the same markets (particularly Japan and the socialist countries). Alternatively, realization of the aspirations of Canada, Australia, and New Zealand is in conflict with the position of the U.S. farmer in the domestic U.S. market and requires changes in current U.S. farm and trade policies, particularly for meats, dairy products, sugar, and wool.

To be specific on the latter matter, Australia and New Zealand exports of beef, veal, and mutton would benefit greatly by the permanent removal of the Meat Import Law or an increased share in U.S. domestic meat consumption. Both countries would be the principal beneficiaries of a relaxation of U.S. (and Canadian) dairy quotas. Australian exports of apparel wools and sugar would be enhanced by a removal of the U.S. wool tariff and an increase in the sugar quota. Canada has few urgent complaints against U.S. import policies since mutual reduction of tariffs on farm products moving mainly on the continent was one of the few accomplishments of the Kennedy Round of agricultural negotiations. There is no particular reason why Canada should expect the United States to replace her own high-cost dairy products with equally high-cost Canadian supplies.

It is clear that competition between the United States and Canada and Australia is likely to be intense for wheat, feed grains, and oilseeds sold to Western Europe, Japan, and the socialist countries. Whatever trade advantages Canada and Australia have had in dealing with China, Russia, and Eastern Europe are likely to be eliminated by recent relaxation of policies governing U.S. trade with the Communist countries. Canada and Australia have several major concerns about this projected competition, including the easier merchandisability of corn and soybeans relative to competing feed grains and oilseeds, the consequences of an overexuberant or permanent release of the 60 million acres of farmland held out of production in the United States, and the impossibility of competing with the long purse of the U.S. Treasury in export aids of various kinds should these be revived. Conversely, the United States takes the view that the flexibility in pricing and international merchandizing enjoyed by Canada and Australia by reason of the monopoly control over exportable supplies of grains enjoyed by the Canadian and Australian Wheat Boards confers a competitive advantage. Whether this advantage is "unfair" will have to be resolved in wider discussions of "state trading" and of the trade-hindering effects of quasi-official national and provincial marketing boards and agencies.

Canada, Australia, and New Zealand all place greater stress on formal action to stabilize international commodity markets than does the United States. Specifically, Australia and New Zealand would welcome a wider international commodity arrangement for dairy products than the minimum export price schemes now confined to whole and skim milk powder, and Australia and Canada appear to be more anxious than is the United States to see a revised international wheat agreement with price provisions and broad supply and purchase commitments.

One further difference may be noted. All three countries recognize, along with the United States, that improvements in the conditions affecting agricultural trade cannot be secured by reciprocal concessions on frontier measures and domestic programs affecting trade in farm products alone, but must, instead, be part of a balanced package of measures leading to freer trade in agricultural products and manufacturers and strengthening of the international monetary system. However, while Canada now seems prepared to participate fully in liberalization of trade in industrial products, it is by no means certain that Australia and New Zealand will have the same freedom, albeit that both seem to have lost some of their enthusiasm for their traditional policies of attempting to industrialize behind formidably high tariff and nontariff barriers. However, this may be a difference of little importance since the initiation, course, and outcome of the major trade negotiations scheduled to begin in 1973 hinge on the willingness and ability of the United States, the EEC, and Japan to enter into meaningful negotiations and reach accords, and not on the participation or offers of three powers of relatively minor economic and political importance.

6

**AGRICULTURAL POLICIES IN JAPAN,
CHINA, THE SOVIET UNION,
AND EASTERN EUROPE**
compiled by
D. Gale Johnson
John A. Schnittker

JAPAN

Japan, now the U.S. farmers' largest customer, increased the importation of foodstuffs sharply during the 1960s. This was not accidental, but a matter of policy. The largest increases were in cereals, feed grains, and oilseeds, but other major categories also increased.

This pattern is expected to continue, possibly at an accelerated rate, during the 1970s. Japan's natural limitations in respect to agricultural production, the changing food demands of her people, the overriding comparative advantage in production of the grain-exporting countries, especially the United States, and Japan's favorable balance of trade with the United States all suggest the continued advantages to a greater reliance on commodity and food imports. This trend has been described in detail in a report by Mr. Michael Tracey* of the Organization for Economic Cooperation and Development (OECD) in Paris.

Events in Japan only serve to strengthen the conclusions cited above. The new government elected in 1973 appears to be moving toward a greater reliance on food imports, despite some resistance. A significant further drop may be expected in the 1970s in the degree of self-sufficiency in food, after a decline from 89 percent to 80 percent in self-sufficiency in the preceding decade.

Speculation regarding the size and the speed of increases in Japanese wheat, feed grain, and oilseed imports lends to a wide range

---

*"Japanese Agriculture at the Crossroads," Trade Policy Research Center, London.

of results. It is conservatively estimated that Japanese wheat imports
will double between 1970 and 2000. Feed grain and soybean exports
may well increase three to four times over in that period, as consumption of livestock products rises from today's low levels of a few
pounds per person toward levels reached long ago in Euopre and the
Western Hemisphere. The United States can expect to get the greatest
export gains in feed grains and oilseeds. Canada and Australia will
benefit more from Japan's larger wheat imports than from feedstuffs,
although the United States will almost surely share heavily in the
growth of wheat imports by Japan.

Japan's food and agricultural policy trend would appear to be
extremely dependable and irreversible. Its causes are so deeply
rooted in Japan's new economic relationships with the rest of the
world and to her own geography that the possibility of a shift back to
greater reliance on home production could probably do no more than
slow the rate at which imports increase. This was recognized in
1973, when Japan protested the imposition of export controls on soybeans by the United States, but recognized also that she could no
longer rely on home production to any degree.

CHINA

The new political and economic relationships begun between the
United States and China in 1971 can be expected to lead to regular
trade between the two countries. No large volume of trade in agricultural products is expected, however, in the short run, since China's
policy line still holds to substantial self-sufficiency in food commodities, and since Canada and Australia have provided the bulk of China's
grain import requirements the past 12 years.

China has imported wheat in a range of 2 to 6 million tons a
year since 1961, principally from Australia and Canada. In 1972-73,
China's grain crop was reported down 5 percent, or about 10 million
tons, from the previous year, and China bought some U.S. grain.

Too little is known about China in 1973 to judge whether large
increases in grain imports might be required before the decade ends.
The most likely prospect, in view of China's past policies in regard
to food production and her limited foreign exchange, is for a slow
climb in food imports as population and income increase. There
would appear to be little prospect, in view of the present level of
income, that China will adopt meat production targets so high that
grain imports will rise sharply, as the USSR has done. Yet no sure
judgment is possible on this score at a time when China has bought
substantial quantities of 1973 grain and soybeans from crops not yet
harvested, and when a sizable and surprising cotton trade has already
begun.

SOVIET UNION

In sharp contrast to previous agricultural plans of the Soviet Union, the Eighth and Ninth Five-Year Plans established reasonable and achievable goals for agriculture. Both emphasized the expansion of livestock and poultry production. The goals of the Eighth Plan for livestock products were slightly exceeded. The Ninth Plan called for increases of about 25 percent in meat production, 15 percent in milk production, and 30 percent in egg production over five years ending in 1975. The planned increase in grain production of 17 percent seemed reasonable in terms of the population's requirements of grain for food and the grain requirements for the expanded livestock output.

The emphasis in the plan upon expanding meat production is understandable when it is realized that per capita meat consumption in the USSR in a recent year, at 43 kilograms per capita, was nearly the lowest in Eastern Europe, compared to 52 kilograms in Poland and 67 kilograms in Czechoslovakia in the same year. Only Romania has a lower per capita consumption—at 42.4 kilograms. Prices to consumers have been high and the quality poor, though the recent increases in beef prices in Western Europe and North America have brought prices there to or above the levels in the USSR.

If consumer prices of meat are high, producer prices are astronomical. Governmental subsidies to collective and state farms that produce meat and milk may now be as much as 13 to 14 billion rubles ($16 to $17 billion) annually. Beef cattle prices paid to collective farms range from 96 to 183 rubles per 100 kilograms (up to $1.00 per pound), and pork prices from 100 to 200 rubles. In addition, a substantial premium of 20 percent is paid for cattle and sheep of better than average fatness. And if livestock sales exceed the annual plan for a farm, a premium of 50 percent is paid for sales in excess of the plan.

Objectives of Agricultural Policy

The USSR has three major objectives for its agricultural policy:
1. to increase per capita food output, with particular emphasis upon livestock and poultry products,
2. to lower the costs of production of farm products, and
3. to achieve a level of income of the farm population not too far below that of the urban population.

The greatest success has been achieved in raising the level of incomes of farm workers. When a concerted effort was made in this direction, starting with Mr. Khrushchev in the mid-1950s, it was hoped that increased incentives would result in more effective use of farm resources, including more timely availability of farm labor and more interested application of effort. Little seems to have been achieved in getting more effective use of farm labor. The money costs of labor-intensive farm products—especially livestock products—appear to have risen sharply as a result of higher guaranteed payments to collective farm workers and higher wages for state farm workers.

Possibility of Reaching Objectives

Before considering the means of achieving the first two objectives, we wish to note that there is a definite possibility that the meat output goal in the Ninth Five-Year Plan represents an underestimate of the growth in demand for meat from 1971 to 1975. During the plan period, meat output was to increase 26 percent. If population growth equals 5 percent, per capita output would increase a little less than 21 percent.

The plan for income growth indicates an increase in per capita income of 35 percent; the plan for income growth (in money terms) is almost always overachieved, and income increases already appear to be in excess of the plan with two years to go. Assuming constant meat prices, the implied plan income elasticity of demand for meat is 0.6. A number of estimates of the income elasticity of demand have been made by Soviet economists, and the range in estimates has been between 0.35 and 2.62 with all but two falling between 0.61 and 2.0. If the income elasticity is one, the planned output growth is less than two-thirds the possible increase in demand. The elimination of the disequilibrium by increasing meat prices in the state retail stores is apparently not an attractive one. The last official increase in meat (and milk) prices was in 1962. Meat prices in the collective farm markets apparently have increased substantially in the last two or three years; this is confirmation of the slower growth of output than demand in recent years and an indication of the problem Soviet planners must face over the next two years.

The meat and milk subsidies referred to earlier were introduced in 1965 as a means of holding retail prices constant and encouraging expansion of output. It is perhaps worthy of note that the subsidies were intended to be temporary, to be removed when the costs of producing livestock products were reduced by improved feed supplies, greater efficiency in labor use, and the completion of a large-scale investment program in facilities. But few farm subsidies ever turn out to be temporary, and instead of being phased out, the subsidies now cost billions of rubles annually—perhaps 13 to 14 billion rubles in 1972.

Increasing meat output by 5 percent annually, as called for in the current plan, is no small task. If the increase must be as much as 6.5 percent to meet demand growth, the task becomes much more difficult and probably unattainable. Either growth rate for output of meat will require a substantial expansion in feed supplies.

The existence of problems in providing adequate feed supplies became evident near the end of 1971. Following the two largest grain crops on record (1970 and 1971), the USSR contracted for imports of 4 million tons of feed grains for delivery in 1971-72. These commitments were made well before there was any knowledge that the 1972 crop would be poor. There is some indication that several million tons of wheat were withdrawn from stocks in 1969 and 1970 for use as feed.

For the 1971-75 plan period, the average grain goal of 195 million tons (bunker weight) is only 17 percent greater than average production in 1966-70. Assuming normal weather, an increase of grain equal to the planned increase seems feasible. The increase during the Eighth Plan was 29 percent, though the Eighth Plan period included two bumper crops (1966 and 1970) and no really poor crop, while the previous plan included two poor crops (1963 and 1965). If the planned increase in grain production occurs, the increase in grain available for feed should be about 40 percent for the Ninth Plan compared to the Eighth Plan.

How can the significant import of feed grains in 1971-72 be explained, given the claimed large grain crops of 1970 and 1971? Several explanations are possible. One is that Soviet planners may have detected a more rapid growth of demand for livestock products, especially meat and eggs, than indicated in the plan. Another is that the poor quality of livestock rations has lowered the effectiveness of additional grain below that anticipated. A third is that it is proving more difficult to increase cattle numbers than originally expected, and more of the beef output requires additional concentrates rather than roughage. Cattle numbers reported on January 1, 1972, were only 5 percent above the level five years earlier. Finally, there has been a significant relative shift toward poultry production, which requires more grain and protein meal relative to other feeds than either milk or beef. Perhaps all of the explanations have some relevance. Without more information it is difficult to say what the real situation is.

1972-73: A Special Case

The large imports of wheat and corn planned during the 1972-73 season should not be taken as a portent for the future. In 1972 both the grain and potato crops were poor, something that has not occurred in recent history. This crisis, and it is a crisis for the USSR, was far more serious than that resulting from the poor grain crop of 1963. In 1962-63 the USSR exported 5.3 million tons of wheat; in the following year net wheat imports were 8.5 million tons for a shift in net trade in wheat of almost 14 million tons. In 1972-73, net grain imports may be 26 million tons, and there are indications that imports will again be substantial in 1973-74 because of reduced stocks and expanding demand despite a good harvest.

With the many events and, one can say, surprises of 1972, it seems the height of folly to project what might happen by 1980 in Soviet imports of agricultural products. The most recent Food and Agricultural Organization (FAO) projection was for net Soviet exports of 5 million tons of grains in 1980, almost all of it wheat, no significant net trade in feed grains, and only very modest imports of oilmeals (200,000 tons). If we had been making such projections in the late 1960s, we would have thought the FAO projections reasonable. But now that new information is available, can one justify a major change in the projections?

It seems probable, assuming normal weather, that the Soviet Union will be a net exporter of wheat in 1980. Assuming an extraction rate of 70 percent, wheat required for milling amounts to about 50 million tons and will probably remain at this level for the decade; seed requirements are high and amount to about 13 million tons. If waste amounts to 15 percent and poor-quality wheat (used for feed) to 10 million tons, wheat production of 85 million tons (bunker weight) would meet all domestic requirements, and any output in excess of that amount would be available for export or feed. Because of commitments to Eastern Europe and certain other regions of the world, net wheat exports of at least 5 million tons seem a reasonable projection. While the Soviet Union will probably import as well as export wheat in 1980, it seems probable that such imports will continue to come primarily from Canada and, to a lesser degree, from Australia and France, with small quantities from the United States.

Whether the United States will export any significant amount of feed grains to the Soviet Union in 1980 is highly uncertain. Exports could be substantial, with regular Soviet imports of feed grains amounting to as much as 20 million tons a year, or such imports could be nominal. As a basis for long-run plans, the assumption of a mid-range of 10 to 12 million tons for Soviet feed grain imports seems the most reasonable. There are substantial potentials for increasing feed grain production and equal or greater potentials for reducing feed use per unit of output of livestock products.

In the long run, the import demand for high protein feeds may well be the most promising export possibility for the United States.

There are significant climatic limitations on the production of high protein feeds in the Soviet Union. One of the apparent reasons for thè high feed use per unit of livestock output is the limited amount and poor quality of protein available. Enormous quantities of low-quality roughage (straw and poor-quality hay) are fed. Adding high protein feeds to such rations would substantially increase livestock output. The importation of oilmeals would also make it possible to reduce the feeding of milk to young animals and thus permit more meat production as a replacement of milk output that is now used for livestock feeding in such large quantities. Soviet imports of 3 to 5 million tons of oilmeal annually by 1980 are possible and, in fact, may well be reached by 1975, unless continuing large grain imports place too heavy a burden on Russia's foreign exchange.

EASTERN EUROPE

Throughout Eastern Europe, agriculture continues to be a significant economic and political problem. Output growth has been slow over the past decade, especially since the mid-1960s. Output of crop products are quite variable from year to year and, largely as a result, so are imports. Following a generally poor grain crop in 1970, net grain imports of the region increased from about 4 million tons to 10 million tons and remained at a high level in 1971/72. Eastern Europe is a substantial net exporter of meat products and live animals, principally to Western Europe, though Poland exports significant amounts of cured pork products to the United States. In 1971 Eastern Europe imported approximately 1 million tons of oilmeals from the United States (including transshipments). In 1971 U.S. exports of farm products to Eastern Europe (excluding transshipments) were approximately $250 million; imports were valued at $91 million.

Import Policy

To a considerable extent, the import policies of the countries of Eastern Euorpe are dictated by four important considerations:
1. the role of livestock and products as important earners of convertible currencies,
2. the year-to-year variability of crop production,
3. the traditional role of meat products in the diets of their citizens and the political importance of adequate supplies at "reasonable" prices, and
4. political, economic, and trade ties with the Soviet Union through the Committee for Mutual Economic Assistance (COMECON).

Maintaining and increasing livestock production are critical as a means of obtaining convertible foreign exchange and of maintaining political and economic stability at home. The Polish riots in 1970-71 apparently had a major impact, not only in Eastern Europe but in the Soviet Union as well. For these reasons Eastern Europe is likely to emphasize feed imports in the years ahead to insure adequate livestock products. If the Soviet Union were a reliable source of feed grain, it would undoubtedly supply most of Eastern Europe's imports, except for Yugoslavia. But it has not been a particularly reliable source in the past and is not likely to be in the future.

U.S. Exports

Exports of agricultural products to Eastern Europe will depend on both our policies and those of Eastern Europe. Only Poland and Yugoslavia receive most-favored-nation (MFN) treatment in the application of our tariff duties. Most types of government credit are not available to the region.

The per capita demand for meat is apparently increasing significantly. This will mean that the demand for feed will continue to grow, and probably only part of this increased demand will be met from internal sources. If recent trends can be taken as an indication, net feed imports will probably increase during the rest of the decade. This does not mean that grain imports will equal the unusual levels of 1970/71 and 1971/72, but could well be substantially above the 4-million-ton average for the three years before 1970/71. Significant growth in oilmeal imports, which increased from about 300,000 tons in the early 1960s to 1.6 million tons in 1970 and 1971, appears probable. The United States, both directly and via transshipments, apparently supplied about two-thirds of oilmeal imports in the past two years.

It will probably continue to be true that when the Soviet Union can supply grain to Eastern Europe, the area's grain imports from the United States and the rest of the world will be adversely affected. But for the rest of this decade, it is reasonable to predict that the availability of grain from the Soviet Union will be smaller than in the past decade, and that the requirements of Eastern Europe for grain will be larger. Thus imports of grain from other sources, including the United States, should increase during the 1970s. Substantial year-to-year variations should be expected, and significant quantities may involve transshipments from Western Europe rather than direct exports from the United States.

There are so many uncertainties about future trade prospects that any projection of export levels can be little more than a guess.

136

The most that we feel can be said is that it would not be surprising if U.S. agricultural exports increased by half from 1970, and we would not rule out a doubling.

7

THE DEVELOPING COUNTRIES
AND U.S. AGRICULTURE
Martin E. Abel

We are concerned in this paper with the interactions of agricultural developments in the developing countries and in the United States. It is difficult to deal with such a broad topic in the space of one relatively short paper. I have chosen, therefore, to focus my remarks on developments in the production, consumption, and trade of a set of commodities that the developing countries and the United States both produce and in which the developing countries have a significant export interest. Emphasis will be on the role of U.S. agricultural trade policies as they affect the world market potential for these products.

We are not concerned with a group of noncompetitive commodities—those that are produced and exported by the developing countries and imported but not produced by the United States. These are mainly tropical products such as coffee, cocoa, tea, bananas, spices, and so on. While the value of noncompetitive agricultural imports by the United States is fairly large—amounting to $2.1 billion in fiscal year 1971 or 37 percent of total U.S. agricultural imports—there are few trade issues involved. Unlike many other developed countries, the United States does not subject imports of noncompetitive commodities to significant levels of tariff and nontariff protection, or to domestic excise taxes. There is, however, one exception to this statement. Some of the tariffs applied to processed forms of noncompetitive agricultural products do discriminate against the processing of these products being done by the developing exporters.

The author would like to thank a number of persons for helpful comments and suggestions during the writing of this paper, namely, Willard W. Cochrane, Vernon W. Ruttan, James P. Houck, W. B. Sundquist, Lauren Soth, and P. G. H. Barter.

The major competitive commodities that have been or are likely to be in the trade picture for both the United States and the developing countries are grains, oilseeds and products, cotton, fruits and vegetables, sugar, tobacco, and meats. Our concern is not just with the raw forms of these products, but also with semiprocessed and processed products based on them. For many agricultural products, the degree of trade protection employed by the United States is higher for processed than for raw products. This means that present trading practices by the United States discourage processing of agricultural products in the developing countries; this is an important trade issue of our time.

There is one large topic in the trade area—generalized trade preferences for the developing countries granted by the developed countries—which is not covered in this paper. This has been an important item of discussion for some time and was a major item at the United Nations Conference on Trade and Development in New Delhi in 1968 (UNCTAD II). It was generally agreed that the question should receive serious study, and efforts should be made to move toward a general system of trade preferences by the developed countries for products from the developing countries. The argument for this kind of reverse discrimination for a very broad range of commodities can be viewed more as a foreign-aid issue than one of trade. The main concern is with the transfer of resources from rich to poor nations, which can be done in many ways. Generalized trade preferences is one such way. Since we consider this topic to fall more appropriately in the foreign-aid rather than in the trade field, we shall not discuss the topic in this paper.

However, foreign-aid prospects are relevant to our discussion in one important sense—the less foreign aid available to the developing countries, the more pressure there is for them to increase export earnings. The developing countries are keenly interested in increasing their access to foreign exchange in order to pay for needed capital imports and service past debts. Basically, there are four ways by which this can be done:
1. Increase the volume of economic aid and private capital transfers from the rich to the poor nations.
2. Relieve the developing countries of part of their debt burden.
3. Increase commercial exports from the developing to the developed countries.
4. Follow policies of import substitution which make the developing countries less dependent on imports.

The prospects for significant increases in flows of foreign aid and private capital to the developing countries in the 1970s are not bright. The Pearson Commission Report[1] refers to a sense of "weariness" in the richer countries toward foreign aid.

The signs are not propitious. In the last years of [the 1960s], the volume of foreign official aid has been stagnant. At no time during this period has it kept pace with the growth of national product in the wealthy nations. In fact, the commitments by the United States, which has been much the largest provider of aid funds, are declining. There, and in some other developed countries, we have encountered a spirit of disenchantment.

With no increase in the annual flow of foreign aid in sight, and a decline being possible, the annual flow of net aid from the developed to the developing countries will decline. This is so because the levels of interest and principal repayments on old debts are scheduled to grow rapidly. Table 7.1 from the Pearson Commission Report illustrates how critical this problem is likely to become. The debt figures in the table refer to the flow of supplier's credits, private and governmental loans, and loans of international agencies, but exclude grants or direct private investment. Clearly, the debt burden is rising and is projected to equal or exceed gross foreign-aid lending in all developing regions of the world by the end of the 1970s. Thus, the 1970s, rather than being the "Nth Development Decade," could very well be the "Decade of Debt Crisis"!

There are two ways out of this problem, assuming the level of gross aid cannot be increased. One is to provide debt relief to the developing countries either through cancellation or rescheduling of old debts. This has the effect of increasing the flow of net aid. This

TABLE 7.1

Debt Service as Percentage of Gross Lending
(1965-67 and 1977)

	Africa	Europe	East Asia	South Asia Middle East	Latin America
1965-67	73	92	52	40	87
1977 with gross flow of new lending unchanged	121	109	134	97	130

Source: Partners in Development: Report of the Commission On International Development (New York: Praeger Publishers, 1969).

140

has been done in the past, and it is inevitable that more of it will be done in the future. But if the donor nations are already in an "owly" mood with respect to foreign aid, the prospects of the developing countries not being able to meet their debt obligations will make them even more parsimonious.

The other alternative is to facilitate a larger and growing volume of exports from the developing to the developed countries. While there is a great deal that would have to be done by both groups of countries to bring this about—much more than is possible to discuss in this paper—we shall focus on what the United States could do to increase the flow of exports from the developing countries, particularly the flow of agricultural products based primarily on agricultural raw materials.

Further import substitution, particularly for nonagricultural products, does not represent a viable alternative. Many developing countries have already pushed such policies to the point where long-term economic growth and development have been adversely affected.[2]

However, there are ample opportunities for developing countries to increase agricultural production in an efficient manner and reduce somewhat their dependence on agricultural imports. Increased production can be accomplished by a shift in agricultural growth based on traditional resource use to one that is science (technology) based. This, of course, requires the development of agricultural research institutions capable of producing a steady stream of technologies that are economically viable in the developing countries.

PRODUCTION AND TRADE IN THE DEVELOPING COUNTRIES

The purpose of this section is to indicate the importance of grains, oilseeds and products, cotton, sugar, fruits and vegetables, meats, and tobacco in world trade, the importance of these commodities in the total value of exports from the developing countries, the extent to which world trade in them is likely to expand, and the position that the United States occupies in world markets as either an exporter or importer of these commodities. From such a perspective, we can get a rough idea of the importance of U.S. trade and trade policies to the export interests of the developing countries.

Grains

We are concerned with wheat, rice, and coarse grains. In 1965 four developing countries—Burma, Cambodia, Thailand, and

Argentina—depended on grain exports for 20 percent or more of their total export earnings. In Burma and Cambodia rice accounted for over 50 percent of export earnings.[3] Thus the number of developing countries that depend heavily on grain exports is small. On the other hand, there are a large number that have become or could become grain-exporters.

Since about 1965 there has been a marked increase in grain production in a number of developing countries, particularly in wheat and rice. The basis for this expansion has been the development and adoption of new, higher-yielding varieties of grain and favorable grain prices. At the same time, excess production capacity continues to exist in the developed grain-exporting countries, while some major developed grain-importing countries like the European Community (EC) continue to increase their output. As a result, there has been a downward pressure on world grain prices in recent years.

But one should view these price developments in a longer-term context. World grain prices at the end of the decade of the 1960s were at about the same level as at the beginning of that decade. Yet wide swings in prices occurred during this period. Let us look at rice, which, of all the grains, exhibited the widest price swings in the 1960s. In 1961 the f.o.b. Bangkok export price of Thai white rice 100 percent was about $135 per metric ton. World rice prices rose sharply in the 1966-68 period; the price for the same grade of rice reached a peak of $250 per ton in October 1967. But by April 1971 the price had fallen to $120 per ton.[4] There was a similar, though less pronounced, swing in wheat prices. The Canadian export price for wheat averaged $64 per metric ton during 1959-61. Export prices reached a high of $71 per ton in 1966 and were back down to $64 per ton in 1969.[5]

There were two important factors in the world grain picture—one transitory and one permanent—which gave rise to the roller coaster behavior of grain prices, and both operated in the developing countries. The transitory element in the picture consisted of two parts:
1. the unprecedented droughts in South Asia during the 1956-66 and 1966-67 crop years, which required record levels of food aid, and
2. the sharp increases in rice imports by South Vietnam in 1966 and 1967, which put considerable pressure on world rice prices.

The more permanent aspect of the grain situation in the developing countries can also be looked at in two parts. During the 1950s and the first half of the 1960s, grain production per capita in the developing countries was increasing at a modest rate, but not fast enough to keep pace with the rate of growth in demand.[6] Consequently, grain imports by the developing countries increased steadily. Starting in about 1965, the new high-yielding varieties of wheat and rice began to be used in many developing countries. And, by the end of the decade, several countries had experienced sharp increases in production of these crops, reducing the need for imports and, in some cases, contributing to export supplies. In a number of countries, significant increases in the production of maize, sorghum, and millets were also experienced. At the same time, the major developed grain-exporting countries continue to have more grain production capacity than can be utilized at current domestic and world prices. For example, in the late 1960s and early 1970s, wheat production in the United States, Canada, and Australia was sharply curtailed in response to sagging exports and growing stocks. It is generally agreed that rapid technological change in grain production in many developing countries and surplus production potential in the developed grain-exporting countries will continue in the 1970s.

World trade in coarse grains grew at a fairly rapid rate in the 1950s and 1960s because of the rapid rates of economic growth and growth in the demand for livestock products in the developed countries. These forces for growth in the trade of coarse grains can also be expected to continue in the future.

What are the trade prospects in grain for the coming decade? A recent study by the Economic Research Service (ERS) of the U.S. Department of Agriculture (USDA) projects world grain production, consumption, and trade to 1980.[7] Trade data for the 1964-66 period and projections to 1980 are summarized in Table 7.2. The study concludes that

For wheat:

> Import demand will be sluggish in the developed area but potentially strong in the developing countries if concessional terms of trade are available. Increased feed use of wheat would reduce downward pressures on prices. Some increase in the share of the world market would be possible for developing country exporters, largely Argentina. Accelerated wheat production in the developing countries could lead to an improved export earnings position if major developed exporters moderated the price effect by withdrawing exportable supplies from the world market. Subsidy costs and quality factors could offset potential export earnings in South Asia.

For rice:

> The Green Revolution would result in lower world import demand, a demand centered in the developing countries. Import demand in the developed area is expected to rise moderately, but the increase is small relative to potential

supplies for export—from both developed and developing exporters. Consequently, continued downward pressure on prices is expected. Since most of the market for the developing country exporters is within the developing countries, prospects for export earnings from rice are poor, particularly under accelerated growth in rice production in the importing developing countries.

For coarse grains:

Import demand in developed areas, particularly Japan, is expected to be strong. Given concessional terms of trade, import demand of the developing countries could increase sharply as a result of a rapidly expanding livestock industry in these countries. Lower internal grain prices in developed importing areas, particularly the EC, could give trade an additional boost. Some developing country exporters might not fully share in the expansion because their port facilities are limited in handling large cargo vessels. On the other hand, maintenance of very high internal prices through limited access could lead to self-sufficiency in total grains in the EC, thereby lowering export prospects.

Thus, the prospects for growth of grain exports from the developing countries are mixed. For wheat and rice especially, much hinges on the policies followed by the developed grain-exporting countries. We shall return to this subject in a later section of the paper with specific reference to the United States.

Oilseeds and Products[8]

Oilseeds and products are important export crops for many developing countries. In 1965 exports of oilseeds, oil nuts, and animal and vegetable oils accounted for more than 20 percent of export earnings in 15 countries. In seven of these countries, these products accounted for more than 50 percent of total export earnings.

World prices of various oilseeds and vegetable oils have followed generally similar patterns since World War II. Prices were relatively high in the early 1950s, declined from about 1951-52 until the early 1960s, and exhibited some upward movement in the mid and late 1960s.

On the other hand, there has been rather continuous growth in the value of world trade in oilseeds and vegetable oils. Between 1951 and 1965, world trade in oilseeds and oil nuts increased from 5.0 to 12.2 million tons. Trade in vegetable oils went from 1.8 to 3.9 million

TABLE 7.2

World Trade in Wheat, Rice, and Coarse Grains, 1964-66: Average and Projections to 1980

Region	Wheat			Coarse Grains			Rice		
	1964-66	1980Aa	1980Bb	1964-66	1980Aa	1980Bb	1964-66	1980Aa	1980b
United States	21.2	19.3	14.8	21.8	30.0	21.0	1527	2063	147
Canada	13.8	11.9	8.7	0.7	1.1	0.4	-45	-64	-66
Central America and Mexico	-1.0	-2.3	-2.1	0.7	-2.2	-0.7	-367	-503	-394
E. South America	-3.0	-4.9	-5.0	0.2	1.0	3.0	382	158	379
W. South America	-1.2	-3.4	-3.5	-0.1	-1.2	-1.2	-71	-22	100
Argentina	5.1	5.2	6.2	5.2	7.0	8.4	29	43	81
N. Africa	-3.6	-8.9	-9.6	0.1	-1.0	-0.4	341	538	662
E. Africa	-0.3	-0.7	-0.7	-0.1	1.2	3.3	-177	-454	-437
W. Africa	-0.6	-1.5	-1.6	0.1	-2.8	-2.2	-428	-791	-637
S. Africa, Rep. of	-0.4	-0.5	-0.5	0.5	3.9	3.4	-73	-132	-137
W. Asia	-1.9	-5.0	-4.3	-0.5	-2.8	-2.6	-354	-575	-464
S. Asia	-9.3	-2.4	7.1	-1.3	-2.8	-2.4	-1137	-770	-117
SE Asia	-0.2	-0.4	-0.4	1.3	1.6	2.9	2419	2480	2791
E. Asia and Pacific Is.	-2.1	-4.2	-4.4	-0.3	-3.7	-1.3	-1728	-1627	-1046
Australia and New Zealand	6.3	7.8	6.8	0.7	2.8	2.7	71	158	140
Eastern Europe	-5.7	-1.8	-1.8	-0.4	1.1	1.0	-290	-354	-367
USSR	-2.4	4.6	4.6	0.3	0.7	0.6	-247	-266	-287
Communist Asia	-5.7	-6.1	-6.1	0.1	-0.3	-0.4	903	768	574
Japan	-3.6	-6.5	-6.5	-6.0	-16.7	-17.2	-750	-170	-365
E C	1.3	3.9	2.4	-11.9	-10.0	-9.3	-199	-302	-336
United Kingdom	-4.3	-4.5	-4.6	-3.5	-1.7	-2.9	-109	-134	-140
Other Western Europe	-1.3	0.5	0.6	-5.6	-5.1	-6.2	-29	-40	-82

Note: Figures for wheat and coarse grains are in million metric tons; figures for rice are in 1,000 metric tons.

aAssumes a continuation of present food and fiber policies, allowing for moderate gains in productivity in the developing countries.

bAssumes that agricultural productivity and economic growth in the developing countries would be higher than projected under 1980A.

Source: Anthony S. Rojko, Francis S. Urban, and James J. Naive, "World Demand Prospects for Grains in 1980 with Emphasis on Trade by the Less Developed Countries," Foreign Agricultural Economics Report (FAER) No 75, ERS, USDA, December 1971.

tons during the same period. Most of this growth has been in oilseeds and vegetable oils produced in the temperate zone developed countries; the exports from tropical developing countries have not fared that well. Within the category of oilseeds and oil nuts, soybeans, cottonseed, rape and mustard seed, and sesame seed had the most rapid rate of increase in trade. On the other hand, ground nuts, palm and palm kernel, and copra—commodities important to the developing countries—had either no growth or suffered some decline in world trade. A similar pattern existed for vegetable oils, although the picture was a little less pessimistic for the developing countries because there was a modest increase in exports of ground nut and coconut oil while exports of palm oil and palm kernel oil declined or remained about constant.

Looking to the future (1980),[9] production of major oilseeds is expected to increase steadily. In terms of oil equivalent, world production is expected to grow by 3.5 percent a year through 1980. A slightly faster rate of growth is expected in the developed than in the developing countries. For vegetable oils, prices are expected to decline by as much as 20 percent. Of equal importance to many developing countries, growth in their domestic consumption will hold down exportable supplies. On the other hand, import demands for oil cake, particularly in the developed countries, are expected to increase at a substantial rate. Since production of oil cake in the developing countries will increase faster than domestic demands, exportable supplies of oil cake should increase.

Cotton[10]

Cotton is another agricultural commodity that is a major earner of foreign exchange for a number of developing countries, and a potential earner of foreign exchange in a number of other developing countries. In 1966 a total of 15 developing countries earned more than 10 percent of their total export earnings from lint cotton. Of these, cotton accounted for more than 20 percent of total exports in eight countries and for more than 50 percent of total exports in three countries (Table 7.3).

A number of other countries depend heavily on cotton textiles for foreign-exchange earnings. In 1968 cotton textiles accounted for 15 percent or more of total exports in four countries—Hong Kong, United Arab Republic (UAR), Portugal, and Pakistan (Table 7.4). The combined exports of lint cotton and cotton textiles accounted for about 75 percent of total exports from the UAR. The prospects for future world trade in lint cotton and cotton textiles are of significant interest to a large number of developing countries.

TABLE 7.3

Cotton Lint Exports as a Percentage of
Total Merchandise Exports (Selected Countries, 1966)

Country	Percent
Chad	77.2
United Arab Republic	55.0
Syria	51.6
Sudan	49.9
Nicaragua	41.5
Turkey	25.8
Uganda	22.9
Tanzania	20.9
Guatemala	19.2
Afghanistan	17.0
Mozambique	15.4
Central African Republic	14.6
Mexico	13.5
El Salvador	12.6
Peru	11.1
Cameroon	7.3
Pakistan	6.9
Greece	6.7
Brazil	6.4
USSR	4.2
Honduras	4.0
Paraguay	3.8
Togo	3.1
Iran	2.9
Angola	1.7
Kenya	1.4
United States	1.4
Costa Rica	1.4
Nigeria	1.2

Source: Richard S. Magleby and Edmond Missiaen, "World Demand Prospects for Cotton in 1980 with Emphasis on Trade by Less Developed Countries," FAER No. 68, ERS, USDA, January 1971.

TABLE 7.4

Cotton Textile Exports as a Percentage of
Total Merchandise Exports (Selected Countries, 1968)

Country	Percent
Hong Kong	20.5
United Arab Republic	19.3
Portugal	15.4
Pakistan	15.3
Taiwan	8.1
India	7.2
South Korea	4.6
Israel	3.3
Japan	3.1
Greece	2.6
Poland	1.5
EC (total)	1.2
Turkey	1.0
United Kingdom	0.8
Mexico	0.7
United States	0.7

Source: Magleby and Missiaen, op. cit.

While cotton use has increased from 7.7 million metric tons in 1952 to 11.4 million metric tons in 1968, its share in total fibers used for textiles declined from 73 to 57 percent during the same period. This was the result of proportionately greater growth in the use of man-made fibers.

World prices of cotton declined sharply in the 1950s and continued to decline at a moderate rate in the 1960s. In 1952 the price of strict middling 1 1/16-inch cotton at Liverpool was about 38 cents a pound. By 1960 it was down to 30 1/2 cents a pound and declined further to about 28 cents a pound for the 1970-71 crop year.

World cotton trade has grown steadily over the years in both volume and value, despite the decline in world cotton prices. The volume of total cotton exports (lint and textiles) went from 3.4 million tons in 1952 to 5.4 million tons in 1967 (Table 7.5). Textile exports had a faster rate of growth, from 0.8 to 1.6 million tons, than lint cotton, which went from 2.6 to 3.8 million tons. In 1967 world exports of lint cotton and cotton textiles were valued at $6.1 billion.

TABLE 7.5

World Cotton Trade and Textile-Lint Mix, 1952-67

Calender	Exports			Share of Total		
Year	Textiles	Lint[a]	Total	Textiles	Lint	Total
Volume	(thousand metric tons)			(percent)		
1952	798	2617	3415	23	77	100
1953	795	2681	3476	23	77	100
1954	883	2949	3832	23	77	100
1955	843	2838	3681	23	77	100
1956	893	3084	3977	22	78	100
1957	960	3395	4355	22	78	100
1958	871	2930	3801	23	77	100
1959	1045	3325	4370	24	76	100
1960	1219	3943	5162	24	76	100
1961	1133	3729	4862	23	77	100
1962	1133	3508	4641	24	76	100
1963	1168	3705	4873	24	76	100
1964	1480[b]	3890	5370	24	76	100
1965	1462[b]	3778	5240	28	72	100
1966	1579[b]	3917	5496	29	71	100
1967	1556[b]	3813	5369	29	71	100
Value	(million dollars)			(percent)		
1952-58	not available (n.a.)			not available (n.a.)		
1959	n.a.	1891	n.a.	n.a.	n.a.	n.a.
1960	3100	2569	5669	55	45	100
1961	3020	2362	5382	56	44	100
1962	3030	2054	5084	60	40	100
1963	3190	2257	5447	59	41	100
1964	3470	2372	5842	59	41	100
1965	3600	2295	5895	61	39	100
1966	3790	2307	6097	62	38	100
1967	3815	2238	6053	63	37	100

[a]Volume data 1952-65 are USDA/FAS. Other figures and all lint value data are FAO.
[b]These data are more inclusive of clothing than previously.

Source: Magleby and Missiaen, op. cit.

The developing countries are very interested in exporting cotton textiles rather than lint cotton because of the increased possibilities for earning foreign exchange and expanding domestic income and employment. The value of cotton textiles over the value of lint cotton ranges from over 1.5 times for yarn to 3 to 6 times for clothing exports.

The long-term outlook for world cotton trade is reasonably favorable. While prices are expected to decline slightly in the 1970s, world cotton production, consumption, and trade are expected to grow at a moderately rapid rate. Rojko and Mackie[11] conclude:

> The developing countries would increase their share of world cotton lint and textile exports by 1980, and the developed countries would increase their net imports. . . . The greatest changes for the developing countries are projected for cotton textile trade . . . net cotton textile imports of the developed [areas] should increase from a little over 100,000 tons in 1965-67 to almost 600,000 tons in 1980.

Sugar

The volume of world trade in sugar has grown steadily from a level of 10.5 million tons in 1951 to 18.5 million tons in 1965. On the other hand, world prices of sugar varied considerably during this same period (Table 7.6), giving rise to significant variation in the value of world trade.

In 1965 some 14 countries[12] depended upon sugar for over 20 percent of their total export earnings. In eight of these countries,[13] sugar accounted for over 50 percent of total export earnings. Sugar exports were valued at $2.6 billion or about 7.0 percent of world agricultural trade in 1965.

Regionally, Latin America, Australia, New Zealand, South Africa, Eastern Europe, and other East Asian countries accounted for 73 percent of world sugar exports in 1964. Latin America alone accounted for 45 percent of world sugar exports. The major importers are the United States, Japan, Western Europe, and the USSR. They accounted for 65 percent of world imports of sugar. The United States is the second largest importer in this group, accounting for 20 percent of world sugar imports.

Most of the major developed importers have followed high domestic price policies aimed at ensuring a high degree of self-sufficiency in sugar. While the world demand for sugar can be expected to grow at a modest rate, the future trade prospects depend heavily on future

TABLE 7.6

World Trade in Sugar, 1951-65

Year	Volume (thousand metric tons)	Price per Metric ton (U.S. dollars)
1951	10,542	116.1
1952	10,960	110.0
1953	12,728	97.4
1954	13,042	99.0
1955	14,177	95.1
1956	13,549	95.4
1957	14,791	116.4
1958	14,902	99.8
1959	14,174	94.5
1960	17,039	89.5
1961	19,902	92.7
1962	18,763	93.9
1963	17,255	135.7
1964	16,771	135.0
1965	18,476	102.4

Source: Arthur B. Mackie and J. Lawrence Blum, "World Trade in Selected Agricultural Commodities, 1951-65; Vol. IV—Sugar, Fruits, and Vegetables," FAER No. 44, ERS, USDA, June 1968.

sugar policies in the developed countries. We shall return to a more detailed discussion of this matter for the United States in a later section of the paper.

Fruits and Vegetables

As discussed earlier, we shall concentrate on those fruits and vegetables that are produced in both developed and developing countries. This eliminates from our discussion such important tropical fruits as bananas and pineapple.

In 1965 there were 20 developing countries in which exports of fruits and vegetables accounted for 20 percent or more of their total exports.[14] World trade in fruits and nuts increased from 6.1 million tons in 1951 to 15.2 million tons in 1965. During the same period, trade in vegetables went from 3.1 to 10.9 million metric tons. These commodities have experienced rapid growth in world trade, and future trade prospects are also bright.

The major importers of fruits and vegetables are the United States, Western Europe, and Eastern Europe. These three areas accounted for 74 percent of world imports of fresh fruits and 71 percent of vegetable imports in 1964. Western Europe is by far the biggest importing region, accounting for 57 percent of total world imports of fruits and vegetables.

Meats

World trade in meats has increased rapidly. We shall focus on trade in beef, since this is the meat that is generally of most interest to the developing countries. Between 1954 and 1969, total world exports of beef went up from 530,000 to 1,857,902 tons, or by 350 percent (Table 7.7).

Among the developing regions of the world, beef exports expanded most rapidly in Central and South America. Exports from Central America increased 18-fold, from Argentina nearly 4-fold, from Uruguay by over 2-fold, and from other South American countries by 120-fold. Africa is the only other developing region of the world where beef exports increased significantly, from 20,000 tons in 1954 to 45,596 tons in 1969. In value terms, beef exports in 1969 from Central America, South America, and Africa were $97, $333, and $30 million, respectively.

Europe and the United States are the major beef importers. Imports into Europe increased from 380,000 tons in 1954 to 1,203,952 tons in 1969, or by nearly 320 percent. United States imports during the same period went from 7800 to 470,160 tons, an increase of 600 percent. Imports in Asia also increased rapidly, from 11,000 to 74,342 tons, or by 675 percent.

The United States has been and is likely to continue to be a major importer of beef. In 1969 the value of beef imports into the United States was $483 million. Policies affecting U.S. meat imports have an important bearing on the export-earning potential of a large number of developing countries exporting beef.

The above data are for fresh, chilled, and frozen beef only. They do not include U.S. imports of beef in processed form. Unfortunately, the available data do not permit us to look at the world trade picture for processed beef separately from all processed meats. However, we should keep in mind that processed beef is also a significant import item for the United States.

TABLE 7.7

World Trade in Beef for Selected Regions and Years

Region	Exports 1954	Exports 1969	Imports 1954	Imports 1969
		(metric tons)		
Europe	167,000	695,823	380,000	1,203,952
Canada	8,400	21,522	1,500	49,252
United States	5,900	7,609	7,800	470,160
Central America	5,700	100,925	7,700	18,773
South America	—	—	15,000	26,362[a]
Argentina	105,200	404,570		
Uruguay	45,100	106,461		
Other South American countries	700	84,175		
Asia	—	1,844	11,000	74,342
Africa	20,000	45,596	18,000	43,439
Oceania	175,000	389,377	2,000	3,544[a]
World	530,000	1,857,902	500,000	1,887,120

[a]Numbers are for 1968.

Source: FAO Yearbook of Trade, various issues.

Tobacco

World trade in tobacco has grown steadily during the past two decades. World exports increased from 620,000 metric tons in 1951 to 1 million metric tons in 1969, or by 5.5 percent a year. Between 1959 and 1969 quantities exported increased by 3.3 percent a year, while the value of exports increased by 3.7 percent, indicating a modest rise in world tobacco prices. The United States accounted for 26 percent of world exports in 1969.

Europe is by far the largest importing region, accounting for 68 percent of world imports in 1969. The United States accounted for 10 percent.

The principal tobacco-exporting developing countries are Cuba, Dominican Republic, India, Indonesia, Philippines, Turkey, Rhodesia, Malawi, and Zambia. (The People's Republic of China also exports significant quantities.) Based on historical trends, one would expect world trade in tobacco to continue to grow at a moderate rate.

IMPACT OF U.S. AGRICULTURAL POLICIES
ON THE DEVELOPING COUNTRIES

The developing countries probably have at least one overriding common interest—to increase foreign-exchange earnings from trade, especially from primary products. But while the bulk of trade in these products is from the developing to the developed countries, we have to be mindful of the fact that all poor countries are not exporters of the commodities being considered; some are net importers. Thus it is difficult for a country like the United States to be all things to all developing countries with respect to her present or future agricultural trade policies. Changes in trade policies that increase U.S. imports and raise world prices would be beneficial to the developing exporters but work against the interest of the developing importers.

In addition, many developing countries are striving to reduce their dependence on agricultural imports. In the process they have supported domestic prices of some commodities at well above world levels. Thus the developing countries are contributing to distortions in world prices of certain agricultural commodities.

In a world in which trade is distorted by policies of both the developed and developing countries, it is difficult to define quantitative norms of good economic behavior. Of course, we can invoke the principles of comparative advantage and free trade. However, it is difficult to estimate what a world operating on these principles would look like and unrealistic to think that such a world would come to pass very quickly. What we can do is to estimate, however roughly, the impact of changes in U.S. agricultural trade policies on the volume and value of world trade and on the value of agricultural exports from the developing countries.

To examine the impact of U.S. agricultural policies on the agricultural trade of developing countries, we have to do three things:

1. Assess the comparative advantage of the United States in the production of each of the commodities or commodity groups with which we are concerned.
2. Determine the extent to which U.S. agricultural trade policies restrict exports from developing countries.
3. Evaluate the benefit to developing countries from less restrictive policies for the United States. We shall concern ourselves with policies that encourage U.S. exports as well as those that restrict imports.

We can get a fairly good, though not precise, idea of the extent to which agricultural production in the United States is insulated from world markets by looking at both the nominal and effective degrees of protection for different commodities. The nominal rate of protection tells us the extent to which tariff and nontariff barriers, payments to producers, and so on, keep domestic product prices above world prices. The effective rate of protection given to a particular product depends not only on the levels of tariff and nontariff protection of the final product, but also on the value added in production and the tariff and nontariff protection given to production inputs.

In a recent study, Wipf[15] has calculated the levels of nominal and effective rates of protection for a number of agricultural products at the farm level in 1968. These data are presented in Table 7.8. Four commodities stand out as having very high rates of effective protection—sugar (662.2 percent), cotton (100.8 percent), food grains (143.5 percent), and dairy products (48.2 percent). Of these, we are interested in all but dairy products. The other products that we are concerned with in this paper—oilseeds, fruits, vegetables, meats, and tobacco—do not appear to have excessively high rates of protection. If we accept these measures as a rough guide to the competitive position of the United States in world agricultural trade, we can focus our

TABLE 7.8

Nominal and Effective Rates of Protection in the U.S.
Farm Production Sector, 1968

Farm-Level Sector	Total Nominal	Total Effective	Effective Tariff	Effective Nontariff
		(percent)		
Meat animals	7.5	13.8	13.2	0.6
Poultry and eggs	0.8	-19.6	-16.6	-3.0
Farm dairy products	16.8	48.2	-3.4	51.6
Other livestock products	2.5	3.3	3.5	-0.2
Food grains	8.4	143.5	2.7	146.2
Feed crops	0.4	8.1	0.0	8.1
Cotton	0.3	100.8	-1.3	102.1
Tobacco	17.0	28.2	24.5	3.7
Oil-bearing crops	11.3	16.4	-0.8	17.2
Vegetables	12.4	17.9	20.8	-2.9
Fruits	8.4	9.1	11.8	-2.7
Tree nuts	20.1	25.5	35.2	-9.7
Sugar and syrup crops	195.8	662.2	72.2	590.0

Source: Larry J. Wipf, "Tariffs, Nontariff Distortions, and Effective Protection in U.S. Agriculture," American Journal of Agricultural Economics 53, no. 3 (August 1971).

analysis on wheat, rice, sugar, and cotton. While it would appear that the United States has a comparative advantage in oilseeds (primarily soybeans), we could add peanuts to our list because they are a highly protected commodity. In 1968 the nominal and effective rates of protection on peanuts were 69.3 and 204.0 percent, respectively.[16]

Wheat

With the exception of Argentina, and possibly Mexico, the developing countries have not historically had a significant interest in wheat exports. They have, in the main, been importers (Table 7.9). In the 1960s most of U.S. wheat exports were to the developing countries under government programs, mainly PL 480. About 70 percent of wheat exports were under government programs in the first half of the decade, and between 50 and 60 percent during the last half. Thus the developing countries, being mainly importers of wheat, benefited greatly from the soft terms under which they received wheat from the United States.

In recent years a large number of developing countries have increased their wheat production through the use of the new high-yielding varieties, related production inputs, and price support programs. These developments have greatly reduced the need for imports in several of these countries and even created some small exportable surpluses. In the main, however, it does not look as if the traditional developing country importers of wheat will contribute significantly to world wheat exports. Growing domestic demands resulting from increases in population and per capita incomes will keep pace with increased production. Those few countries that have produced or will produce exportable surpluses will find difficulty selling in world markets because

1. they lack adequate marketing and grading facilities;
2. their domestic prices are well above world levels, requiring costly export subsidies.[17]

Nonetheless, increased self-sufficiency in wheat for a number of the historically large wheat-importing countries in the developing world will sharply reduce the size of world wheat trade and U.S. exports.

Needed adjustments in wheat production and consumption in the United States as well as in the other developed exporting countries and Western Europe would call for, among other things, pricing of wheat basically as a feed grain. If this were done, the effective supply of feed grains would be expanded, and world prices would probably move downward. It is difficult to judge the extent of this downward pressure because we do not know how much wheat production would decline with the decline in prices. In any event, bringing about more

TABLE 7.9

World Trade in Wheat and Wheat Flours, 1967

Region	Imports (thousand metric tons)	Exports
Europe	18,077	12,112
USSR	418	6,802
Canada	—	7,333
United States	38	13,774
Mexico	1	253
Other Central America and Caribbean	1,990	—
Argentina	—	2,462
Uruguay	—	68
Other S. America	4,566	—
N. Asia	1,709	62
S. Asia	3,734	2
SE Asia[a]	2,403	111
E. Asia[b]	10,308	82
Africa	3,914	71
Oceania	931	5,343
Total	48,039	48,697

[a]Includes Republic of North Vietnam.

[b]Includes People's Republic of China, Mongolia, and Republic of North Vietnam.

Source: Trade Yearbook, 1970 (Rome: FAO, 1971).

competitive pricing of wheat in many of the developed countries would affect the world market prices for feed grains and the market prospects for the developing countries that are feed grain exporters. This would tend to work against the interests of those developing countries that are now or have the potential of becoming major exporters of coarse grains such as Mexico, Argentina, Brazil, Kenya, Thailand, and Indonesia.

Sugar

Of all the agricultural commodities that the United States imports from the developing countries, sugar undoubtedly is the most protected.

Detailed descriptions of the U.S. sugar program can be found in Johnson[18] and Horton[19] and will not be repeated here. We are interested in looking at the cost of sugar programs and what alternative programs would mean to both the United States and to the developing countries.

Over the last 40 years, the United States has relied increasingly on domestic sugar production. During the period 1925-29, about 37 percent of U.S. sugar consumption was produced on the mainland, Puerto Rico, Hawaii, and the Virgin Islands. By the late 1960s, about 60 percent of U.S. consumption came from these same sources. Johnson points out that "the net effect of the Sugar Acts has been to reserve all—or more than all—of the growth in domestic use for domestic producers."[20]

The United States is a very high-cost producer of sugar. Various estimates have been made of U.S. production, consumption, and imports under alternative price and program assumptions. They all point to substantial gains to both the United States and the developing countries from a more liberal U.S. sugar policy.

Johnson has estimated that in 1970 the U.S. sugar program cost U.S. consumers and taxpayers $1 billion, compared with total cash receipts from sugarcane and sugar beets in domestic areas of $700 million.[21] Thus U.S. consumers and taxpayers could afford to completely subsidize domestic producers for not producing at all and still be left with a substantial net benefit.

It has been estimated that if the United States were to follow a completely free trade policy for sugar, the domestically produced share of consumption would decline from 60 percent to 20 percent. Free trade in sugar would increase the gross earnings of developing countries by about $400 million,[22] not an insignificant sum.

Harry Johnson,[23] refining some earlier work by Snape,[24] has estimated that in 1959 if the United States allowed free imports of sugar but made a deficiency payment to domestic producers, the increased consumption and imports of sugar would be worth about $250 million to the developing country exporters. The assumptions about deficiency payments are less extreme from the point of view of domestic producers than a totally free trade situation. Yet they illustrate once again the large gains to U.S. consumers and sugar exporters from more liberal import policies without imposing undue burdens on domestic producers.

Cotton

Cotton is also one of the highly protected agricultural commodities in the United States. It is estimated that in 1968 the effective rate of protection for U.S. cotton production was just over 100 percent.

158

United States production and exports have declined in recent years (Table 7.10) to the point where production has been around 10 million bales a year and exports about 3 million bales. This has worked to the benefit of developing country exporters.

Under a situation of no-government programs for cotton in the United States and a domestic farm price of 19.5 cents a pound, production is estimated at 9.4 million bales, lower than the level prevailing in recent years.[25] Under such conditions, exports would be at a modest level, probably not over 1.5 million bales. Such further reduction in U.S. cotton exports would add to the foreign-exchange earnings of a large number of developing countries with exportable supplies of cotton.

TABLE 7.10

Production and Export of Cotton
(United States, 1955-70)

Year	Production[a]	Exports[a]
	(million bales)	
1955	14.7	2.3
1956	13.3	7.9
1957	11.0	6.0
1958	11.5	2.9
1959	14.6	7.4
1960	14.3	6.9
1961	14.3	5.1
1962	14.9	3.4
1963	15.3	5.8
1964	15.2	4.2
1965	15.0	3.0
1966	9.6	4.8
1967	7.5	4.4
1968	11.0	2.4
1969	10.0	2.9
1970	10.3	3.7

[a]These are 500-pound bales.

Source: Agricultural Statistics, 1971, (Washington, D.C.: USDA, 1971).

Rice

The United States has been the largest exporter of rice in recent years, accounting for nearly 30 percent of world exports in 1968 and 1969. Italy, Australia, and, very recently, Japan are the only other developed countries that export any significant amount of rice, and their exports are small. Both the nominal and effective rates of protection for U.S. rice producers have been very high—36.4 and 120.4 percent, respectively, in 1963.[26]

The level of rice production in the United States is controlled through acreage restrictions, and domestic prices are well above world market levels. Thus sizable export subsidies are required for commercial exports. Even more important, exports under the PL 480 program have accounted for between 38 to 57 percent of total rice exports between 1961 and 1970. The United States is the largest competitor that the developing rice-exporting countries face. And they are not competing with U.S. rice producers, but with the U.S. Treasury.

On a milled basis, farm prices of long-grain rice have averaged about $220 per metric ton. The export subsidy has been running at $44 per metric ton, or about 20 percent of the domestic price.[27] Continued protection of domestic rice production and aggressive use of export subsidies provide stiff competition for the developing exporters. Because of her dominant position in world rice trade, the United States can exert considerable influence on the level of world prices and export earnings of rice.

Estimates of rice production in the United States under free-market conditions are difficult to come by.[28] It is the author's best guess that, given the outlook for relatively low world prices in the 1970s, production in the United States would decline somewhat under a free-market situation, U.S. exports would decline, and the position of developing rice-exporting countries would improve.

Effective Rates of Protection on
Processed Agricultural Products

Access to the markets for raw agricultural products in developed countries, such as the United States, by the developing countries is only one part of a larger set of agricultural trade issues. Another is the ability of the developing countries to penetrate the market in the United States for semimanufactured and manufactured products based on agricultural raw materials. The developing nations would like to do as much processing as possible of the raw product. This generates much needed employment and incomes domestically and increases the value of and, therefore, the foreign-exchange earnings from agricultural exports.

It is typical for developed countries to have higher degrees of protection for manufactured products than for raw materials, and the United States is no exception. Tariff structure of this type biases imports in favor of raw materials and provides added protection to domestic manufacture in the developed countries. In other words, the effective rate of protection for manufactured products can be much larger (or smaller) than the value of the nominal tariff. This is illustrated in Table 7.11 for a few commodities; the effective tariff rate is about 2 to 3 times the nominal tariff for some of the commodities listed and 10 times higher for one product, coconut oil. The effective rate of protection is further enhanced when nontariff trade barriers such as quotas are employed in addition to tariffs.

To further illustrate the point, Belassa[29] calculated the effective rates of protection for 22 primary products for the United States, the United Kingdom (UK), the EC, Sweden, and Japan. The commodities covered in the study are meat, fish, fruits, vegetables, cocoa, leather, groundnuts, copra, palm kernel, palm oil, rubber, wood, pulpwood, wool, cotton, jute, sisal and henequen, iron, copper, aluminum, lead, and zinc. Four stages of processing were considered. The results for the United States are presented in Table 7.12.

Clearly the degree of protection, both nominal and effective, increases rapidly as we move to higher stages of processing. Furthermore, the distribution of imports by stage of processing follows from the nature of protection. Of the total value of the 22 commodities imported by the United States from the developing countries in all stages of processing, over one-half—56.6 percent—was imported in the primary stage. An additional 33.2 percent was imported with the first stage of processing. Only 10.2 percent was imported in the third and fourth stages of processing. Clearly, the United States (and other industrialized countries as well) is discriminating against the import of processed products from the developing countries.

All this is not insignificant for the developing countries that are hungry for foreign exchange and are not getting as much as they need or want in the form of economic aid. In 1964 the value of U.S. imports from developing countries of the 22 commodities that Belassa studied amounted to $2.3 billion. The amount is even larger today. Removal of discrimination against imports of processed primary products by developed countries should be given serious attention in future trade negotiations.

TABLE 7.11

Nominal and Effective Tariff Rates for Selected Commodities
(United States, 1962)

Item	Nominal Tariff	Effective Tariff
	(percent)	
Thread and yarn	11.7	31.8
Textile fabrics	24.1	50.6
Hosiery	25.6	48.7
Clothing	25.1	35.9
Other textile articles	19.0	22.7
Shoes	16.6	25.3
Coconut oil (refined)	5.7	57.5
Jute fabrics	3.1	5.3
Cigarettes	47.2	89.0
Hard fiber mfg.	15.1	38.0

Source: Bela Belassa, "Tariff Protection in Industrial Countries: An Evaluation," The Journal of Political Economy LXXIII, no. 6 (December 1965); and Harry G. Johnson, Economic Policies Toward Less Developed Countries (Washington, D.C.: The Brookings Institution, 1967).

TABLE 7.12

Weighted Averages of Nominal and Effective Tariffs and Imports
from Developing Countries
(United States, 1964)

Stage of Processing	Nominal Tariff	Effective Tariff	Value of Imports ($ million)	Distribution of Imports (percent)
	(percent)			
I	4.0		1311.1	56.6
II	6.0	19.5	768.9	33.2
III	16.6	30.7	114.9	4.9
IV	24.0	42.7	123.7[a]	5.3[a]
Total			2318.6	100.0

[a]A fifth stage of processing was listed for value of imports. The amount of trade in this category was small ($7.1 million), and it was added to Stage IV.

Source: Bela Belassa, "Tariff Protection in Industrial Nations and Its Effects on the Export of Processed Goods from Developing Countries," Canadian Journal of Economics vol. 1, no. 3 (August 1968).

THE DEVELOPING COUNTRIES AS A MARKET
FOR U.S. EXPORTS

The interest of the United States in promoting economic development in the developing countries should go beyond moral and political considerations; economic benefits should not be overlooked. Certainly, changes in U.S. trade policies that would stimulate imports of agricultural raw materials and processed agricultural commodities from the developing countries would contribute to their earning of foreign exchange and their ability to finance imports and future development.

There has been a positive association between the rate of economic growth in developing countries and growth of U.S. agricultural exports to them, to say nothing of nonagricultural products. Mackie[30] has shown that between 1955/56 and 1961/62 there was a positive relationship between the rate of growth of national income in the developing countries and the rate of growth of commercial imports of agricultural products from the United States. For all developing countries, national income grew at 4.0 percent a year, total agricultural imports from the United States by 11.0 percent, and commercial agricultural imports by 8.4 percent. One group of developing countries with a rapid rate of growth of national income of 8.1 percent per year[31] had a rate of growth for total agricultural imports of 7.6 percent a year, while commercial imports grew at 14.0 percent a year. On the other hand, the remaining low-income countries had annual average growth rates of 2.4 percent for national income, 13.0 percent for total agricultural imports from the United States, and 2.8 percent for commercial agricultural imports. Furthermore, an analysis of agricultural imports from the United States by a group of 24 countries in the 1959-61 period showed that the proportion of commercial imports was positively associated with the levels of per capita incomes in these nations.

During the 1960s, U.S. agricultural exports to the developing countries continued to grow at a rapid rate. In general, exports under government programs (mainly PL 480) declined, while commercial exports rose rapidly (Table 7.13). From 1962 to 1971, agricultural exports under government programs declined from $1512.8 million to $1057.1 million. On the other hand, total commercial exports increased from $3518.6 million to $6637.8 million, or by 7.3 percent a year. Asia was the only region of the world to which exports under government programs increased. In general, commercial exports to the developing countries increased at a faster rate than commercial exports to the developed countries: by 7.1 percent a year for exports to Latin America and the Caribbean, by 13.6 percent a year to Asia (excluding Japan), and by 12.1 percent a year to Africa. In fact, the developing regions of the world accounted for 43 percent of the growth in U.S. commercial agricultural exports during the 1962-71 period.

163

TABLE 7.13

U.S. Agricultural Exports, by Region and
Terms of Sale, 1962 and 1971
(in millions of dollars)

Region	Government Programs		Commercial	
	1962	1971	1962	1971
Latin America and Caribbean	148.9	110.3	288.8	535.3
Asia (excluding Japan)	663.1	761.9	251.0	792.1
Africa	310.9	115.7	63.6	177.9
Total	1512.8	1057.1	3518.6	6637.8

Source: "Foreign Agricultural Trade of the United States,"
ERS, USDA (October 1972).

The United States should not overlook the rapid growth of her
agricultural exports to the developing countries. There is evidence
of a strong association between rapid economic development in the
poor countries and rapid growth in their agricultural imports, particularly commercial imports. To the extent that the United States pursues
trade and aid policies that contribute to economic growth in the developing countries, it is helping to build markets for U.S. farm and nonfarm
products.

ALTERNATIVE AGRICULTURAL POLICIES FOR
THE UNITED STATES

We confine our discussion of changes in agricultural policies
to wheat, rice, cotton, and sugar—commodities that are of great importance in the export trade of developing countries and that are highly
protected in the United States. More general discussions of U.S. agricultural policies and their impact on world agricultural trade can be
found elsewhere.[32]

Guiding Principles

Before turning to a discussion of specific commodities, we
should spell out certain guiding principles that will be employed in

the discussion of agricultural trade policies. First, the welfare of consumers should be a major concern of trade policy. The improvement of consumer welfare is one of the major underpinnings of the arguments in favor of freer trade. We can further argue that trade policies that place a relatively heavy burden on the poor compared with the rich represent one of the worst forms of protectionism. The "ability-to-pay" argument, which is applied (sometimes) to domestic policy considerations, should also be applied to foreign trade and aid policies. As one author has commented about the highly protectionistic U.S. sugar program, "To the extent that sugar quotas can be justified as a form of foreign aid they appear to be a case of 'poor people in rich countries giving money to rich people in poor countries.'"[33] Another writer[34] has pointed out that it is one of the ironies of protectionism that the burden of such policies falls on the very poor and the very rich.

> The man who eats Kobe beef and the one who eats at McDonald's have something in common, just as the one with the $25 English cotton shirt and the one with the $1.95 discount house shirt from Hong Kong. Both are consumers for whom the mass market is not large enough to activate the U.S. production process, and in the absence of imports they would be forced into less satisfactory consumption patterns.

The rich can afford it, but the poor cannot.

Second, trade policies should promote efficient use of resources from the point of view of national output and productivity. This, after all, is what the free trade argument is all about. In moving from a protectionistic set of policies to ones that are more free trade oriented, one has to keep in mind the kind of resource adjustments that could be expected to occur and their impact on total output and productivity. In particular, special attention has to be given to moving resources out of inefficient production processes into efficient ones.

Third, the benefits to producers from past agricultural programs have been capitalized into the value of land or allotments. Policies that would reduce prices received (without compensating income payments) would, in the short run, lead to lower incomes based on current land values and, in the longer run, to lower land prices. This would represent a depreciation of an important capital asset. If there is a real saving to consumers and taxpayers from more liberal agricultural trade policy, considerations of fairness and political feasibility might dictate compensation to producers for part or all of the capital losses associated with a liberalization of trade policies and resulting adjustments of resource use in agriculture. But unlike present income transfers which perpetuate inefficient resource use, this would be a compensation that would bring about desired resource adjustments.

Fourth, there are those who would argue, with considerable justification, that there are surplus resources employed in U.S. agriculture, and shifting resources out of the production of one set of agricultural commodities into the production of others is merely shuffling around redundant resources. In the short run, this is probably true. But in the long run, something of value would be accomplished— resources would be moved into the production of those agricultural commodities in which the United States has a comparative advantage and for which world markets are growing at reasonably rapid rates, for example, feed grains and soybeans. And, with competitive prices, the United States would assure herself of a "fair" share of this growth. There would undoubtedly still be a need for controlling output of U.S. agriculture after all these resource adjustments took place. But with more efficient resource use, the cost to society of withholding a given amount of resources from production in agriculture and meeting a given income objective for farmers would be less than it presently is.

Fifth, changes in U.S. trade policies that are clearly to the benefit of the United States should not be made conditional upon actions by other countries. We have been conditioned to think in terms of balanced, multilateral trade negotiations, primarily concerning tariffs. But if it is clearly in the national interest to change some agricultural policies, one cannot justify asking other countries to do something of "equal value" in return. Furthermore, tenacious adherence to a reciprocity approach provides opponents to trade liberalization with a justification for continuing protectionistic policies.

Sixth, changes in agricultural policies are always difficult; they are especially so when the removal of a significant degree of protection is involved. It is doubtful that much can be achieved by relying solely on voluntary surrender of such protection. But decisions should be made, and they should take into account the interests of consumers, taxpayers, and national economic growth as well as those of the agricultural producers concerned. This means that responsibility for agricultural policy changes that lead to trade liberalization should rest at sufficiently high levels of government to permit the views of all the aforementioned groups to be fairly represented.

Policy Alternatives

With these principles in mind, let us now look at some policy alternatives for the four commodities in which we are principally interested—wheat, rice, cotton, and sugar.

From the point of view of the developing countries, movements toward less protectionistic wheat policies in the United States present some vexing problems. We shall highlight these problems by assuming that the United States moves toward a set of policies for wheat that lower domestic and world market prices and make wheat competitive with feed grains for feed uses, as some have suggested.

First, with the exception of Argentina and possibly Mexico, the developing countries do not have a major export interest in wheat. Thus actions on the part of the United States that would lower world wheat prices would adversely affect only a few developing countries.

Second, since most developing countries are net wheat importers, lower world prices would work to their benefit by reducing their import bill. However, the extent of this benefit must be tempered by the fact that many developing countries have availed themselves of the new wheat technology, have succeeded in expanding their production, and have substantially reduced their reliance on wheat imports. These developments are likely to continue in the future, and this is one of the reasons why export prospects for wheat are not bright. Thus one would have to think of the benefits of lower world wheat prices to the developing countries in terms of a lower import level than prevailed in, say, the 1960s.

Third, to the extent that lower wheat prices lowered the price of feed grains in world markets, this would work against the interests of developing countries that have a stake in feed grain exports. To them, the United States would become an even more awesome competitor in the world feed grain market.

Thus it is difficult, if not impossible, to come to any conclusion about the net benefit to the developing countries of less protectionistic U.S. wheat policies that lowered world wheat and feed grain prices. How does one weigh the benefits of lower world grain prices to the developing net grain importers against the losses to developing grain exporters?

But what about the benefit to domestic consumers and taxpayers from lower wheat prices? Certainly consumers would gain. But the gain to taxpayers is not obvious, or at least not overwhelmingly so. There is excess production capacity in both wheat and feed grains at current prices. And this would continue to exist, at modestly lower prices. There would continue to be a need to control grain output. In this situation, expanded production of wheat would call for less production of feed grains. There is no obviously large saving in government program costs from pricing wheat competitively with feed grains at current or even modestly lower support rates for feed grains.

Some have argued that the current level of support for wheat is above that which is required to withhold current acreage from production; that is, there is a net income transfer to producers.

This net income transfer might be eliminated, but it would not affect output levels, only incomes of wheat producers. But this is a domestic policy consideration that has little bearing on trade.

We are left then with one policy consideration for wheat which may have some significance for agricultural trade. The one agricultural commodity in which the United States does not have surplus production capacity is beef. To the extent that land currently could be shifted into forage and beef production, U.S. consumers would be better off, and in the long run, so would taxpayers.

The value of land presently in wheat production reflects past high prices of wheat. A combination of somewhat lower wheat prices (including payments), lower acreage allotments for wheat, and payments to producers for all or part of the cost of shifting land out of wheat into forage production should be considered. The amount of resource adjustment that can be achieved and its cost are matters for careful study.

The situation for rice is more clear-cut than for wheat. Its production in the United States is highly protected; the U.S. is a major exporter competing directly with developing rice exporters; and reduced production in the United States would greatly expand the export market for low-cost producers in the developing countries.

Adjustment of acreage out of rice production would, to a large extent, free resources for the production of commodities for which there are no surpluses, and additional output would be welcomed at home and for export, for example, beef and soybeans.

The United States should move toward a policy for rice under which production would take place at competitive world market prices. During a transition period, rice producers should be compensated for losses in land values as a result of shifting land out of rice production and the lower rice prices. In the long run, there would be some benefit to domestic consumers, appreciable benefit to taxpayers, and substantial benefit to the rice-exporting developing countries.

The case of cotton appears to be quite different from that of either wheat or rice. The United States has ceased to be a major factor in the world cotton market. At the same time, the United States has become a major importer of cotton textiles. As we have seen, world market prices for cotton in the United States would reduce production in, and exports from, the United States. This would be a benefit to the developing countries. Reliance on world market prices to guide production of cotton is recommended with resource adjustment payments similar to those for wheat and rice. But the United States should go beyond questions of lint cotton production and trade. The United States has high rates of effective protection against imports of cotton manufactures through the use of tariffs and quotas. It is in the area of manufactures rather than lint cotton that the developing countries have the greatest export interest in the U.S. market.

Clearly, the efforts of U.S. textile manufacturers to limit cotton textile imports indicate that the U.S. industry is not fully competitive with foreign suppliers. The present voluntary import quotas on textiles attest to this fact. Every effort should be made to liberalize textile imports into the United States. Mindful of the dislocation that such liberalization would cause to the domestic industry, consideration should be given to financial assistance to relocate textile workers in other industries and for manufacturers to shift investments, where feasible, to other lines of production.

The case of sugar is in a category all by itself when it comes to the degree of protection afforded domestic producers. In addition, there is the procedure by which the United States allocates sugar quotas to foreign suppliers. The United States should dispense with all quota allocations, making the U.S. market for sugar available to all suppliers on an equal basis.[35] Furthermore, the United States should move to a free-market price for both domestic consumers and producers. As we have seen, the savings would be great enough to buy U.S. producers out and still have a net benefit to the economy to show for the effort. If it were not politically possible to move to a free market, even in the long run, it would still be beneficial to U.S. consumers and taxpayers and to developing country exporters for the United States to move to a deficiency payment system that would support a limited amount of domestic production, but allow domestic market prices to decline to world levels.

In the short run, resources freed from the production of wheat, rice, cotton, and sugar as a result of less protectionistic policies would go into the production of other commodities and put downward pressure on their prices. The extent to which this occurs is a matter for detailed analysis. In the longer run, however, we would be producing agricultural commodities that have high and more rapidly growing domestic demands—feed grains, soybeans, beef, and so on. This would aid in adjusting resources and help the United States meet domestic needs as well as stimulate exports.

One final comment. The United States has had quotas on meat imports for several years. They have recently been suspended because of the high domestic meat prices. While it can be argued that these quotas have not been overly restrictive, they nonetheless should be suspended permanently to the benefit of U.S. consumers and meat exporters.

The previous discussion on proposed policy changes for wheat, rice, cotton, and sugar is primarily, though not entirely, in the context of an idealized economic world—one that does not give full weight to the politics of American agriculture (and agriculture in other developed countries as well). When one considers some of the political realities, there does not appear to be much hope for moving away from high levels of protection afforded domestic producers.

Clearly, the producers of the commodities in question had sufficient political power to get and retain the present set of policies. There is no evidence to indicate that they have lost, in any measurable degree, the political power to protect present programs. In fact, the growing mood of protectionism in many quarters of the United States—both in and out of agriculture—is working to strengthen rather than reduce protective agricultural policies.

The main beneficiaries of more liberal agricultural trade policies in the context of this paper are domestic consumers and taxpayers and the developing countries. Yet none of these groups has the political strength or willingness to focus on specific policy questions of the type we have discussed and bring about policy changes.

All this argues in favor of basically more of the same; economic rationality does not carry a high premium. This is not to say that efforts should not be made to put forth arguments in favor of the benefits to be derived from more efficient resource use and trade policies. But we should recognize that much more than the logical merits of alternative agricultural policies will be needed to bring them into being.

Food and Fiber Assistance Programs—PL 480

Exports of agricultural commodities under PL 480 have been an important factor in U.S. trade and of considerable importance to the developing countries. The developing countries benefited from food and fiber imports that required very little foreign exchange, and the PL 480 program helped to export some of the U.S. surplus agricultural production (capacity).

In the early 1960s, exports of agricultural commodities under PL 480 were valued at about $1.4 billion, rose to $1.6 billion in 1966, and have been around $1.0 billion in recent years. The major commodities involved have been wheat and wheat products, rice, cotton, and dairy products.[36]

The decline in exports under the PL 480 program reflects two basic developments in the developing countries. One is that several developing countries have achieved rapid rates of economic development, have ceased to be eligible for the soft credit terms of the PL 480 program, and have become commercial importers. The other is that a number of formerly large recipients of PL 480 have benefitted from the Green Revolution and now require less in the way of imports. This has been particularly true for a country like India and for a commodity like wheat.

With continued progress in agricultural development in the developing countries, there will be a smaller market for PL 480 commodities in the 1970s than there was in the 1960s. Nevertheless, there will be a need for commodity assistance to the developing countries. Droughts, typhoons, floods, and wars will still occur in the developing nations, causing dislocation in their agricultural production. There will be need for temporary food assistance. Further, not all developing countries are going to become "rich" and self-sufficient in agricultural production in either the near or distant future. There will be countries that could benefit from food and fiber assistance on a long-term basis.

It is recommended that the United States continue to supply such assistance whether under bilateral programs such as PL 480 or through multilateral international programs. But because of the limited and uncertain size of this market, food and fiber assistance should be provided out of a commodity reserve for that purpose; it should not be viewed as a surplus disposal program, as it has been through most of the life of the PL 480 program.

Since the PL 480 market has been so important for wheat, rice, and cotton, and since the commercial as well as PL 480 export prospects for them are not bright, there is all the more reason for policies that will adjust resources out of the production of these commodities.

Commodity Price Stabilization

One cannot discuss the interests of developing countries in exporting agricultural commodities without at least referring to the problem of commodity price instability in world markets. This has been a subject of a great deal of discussion and study. The main thrust has been to establish international commodity agreements that would stabilize prices and foreign-exchange earnings of exporters.[37]

The exports of primary commodities account for a very large proportion of total exports from the developing countries. And most of these exports are to the developed countries. The following is a good summary of the problem.

> With limited but important exceptions, [world commodity markets] have shown two major unfavorable characteristics. First, their absorptive capacity has grown only slowly, so that increased sales have often been possible only at falling prices. Second, these markets have been subject to particularly wide price fluctuations which themselves sometimes contribute to adverse longer-term trends.
>
> Demand for most primary products is growing relatively slowly as a result of both technological developments and changes in consumer spending patterns. Moreover, world trade in primary products, and

particularly in agricultural products, has been held back by the protection given by industrial countries to their own primary producers. As a result, world commodity markets have in some cases taken on the characteristics of unstable residual markets bearing a disproportionate share of attempted adjustments between production and consumption in domestic as well as international markets.

The necessary remedial action has to extend over a broad front. Commodity arrangements have a part to play. To be effective, these will need to be associated with action by the developing countries in the field of development policy and of domestic and external financial policies. Industrial countries could make a major contribution by providing access to their markets and opening their domestic primary production to international competition, as well as by the extension of financial assistance of a high and stable level of aggregate demand.[38]

We have argued in this paper for less protectionistic policies by the United States for some agricultural commodities. This would either provide the developed countries with greater access to the U.S. market or spare them from undue competition from subsidized U.S. exports. While these policy changes would significantly increase the size of the market for a number of exports from the developing countries, they would not necessarily lead to greater stability in world prices and export earnings.

First, there is considerable evidence to indicate that instability in world markets for primary products results primarily from fluctuations in supply rather than demand.[39] This being the case, some form of effective control over output or management of the quantities marketed would be required to stabilize prices. That the developing countries have been unable to do this, except in a few cases, is one of the reasons why there have been so few successful international commodity agreements. This is particularly true when price stabilization efforts have also involved attempts to raise world prices. The near-term prospects for improvements in this situation are not bright.

Second, stabilization of world market prices does not necessarily lead to stabilization or increases in foreign-exchange earnings.[40] Much depends on the price elasticities of demands for the products in question.

Third, while it has been generally assumed that fluctuating world prices of primary products have been detrimental to the development interests of the poor countries, a recent study concludes that "the statistical evidence . . . appears to contradict the consensus that export fluctuations inflict significant damage on the stability and growth of the average underdeveloped country."[41] The same author does not, however, jump to the conclusion that this is no place for price stabilization schemes. Rather, he suggests a careful analysis of each proposal.[42]

While international commodity arrangements for stabilizing world prices (and earnings) do not appear to be all that has been claimed for them, and the history of negotiating successful agreements has not been good, there are reasons why the United States should take a sympathetic posture with respect to the developing countries' interests in such arrangements. There are a number of agricultural commodities that face intense competition from synthetics, that is, cotton and jute. With wide swings in their prices, synthetics are substituted for the primary product during periods of high prices, but the reverse does not occur when primary product prices fall. Thus there tends to be a cumulative loss of markets. Stabilization of primary product prices at modest levels would tend to lessen the inroads made by snythetic prices.

For other products, the developing countries do not have the financial resources to store commodities and follow orderly marketing practices. To the extent that market conditions are such as to stabilize (and possibly increase) earnings from stabilizing marketings, the United States ought to support efforts to achieve this goal.

Finally, in some cases the developing countries have too many resources locked into the production of a few primary commodities. Sensible efforts to diversify their output mix should be encouraged since this may add stability to total export earnings. The present International Coffee Agreement provides for restructuring of the agricultural sector. The United States should encourage and provide financial support to such efforts.

The above recommended changes in domestic U.S. agricultural policies and suggested U.S. posture with respect to food aid and international commodity agreements are in general, though not complete, accord with the recent recommendations of several high-level groups within government.[43] For the commodities concerned, however, the recommendations in this paper go beyond those contained in the recent recommendations to the U.S. government in both the extent of resource adjustment suggested and explicit means for bringing these adjustments about. Furthermore, the interests of U.S. consumers and taxpayers have been treated in a more explicit manner.

Also, trade can be treated as either an alternative or, hopefully, as a complement to foreign aid. Certain U.S. agricultural policies loom large in this arena; the developing countries have much to gain from alternative policies that provide a more liberal trade environment.

173

Thus there is ample opportunity for the United States, through significant changes in her policies for a few agricultural products and for a few manufactured products based primarily on raw agricultural products, to

1. improve the lot of domestic consumers and taxpayers,
2. contribute to more efficient domestic resource use and stimulate total domestic economic growth,
3. contribute to the economic development of numerous poor countries, and
4. indirectly expand the market for U.S. farm and nonfarm products in the poor regions of the world.

MEANING OF AGRICULTURAL TRADE NEGOTIATIONS WITH DEVELOPING COUNTRIES

Our discussion of agricultural trade policies of the United States as they affect trade with the developing countries involves changes in domestic agricultural policies in order to bring about changes in trade policies. Historically, international trade negotiations have primarily dealt with tariff barriers. An institutional mechanism— General Agreements on Tariffs and Trade (GATT)—has provided clearly defined procedures for carrying out these negotiations. But no such institution exists for negotiating nontariff barriers, particularly those that are an integral part of domestic agricultural policies. Schnittker has said:

I am pessimistic to the core about "negotiating major elements of domestic agricultural policies." Here again, we move from a conventional stance associated with tariff negotiations to a situation where such an approach is scarcely applicable. About 10 years ago, it came to be generally understood that domestic agricultural policies may and do interfere with an efficient and fair world trade pattern, just as excessive and uneven tariffs do. So, people said, let's negotiate. Such a stance neglects entirely the sensitive political nature of agricultural policies in most countries, even where farmers represent a very small percentage of the population.[44]

The above quotation refers mainly to the developed countries where, with respect to domestic and foreign agricultural policies, none is without sin—some are just more sinful than others. In such a situation, domestic political considerations aside, there is or should be a mutual interest among countries to move toward less trade-restrictive agricultural policies. One can visualize a "give-and-take" approach for all the countries, although the actual trade results might be hard to predict with any reasonable degree of precision.

But when we look at agricultural trade relations between a major developed country like the United States and the developing nations, we have quite a different situation. In the first place, most developing countries are not that far away from the period of colonial rule that they do not feel strongly about past exploitation of their economies by the developed, ex-colonial powers. Second, the economic development of the developing countries is dependent upon export earnings of primary products, and the "irrational" and trade restrictive policies of most of the developed countries are a matter of serious, immediate concern.[45] Third, because the developing countries are poor and disadvantaged, they would argue that the developed countries have moral, political, and economic obligations to assist them in their development through economic aid and expanded trade opportunities. This the developed countries should do as a matter of course, without extracting concessions from the developing countries. A poor trade policy is just that, and policies should be improved as quickly as possible. The fact that most developing countries also follow restrictive trade policies, they would argue, is a matter of necessity in order to husband scarce foreign exchange. Less restrictive trade policies by the developed countries would expand exports from the developing countries, increase their foreign-exchange earnings, and lead to a liberalization of their import policies.

In the situation described above, it is difficult to imagine the United States changing certain of her agricultural policies in favor of the developing countries on the basis of concessions granted to the United States by the poor nations. This does not mean that in a process of discussions between the United States and the developing countries that certain understandings could not be reached concerning improvements in the domestic economic and trade policies of the developing countries that might result from expanded exports. But these should be understandings, and not commitments. At present the UNCTAD and Food and Agricultural Organization (FAO) provide well-suited institutional frameworks within which such discussions could take place.

It would seem then that the benefits to the United States from less protectionistic agricultural policies are the main justification for changing U.S. agricultural policies. This being the case, unilateral action by the United States is called for, that is, action that is not only independent of steps taken by the developing countries, but may also be independent of any actions or lack of actions by other developed countries. The negotiation of trade policies between the developed countries as a group and the developing countries as another block generates numerous reasons for inaction. This was evident in UNCTAD I and especially in UNCTAD II, where there was a high degree of polarization between rich and poor countries. This approach should be avoided, except for those trade questions where there is a clear advantage to a multilateral approach.

Unilateral action by the United States would have one very important implication for future multilateral negotiations; it would demonstrate that a leading industrial country has both the will and ability to rationalize its agricultural policies, and it would support those legitimate claims of the developing countries with respect to their disadvantages in world trade. This could well strengthen the present case for other developed countries to liberalize their agricultural trade policies, which would be of general benefit to world agricultural trade.

SUMMARY AND CONCLUSIONS

We have looked at world trade in a number of agricultural commodities in which the United States and the developing countries have competitive interests. Of these, four stand out as being highly protected in the United States—wheat, rice, cotton, and sugar. With respect to rice and sugar, the developing countries stand to gain much from less protective U.S. policies. The benefits to be gained by the developing countries from less protective U.S. wheat and cotton policies are less clear.

While a case can be made to alter domestic agricultural policies for these four commodities in ways that will liberalize trade, benefit the developing countries, and benefit domestic consumers and taxpayers, it is not at all clear that the freer trade forces have sufficient political power to overcome the interests of specific producer groups and other forces for protection of U.S. markets from foreign competition. Nonetheless, continued efforts should be made to put forth the case for more efficient resource use in U.S. agriculture and the benefits of less protectionistic agricultural trade policies. The odds for success in these fields are not high, but the battle is worth fighting.

We have also seen that the United States (as well as other developed countries) discriminates more against imports of processed primary products than against imports of raw materials. This tends to deprive developing countries of an important source of export growth.

We also looked at two other issues of concern to the developing countries—food aid and commodity price stabilization. The future levels of food aid are not likely to be as high as they were during the past decade. The developing countries are making progress toward meeting more of their domestic food needs or are gaining the economic capacity to import food and fiber on commercial terms. There will continue to be a need for food and fiber assistance. But such aid should be geared to the needs of the recipient countries and not be used as a method of surplus disposal by the United States.

There has long been a desire on the part of developing countries to stabilize world prices of agricultural products through the use of international commodity agreements. There have been a few successful agreements and many ill-fated ones. The United States should support efforts to develop realistic international commodity agreements that bring stability to world prices or to export earnings of developing countries. Care must be taken to stabilize prices at realistic levels so that some agricultural products are not replaced by synthetic substitutes and surplus production is avoided.

There is ample opportunity for the United States, through significant changes in her policies for a few agricultural products and for a few manufactured products based primarily on raw agricultural products, to

1. improve the lot of domestic consumers and taxpayers,
2. contribute to more efficient domestic resource use and stimulate total domestic economic growth,
3. contribute to the economic development of numerous poor countries, and
4. indirectly expand the market for U.S. farm and nonfarm products in the poor regions of the world.

There does not now exist an international forum adequately suited for the discussion and "negotiation" of national agricultural production and trade policies. This is true among the developed countries as well as between developed and developing countries. Such an institution is badly needed. But until one comes into existence, the United States should make efforts to unilaterally alter those of her agricultural policies that clearly are harmful to the trade and development interests of the developing countries, as well as to domestic consumers, taxpayers, economic growth, and efficiency of resource use.

NOTES

1. Partners in Development: Report of the Commission on International Development (New York: Praeger Publishers, 1969).
2. For an excellent discussion of this topic, see Ian Little, Tibor Scitovsky, and Maurice Scott, Industry and Trade in Some Developing Countries: A Comparative Study (London: Oxford University Press, 1970).

3. Arthur B. Mackie, A. Nicholas Filippello, John E. Hutchison, and James F. Kiefer, "World Agricultural Trade in Selected Agricultural Commodities, 1951-65: Vol. II—Food and Feed Grains," Foreign Agricultural Economics Report (FAER) No. 45, ERS, USDA, June 1968.

4. Delane Welsch and Sopin Tongpan, "Rice in Thailand," staff paper P71-32, Department of Agricultural and Applied Economics, University of Minnesota (December 1971), and unpublished data on Thai rice prices provided by Delane Welsch.

5. Production Yearbook, 1970 (New York: Food and Agricultural Organization of the United Nations, 1971), vol. 24.

6. Willard W. Cochrane, The World Food Problem: A Guardedly Optimistic View (New York: Thomas Y. Crowell Co., 1969).

7. Anthony S. Rojko, Francis S. Urban, and James J. Naive, "World Demand Prospects for Grains in 1980 with Emphasis on Trade by the Developing Countries," FAER No. 75, ERS, USDA, December 1971.

8. This section draws heavily upon data contained in Arthur B. Mackie, Tom E. Full, and Jon E. Falck, "World Trade in Selected Agricultural Commodities, 1951-65: Vol. V—Oilseeds, Oil Nuts, and Animal and Vegetable Oils," FAER No. 47, ERS, USDA, August 1968.

9. Anthony S. Rojko and Arthur B. Mackie, "World Demand Prospects for Agricultural Exports of Less Developed Countries in 1980," FAER No. 60, ERS, USDA, June 1970.

10. This section draws heavily on Richard S. Magleby and Edmond Missiaen, "World Demand Prospects for Cotton in 1980 with Emphasis on Trade by Less Developed Countries," FAER No. 68, ERS, USDA, January 1971.

11. Rojko and Mackie, op. cit.

12. Fiji, Mauritius, Reunion, Antigua, Barbados, Cuba, Dominican Republic, Guadeloupe, Guyana, British Honduras, Jamaica, Martinique, Philippines, and Taiwan.

13. The first eight countries listed in footnote 12.

14. Arthur B. Mackie and J. Lawrence Blum, "World Trade in Selected Agricultural Commodities, 1951-65; Vol. IV—Sugar, Fruits, and Vegetables," FAER No. 44, ERS, USDA, June 1968.

15. Larry J. Wipf, "Tariffs, Nontariff Distortions, and Effective Protection in U.S. Agriculture," American Journal of Agricultural Economics 53, no. 3 (August 1971).

16. Ibid.

17. James P. Houck, "The Green Revolution: Its Impact on Trade and Agricultural Policy in Developed Nations," staff paper P71-20, Department of Agricultural and Applied Economics, University of Minnesota (November 1971).

18. D. Gale Johnson, "Sugar Program: Costs and Benefits," Foreign Trade and Agricultural Policy, Technical Papers—Vol. VI

(Washington: National Advisory Commission on Food and Fiber, August 1967).

19. Donald C. Horton, "Policy Directions for the United States Sugar Program," American Journal of Agricultural Economics 52, no. 2 (May 1970).

20. D. Gale Johnson, op. cit.

21. D. Gale Johnson, "Comparative Advantage and U.S. Exports and Imports, of Farm Products," paper no. 72:1, Office of Agricultural Economics Research, University of Chicago (February 15, 1971). The program cost estimates are based on higher world prices that would result from increased imports by the United States.

22. Thomas H. Bates, "The Long-Run Efficiency of United States Sugar Policy," American Journal of Agricultural Economics 50, no. 2, (August 1968); and Donald C. Horton, "Policy Directions for the United States Sugar Program," American Journal of Agricultural Economics 52, no. 2 (May 1970). See also R. H. Snape, "Sugar: Costs of Protection and Taxation," Economica XXXVI, no. 141 (February 1969).

23. Harry G. Johnson, "Sugar Protectionism and the Export Earnings of Less Developed Countries: Variations on a Theme by Snape," Economica XXXIII, no. 129 (February 1966).

24. R. H. Snape, "Some Effects of Protection in the World Sugar Industry," Economica XXX, no. 117 (February 1963).

25. P. L. Strickland, W. H. Brown, W. C. McArthur, and W. W. Pawson, "Cotton Production and Farm Income Estimates under Selected Alternative Farm Programs," FAER No. 212, ERS, USDA (September 1971).

26. Wipf, op. cit. The calculated rates of protection were much lower in 1968 because of unusually high world market prices. With present much lower world prices, we would expect current rates of protection to be as high if not higher than in 1963.

27. "Rice Situation," ERS, USDA (March 1972).

28. A recent study by Warren R. Grant and D. S. Moore, "Alternative Government Rice Programs: An Economic Evaluation," FAER No. 187, ERS, USDA (June 1970) concludes that rice production in the United States in a free-market situation would be 138.7 million hundredweight (cwt) at an equilibrium price of $3.40 per cwt for rough rice. This is a much larger amount than the peak production of 104 million cwt produced in 1968 and way above the 1970 level of production of 83 million cwt. This increase is predicted in spite of a sharp drop in net returns from rice production in the short run (actually negative returns) and a significant reduction in land values required in the long run. The author finds these results hard to accept for such a protected commodity.

29. Bela Belassa, "Tariff Protection in Industrial Nations and Its Effects on the Exports of Processed Goods from Developing Countries," Canadian Journal of Economics vol. 1, no. 3 (August 1968).

30. Arthur B. Mackie, "Foreign Economic Growth and Market Potentials for U.S. Agricultural Products," FAER No. 24, ERS, USDA (April 1965).

31. Japan, Venezuela, Israel, Chile, Cyprus, Ghana, Iraq, Thailand, and Mexico.

32. D. Gale Johnson, "Where U.S. Agricultural Comparative Advantage Lies," and John Schnittker, "U.S. Agricultural Policy in Relation to World Trade," papers prepared for the Atlantic Council of the United States study, U.S. Agriculture in a World Context (New York: Praeger Publishers, 1974).

33. H. S. Houthakker, "Domestic Farm Policy and International Trade," American Journal of Agricultural Economics 53, no. 5 (December 1971): 764.

34. Dale E. Hathaway, "Trade Restrictions and U.S. Consumers," paper presented at the U.S. Trade Policy and Agricultural Exports Conference, Ames, Iowa, June 2, 1971.

35. If for political reasons the United States deems it undesirable to trade with a country, then trade should be restricted for all commodities, not just one commodity like sugar.

36. Willard W. Cochrane, "Agricultural Aspects of U.S. Economic Relations with Developing Countries," United States International Economic Policy in an Interdependent World, papers submitted to the Commission on International and Investment Policy, Vol. II (Washington, D.C.: GPO, July 1971), p. 264.

37. "International Commodity Arrangements and Policies," FAO Commodity Policy Studies No. 16, Special Studies Program No. 1, FAO, Rome, 1964. "The Problem of Stabilization of Prices of Primary Products," joint staff study of the International Monetary Fund and the International Bank for Reconstruction and Development, Washington, D.C., 1969.

38. "The Problem of Stabilization of Prices of Primary Products"—see note 37.

39. R.C. Porter, "Who Destabilizes Primary Product Prices?" The Indian Economic Journal XVI, no. 4 (April-June 1969).

40. Herbert G. Grubel, "Foreign Exchange Earnings and Price Stabilization Schemes," The American Economic Review LIV, no. 4 (June 1964).

41. Alasdair I. McBean, Export Instability and Economic Development (Cambridge: Harvard University Press, 1966), p. 32.

42. Ibid., p. 341.

43. See, for example, "Future United States Foreign Trade Policy," report to the president submitted by the Special Representative

for Trade Negotiations, Washington, D.C. (January 14, 1969), and "United States International Economic Policy in an Interdependent World," report to the president submitted by the Commission on International Trade and Investment Policy, Washington, D.C. (July 1971).

44. John Schnittker, "A Look Ahead—Trade Policy Recommendations," United States International Economic Policy in an Interdependent World, papers submitted to the Commission on International Trade and Investment Policy, Vol. I (Washington, D.C.: GPO, July 1971), p. 905.

45. There is some convincing evidence that exporting agricultural products is one way a developing country can extract an economic surplus from the agricultural sector with which to finance general economic development. See George L. Hicks and Geoffrey NcNicoll, Trade and Growth in the Philippines: An Open Dual Economy (Ithaca: Cornell University Press, 1971).

8

TECHNIQUES AND MODALITIES
OF AGRICULTURAL NEGOTIATIONS
Harald B. Malmgren

The liberalization of trade in recent decades has not covered trade in agricultural products to any significant degree. There is continued widespread use of quantitative restrictions, export subsidies, special protective levies, and nontariff restrictions of other types. The international rules governing trade in agricultural products, insofar as they exist, are more ambiguous and less strict than those governing industrial trade, and where there are rules they are often ignored.

Essentially, the General Agreement on Tariffs and Trade (GATT) rules out special measures of protection even for agriculture, except where there are domestic production restraint measures being applied. (The relevant article—Article XI—is appended at the end of this paper.) The idea behind the GATT exception is simply that a support program backed up by production controls is better than a support program without production restraint. If domestic production is restrained, then imports should not be allowed to undermine the domestic supports by the "free ride" into the market provided by the policy limitation on domestic supply.

The basic problems in world agriculture, however, obviously go much deeper than the conflicts in trade policies. All major trading

---

This exploratory paper was prepared before the author returned to government service. It is meant to provoke the development of new ideas and to suggest topics for research. It should not be interpreted as an official paper reflecting the views of the U.S. government. As regards the author's own conclusions, the author held them only tentatively, at the time this paper was written. Footnotes have been added in 1973 to update the factual background.

countries, and many of the developing countries, have government policies for intervention in agricultural markets, technological innovation, land utilization, incomes of farmers, and other aspects of farming. These policies are not only aimed at technical and economic objectives, they are also oriented toward social and political objectives. Among the social and political considerations that governments often give heavy weight to are the balance between rural and urban income levels, the employment opportunities available as alternatives to farming, the conservation of land and the rural environment, the stable supply of food for national populations including the insuring against shortages generated in other parts of the world, and the basic political balance between rural and urban areas. These are critical determinants of policies, and trade measures are often only instruments of the more basic domestic policies.

Consequently, improving the circumstances under which world agricultural production and trade take place must involve actions that take into account the basic social and political limitations. In particular, the governments of a number of countries could not accept implementation of measures that would have the effect of reducing family incomes in agricultural areas. Indeed, some governments believe it essential to pursue in the long run the objective of raising farmers' incomes, so that the remuneration for farm work becomes closer to that for comparable work in industry or services. (However, it is usually recognized that this objective cannot be achieved without reduction in the number of people engaged in or dependent on farm production.)

Looking at the world as a whole, proposals for trade policy changes must also recognize that there is a problem of balancing world production and world demand and that there is an even more important problem of ensuring that the food available globally can be distributed equitably among the world's population.

National policies are economically inefficient in a variety of ways, discouraging as often as not the needed adjustments in product mix, land utilization, and labor. These national policies cause distortions abroad as well as at home. The artificial stimulation of production in one country often results not only in a reduction of imports, but also in an increase in exportation, usually with the aid of subsidies, intensifying the adjustment difficulties of other nations. This in turn can, and often does, cause other nations to erect protective mechanisms to insulate their own markets from the artificially depressed prices that are generated. Or other nations react by introducing export aids of their own.

This interaction of measures taken by each country on the nature of measures taken by other countries compounds the problems in trade. Without generally accepted rules to guide them, and in a position to point blame at the policies of other nations, governments have been encouraged to solve agricultural problems without regard to the external implications—and indeed to solve them by pushing some of the required adjustments on to farmers and traders in other nations.

Thus continuing difficulties between nations result from the conflicts between their respective national measures, and from the adjustments caused in some countries as a result of measures taken in other countries.

Viewed from the context of world trade and world efficiency in agriculture, there are two needs:

1. the development of a more efficient agricultural structure in each nation, more oriented toward world market conditions and trends, and

2. harmonization of the various national production and trade policies.

While agricultural policies are aimed at domestic objectives, they also can affect social and political conditions in other countries. These political interactions among nations have lately caused considerable diplomatic friction and brought about deterioration in the atmosphere for international economic cooperation. Moreover, it has been made clear that for some governments, further efforts to improve general trade relations and to liberalize other sectors of world trade depend politically on substantial improvement in agricultural trade conditions. Even more disquieting is the increasing feeling in some quarters that failure to improve the conditions of agricultural trade will result in intensification of protectionist sentiment in world trade generally.

Consequently, there is urgent need to make progress in rationalizing and liberalizing world agricultural trade. At the same time, it has to be realistically recognized that major changes will take time and are likely to require social and political adjustments in all of the major trading nations.

The way may now be a little more open than in the past, because governments are increasingly becoming aware that the measures they employ do not in the end meet the desired social objectives. Moreover, they increasingly recognize the limitations on present measures imposed by budget costs, by substantial increases in production of unwanted products, and by antiinflationary policies. Finally, the monetary perturbations of the last few years have put strains on the policies of some countries and forced the implementation of patchwork measures that vividly demonstrate the need for change in agricultural policies.

SEARCHING FOR BASIC OBJECTIVES
AND PRINCIPLES

In light of these considerations, rationalization of both trade conditions and domestic policies would appear to be desirable from the point of view of the governments maintaining market-distorting policies. General exchanges of views on appropriate shifts in policies, and information exchange on policy intentions, have been of some value to governments in recent years. Such exchanges have taken place in the Organization for Economic Cooperation and Development (OECD), the GATT, the Food and Agricultural Organization (FAO), and in bilateral channels. However, the mood has normally been one of confrontation, with the emphasis on defending existing measures. Even detailed analysis of each country's measures by other countries in the factual confrontation phase of the Kennedy Round did not succeed in more than making available lengthy articulations of the reasons nations believed they were already doing the right thing.

If rationalization of trade and domestic policies is to be achieved, it may be necessary to develop some commonly agreed principles or guidelines for national policies, or some target objectives, which cut across national boundaries and philosophies, so as to avoid at the early stages the past tendency to revert to defense of the existing policies.

One of the simplest long-term target objectives would be to agree that measures should be adjusted so as to provide for a more efficient international divison of labor. While this may at first seem noncontroversial, problems immediately arise in trying to define what it means. Clearly it implies an orientation of policies toward world market mechanisms. But when that is said explicitly, a debate inevitably ensues concerning the meaning of "world market mechanisms" including what the meaning of market economics is when a few suppliers dominate world markets, and when governments intervene internally with the objective of stabilizing supplies or prices. Questions also arise concerning the desirability of a market orientation for what are thought by some people to be social, not economic policies. That kind of debate has proven sterile in the past, at least among government officials. There is a need to get beneath the philosophic level on these questions. There is a need, in other words, for some pragmatic principles that would lead the world in the direction of greater efficiency in resource use but that would be phrased in terms relevant to the concerns of governments.

As regards relations between governments, there certainly is now a strong incentive to moderate the frictions being generated by agricultural questions. Moreover, it is increasingly recognized that the process of action by one country and counteraction by another is an especially costly method of giving assistance to the agricultural sector. On the side of export aids, there is tendency to test whose system can be more generous than the others in subsidizing consumption in the relatively open markets. This, in turn, creates the incentive to introduce new forms of protection by importing countries that are also producing countries.

It would appear to be useful, in this context, to devise a behavioral principle that might channel government actions and provide a basis for meaningful consultation. One possible principle might involve restriction on the spill-over effects of measures on interests in other countries:

> It should be agreed that agricultural measures taken should not involve a transfer of costs of adjustment to farmers and traders of other nations, except on an agreed basis.

As a political declaration, this has appeal. ("My farmers should not have to pay for your farmers' programs.") In practice, it could be given meaning by focusing international discussions on the extent to which a new measure by one country disrupts interests in other countries, or where existing support measures are made more generous relatively to world market prices. Consultation could then cover the timetable of domestic adjustment, which is envisaged in relation to the implementation of special measures. It could cover possible compensatory measures, internal or external, which might be taken by the countries most affected. It could serve also as a means of educating public opinion about the broader consequences of agricultural measures. A grievance procedure of this type has a greater chance of being useful than straightforward diplomatic complaints and confrontations in international institutions without reference to rules or principles.

Such a principle might be applied to those cases where new measures are contemplated, or where the degree of effective protection or of export assistance is being increased. With experience, it might then be applied to more traditional methods of agricultural intervention.

As regards the policies and measures themselves, in relation to the apparent social objectives of governments, some principles might be agreed internationally that would help governments domestically. If such principles could be found, governments would have an incentive to follow them—or at least they would more clearly recognize their own interests if the issues were put this way.

> It is obvious that one such principle would be that structural adjustment should continue and be accelerated wherever possible.

If this were explicitly agreed, however simplistic it might seem, it would provide a basis for international discussion of the nature and effectiveness of alternative structural adjustment measures. As matters now stand, examination or even general discussion of the structural programs of another nation is considered in many quarters to be illegitimate interference in the internal policies of that other nation.

Given agreement on the principle, an effort might be made to define what types of measures can best achieve the desired ends, with minimal adverse effects on other nations.

In this direction, it might be further agreed in principle that measures of support should be tailored more precisely to the social objectives and that an effort should be made to alter their form, to make production and sale more market oriented.
This would be an important principle, because it would result in changing some of the methods of support—but not necessarily in the case of every product nor of every country. It would involve, for example, tailoring support measures to benefit the relatively disadvantaged farmers, or relatively disadvantaged regions, without windfalls and undesirable excessive incentives to stimulate production on the part of wealthy large-scale farmers. In other words, if there is a social problem, measures should be chosen which deal with that problem, in the specific areas it occurs, without providing costly incentives to producers who are not genuine social problems. (Price support measures are particularly inefficient instruments for dealing with social problems, because the greatest rewards go to the largest producers, who rarely need any assistance.) International discussion of how to shift programs in this direction without reducing at the same time the incentives to greater efficiency could be valuable, if governments agreed that such questions were legitimate matters for international deliberation.

One of the problems with most interventions by governments in the agricultural sector is that the measures taken seem to have a permanent character, at least in terms of public discussion of them. While the problems of adjustment in agriculture may often be more profound than those in industry, it should nonetheless be possible to consider them in terms of a timetable of adjustment.

It might be agreed that special policies that favor certain agricultural products, or that favor the agricultural sector generally, should be treated as transitional policies, and take a form that would facilitate the elimination of the need for and use of such policies at some target date in the plannable future.

Looking at these matters from the point of view of the consumer, and therefore of the wage earner in relation to his wage demands, the cost and quality of food are important to any sound national social policies, as well as sound national economic policies. There has been a tendency in recent years to distort the relative incentives as between higher protein foods (especially meats) and the more traditional basic commodities. Production is stimulated in products for which demand is growing relatively slowly with growth in income, while products for which the demand prospects are much better are subject to dis-incentives or trade restrictions. For example, current meat shortages in many countries make little economic or social sense, and an effort to alter the balance of incentives as between cereals and meat would benefit everyone.

Could it not be agreed that a better balance should be developed between the measures used to aid individual commodities, so that products for which there is relatively high prospect for increased demand are given greater encouragement, while those that appear to be in surplus in the light of world market condi-tions and prospects are subject to gradually reduced relative incentives?

Are there other basic principles, guidelines, or long-term policy objectives that could also be articulated in concrete terms, with a view to facilitating and legitimizing international discussion of national measures?

WHAT ARE THE POSSIBLE TECHNIQUES AND MODALITIES FOR NEGOTIATION?

Negotiations on questions of principle have thus far proven fruitless, primarily because the discussions were couched in terms of black and white allegations. Criticisms of the Common Agricultural Policy (CAP), or of the American import quota system on cheese and other dairy products, have always been expressed in terms that en-courage abstract debate on ideological or moralistic grounds. Indeed, in defending themselves, officials have often become convinced by their own arguments and become irritatingly self-righteous—a condi-tion of mind that makes the exploration of pragmatic solutions almost impossible, while encouraging confrontations of political rhetoric.

It would seem wise, therefore, to explore negotiating possibili-ties very pragmatically. In this regard, a challenge to the form of protection maintained by a country is less useful than a challenge to the degree of protection. As the degree of protection is reduced, the question of its form becomes less and less important.

This line of reasoning would suggest that energy be devoted to developing a common yardstick for measuring protection. One such yardstick was the proposal made by the European Common Market during the Kennedy Round trade negotiations that became known as the montant de soutien (MDS). The idea was to measure the difference between the price that a farmer in a given country receives and the world market price. Where the world market price may be lower than what might be reasonably felt to be the cost of efficient producers, because of the distortions resulting from government policies, a negotiated "reference price" could be developed.

The particular form of this proposal was rejected by the United States at the time it was proposed, and the various possible dimensions of the proposal were consequently not discussed during the multilateral trade negotiations. (The proposal at that time was tied by certain limiting conditions, and in particular the condition that negotiated cuts in protection would be "bound" for only three years, and even then be subject to change as a result of escape clauses. The rejection was based on the judgment that acceptance of negotiations on the basis of the MDS would concede acceptance of the principle of the variable levy system, and even tacit endorsement of it, in exchange for three-year concessions of modest degree that were subject to withdrawal even within the three years in exceptional circumstances. This was, when put that way, considered a bad deal by U.S. officials.)

Setting aside questions of accepting or rejecting the morality of certain systems and methods of support (they exist, whether formally accepted or rejected), the problem with the MDS concept is that no one has been able to define it very precisely. Which world prices? That is no easy question to answer. Then, once a price is agreed as the reference point, how long must it stand? Crops vary from year to year, both in volume and quality. The price relationships between qualities of a single commodity change all the time in the world market, and the relationships between one commodity and another also change.

If it is considered as a measure of <u>relative</u> ranking of the degree of protection and inefficiency, it might perhaps provide a basis for meaningful discussion. Then, to make progress in the direction of greater efficiency, it might be agreed that the levels of support for those products with the highest MDS rating in each country would be lowered, with reviews periodically to continue the process of reducing the <u>degree</u> of protection. Used this way, the absolute measurement of the <u>MDS</u> is less important than the relative height among the various products.

This approach could well be coupled with a general commitment to reduce the degree of protection of agriculture as a whole, so that protection in all sectors would be gradually reduced, but in the relatively more protected sectors, the reductions would be larger, or faster.

Explicit commitments to move further in the direction of liberalization at regular intervals could also be linked to measurements of the degree of self-sufficiency. Thus, where there is an increase in the self-sufficiency ratio in the case of a product subject to reductions in relative protection, the pace of reduction in the support level might be accelerated. That is, a rule might be negotiated requiring acceleration of liberalization where trade is harmed by a perverse increase in domestic production.

Operationally meaningful rules could be developed on the same basis for regulation of export subsidies and other aids to exports. This could be done separately, either before or during liberalization, with a view to controlling subsidization as such. At the present time, export aids tend to be determined on the basis of competitive offer prices. In the Community, the original theoretical link between import levies and export restitutions has been cut. In most cases, the managers of the CAP have rewritten the regulations to provide sufficient restitutions so as to meet competition in the market of destination, rather than limit restitutions to some equivalent of the import levies. Thus even the CAP system has turned out to be pragmatic rather than automatic.

In this environment of competition based on subsidies established in relation to what is thought to be (who determines this?) competitors' offer prices, there is no real control of the extent of subsidization. Small sales at distress prices by small traders, or by state-trading enterprises in the process of clearing stocks, and even false reports of competitive circumstances, can call forth enormous subsidization by the major trading countries.

On the export side, European Community (EC) officials have repeatedly indicated that they could not accept limitations on export subsidies (restitutions) in the absence of changes in domestic policies. The reasoning has been that the Community restitution payments were an automatic and integral part of the CAP mechanism. In reality, there has been plenty of room for discretion in establishing restitutions, not only because of the changes in practice noted above, but also because of the room for maneuver in the technical determination of restitution levels. Thus, for example, the restitution on hams or chickens depends on the estimate of the amount of grain, at what price, was used to feed the typical ham-producing pig or chicken. It is probably fair to say in this respect that the temptation to manipulate these "conversion coefficients" has been great, high-level policy scrutiny minimal and abuse of the original philosophic conception of the restitution payment substantial.

It could be argued, therefore, that the question of export aids needs to be examined with a view to introducing collective discipline among the major trading nations in the near term. Even though this may raise philosophic difficulties for the managers of the CAP, it should be recognized that practice has drifted from theory already. Again, it is a matter of moving away from debate about moral or social principles and economic ideologies to pragmatic improvement of the conditions of trade, the efficiency of domestic production, and the circumstances of the relatively disadvantaged farmers.*

Another problem to be tackled is the form of protection in those cases where it is particularly restrictive, of subject to arbitrary discretion in application, or subject to uncertain fluctuations in the size of border charges. In this regard, some basic principles ought to be sought, which might guide the day-to-day management of border protection devices. Quantitative restrictions in particular should be liberalized and phased out on a scheduled, albeit gradual, basis. In this respect, too much attention to the "GATT legality" of such restrictions and not enough to the desirability of expanding the volume of trade and keeping the pressure on protected production has probably, over the years, resulted in less liberalization than there might have been by openly negotiating the size of quantitative restrictions. No nation's agricultural policies, particularly as they affect trade, can be considered to be fully legal in the sense of consistency with the letter and the spirit of the GATT.

A more complex question is the interaction of quantitative restrictions, state-trading market operations, and commercial activity, as in the case of Japan. Here the internal supports are so far above world market levels for rice that what should be the largest rice-importing market is an exporter instead. The general agricultural distortions that result are protected by an array of discretionary devices. But even if rice supports became subject to some form of collective discipline internationally, Japan might well seek to retain the other devices and practices that are so restrictive.

It would seem desirable, to comprehend the special case of Japan and to restrain the arbitrary or unpredictable manipulations of protection by all nations, to develop a code governing forms of protection and the regulations and procedures used in managing them. Complex mechanisms should, wherever possible, be simplified, preferably taking the form of tariffs.

---

*Moreover, on subsidies, world market conditions are in 1973 favorable to the idea of total abolition of export aids, since food price rises and shortages in key developed country markets make the whole notion of export subsidies from those markets seem absurd. The United States abolished most of her export aids and incentives in late 1972 and early 1973. Reciprocal action, perhaps in a context of consultations about reintroduction of export aids under limited circumstances in later years, should be considered by other exporting nations. A dramatic change in policy may, in fact, be negotiable for the next few years, given a degree of reasonableness.

Criteria for valuation, classification, quality requirements, and similar conditions of entry should be established in a form that is publicly explainable, and changes in such criteria should always be subject to prior public notice and equitable public procedures. Licensing and other permissive steps should be made automatic. The discretion of officials regarding import treatment beyond the explicit public criteria should be minimal.

These kinds of techniques or modes of negotiation are different from the more traditional approaches, but the more traditional approaches have failed to secure significant progress in the liberalization of agricultural trade in spite of significant progress in the liberalization of industrial trade in the post-World War II period. In the Kennedy Round, formulas for guaranteed access and for self-sufficiency ratios were explored, but in the end no meaningful package could be put together on that basis. The problem with a self-sufficiency ratio is that it cannot be adhered to without the implementation of a number of measures to moderate production or to store surpluses.

The possibility of managing the swings between lean years and highly productive years has been subject to increased international discussion lately. In the late 1960s, the idea of managing production and stocks in cereals was thought by many governments to be politically unacceptable, or too costly. The International Grains Arrangement broke down over the unwillingness of the major exporting nations to cooperate in the management of sales and to hold stocks. The shift in world production trends became so obvious eventually that the reluctance receded. Canada and Australia took steps to curb production. The Community, however, refused to move in this direction. More recently, a breakthrough in EC thinking occurred with the agreement in late 1971 to withhold and stock wheat, as part of the international monetary package which was concluded at the Smithsonian Institution in December, as supplemented by the joint trade declaration of the EC and the United States of February 1972. It would now seem politically possible to obtain agreement on some internationally agreed stockpiling system, with perhaps greater relative burdens on producers whose supplies were generated with the aid of unduly high price supports.

The Community agricultural system could be described as a mechanism designed to prevent internal market disruption resulting from fluctuations in world markets. Of course, in practice, the CAP has achieved far more than that limited objective, both in stimulating home production and in disrupting the markets of other countries. Nonetheless, it might be possible to work within the "stabilization" philosophy of the Community mechanism and broaden the horizons of international discussion to comprehend collective responsibility for stabilization of world markets, at least in the sense of avoiding swings of major and disruptive consequence and assuring continuity of supplies in lean years. For many years some countries, particularly the United States, were taking land out of production and incurring costs of keeping capacity running at idle, while others were free not only to race their engines but to dart ahead in world markets. That is untenable in the long run. Without collective discipline in some form, the only other reasonable move by the countries carrying the greatest costs of adjustment in relation to world markets would be to ease their restraints on production.*

This leads to the question of commodity arrangements. We have become accustomed to thinking of such arrangements as price-rigging schemes. As such, they are subject to the same kinds of uncertainties as those noted above in relation to the definition of the MDS and the "world market price" or the "reference price." Only in very rare cases have schemes based solely on price schedules been workable, even for short periods. The incentive to cheat by providing ambiguous information, manipulating quality differentials and shipping rates, and generally exploiting the rigidity of price differentials is so great that policy officials charged with policing such arrangements can scarcely keep up with actual transactions.

Such negative considerations are in addition to all the other traditional objections raised over the years. Proposals for "commodity arrangements" would, therefore, have to be far more sophisticated than heretofore if they were to be given any serious consideration. It is a pity in this regard that the European countries most keen on the commodities arrangement approach have offered no real, concrete proposals related to temperate products that might be analyzed by other nations' governments.

It might be possible to conceive of agricultural trade negotiations undertaken within the boundaries of individual commodity groupings, with a view to dealing with the full range of measures internal and external that influence the world market. In other words, proposals, if they are to be useful, have to go well beyond such traditional questions as self-sufficiency ratios and price schedules to the more basic questions of production and supply management, support policies and their long-term objectives, internal structural adjustment as between the commodity in question and other commodities, levels of protection and export aids, and so on.

Among the options new thought needs to be given to international consultations, grievance procedures, and sanctions. The biggest trading

---

*And that is what the United States began to do in early 1973— to take care of rising world demand and at the same time shuck off the burden of moderation of world supplies she had borne so long.

countries sometimes are able to modify a particular abuse by another country simply by asserting their full weight on a narrow issue, through diplomatic channels. These bilateral solutions have been skimpy and far too infrequent. As we have seen, the GATT rules and procedures give little basis for forcing decisions or even for allowing compensatory or counteracting measures. The answer may lie in writing up a chapter of rules for agriculture to be added to the GATT. Or it may lie in a series of concrete actions which, taken together, constitute movement in the desired direction. Either would be far better than what exists now.

A middle ground might be found within the framework of some general principles of the type laid out in this paper, with a multilateral consultative mechanism which would meet regularly to hear grievances and to assess progress. Reductions in the degree of distortion (protection, subsidy, production incentive) could then be negotiated within a framework of multilateral procedures that would supplement and facilitate liberalization actions. Under such a multilateral framework, countries will always maintain certain rights of unilateral action. But in such cases, a consultative committee might make judgments that other countries are adversely affected, and that they might therefore be given freedom to take some type of compensatory action of their own—preferably on a discriminatory basis.

It might also be possible to reinforce agricultural negotiations that are conducted in the framework of more general trade negotiations by providing for a kind of "conditional MFN" provision of concessions. Thus multilaterally agreed concessions might be denied those supplier nations that maintain specific policies of direct, adverse consequence to the nation granting concessions, for a period directly linked to an agreed liberalization schedule or to the period of maintenance of the adverse measure. This sounds like strong stuff, but it may be necessary to dislodge certain special interests and to force industrial interests to take greater interest in the economic impact of agricultural support and trade policies. The problems in agriculture are, to a significant extent, the consequence of inattention by the public and by officials who characteristically seem to shy away from the details of agricultural policies. In the end, the checks and balances of broadbased political forces and processes just do not seem to bear upon agriculture, while a very small number of farm-based people have an inordinate political weight. If that weight were applied to the development of policies that really achieved the apparent objectives, there would also be less of a problem. But it is not always easy to design policy for the benefit of a particular group by consulting only the members of that group. On the contrary, their best interests might better be served by balancing particular measures against measures taken elsewhere in the economy.

In any event, it seems wise to conclude at this stage in international relations that gradual movement in the direction of more efficient use of world resources is better than movement in other directions, that control of political conflicts and moderation of mercantilistic tendencies is better than a vicious circle of actions and counteractions, and that aiming social policies at those who need help is better than wasting scarce economic resources through vaguely defined policies that provide most of their benefits to those who need them least.

The stipulation of general long-term objectives, together with a series of individually small but concrete steps to be taken each year in the direction of achieving those objectives, might be the best way to get moving, for this approach would recognize the fact that change will come slowly.*

The objectives would provide a target and guidelines for international consultation. A commitment to the target would be only one part of the negotiation, however. The other critical part would be the sequence of agreed phased steps which would lead in the direction of greater market orientation and liberalization of trade. If multilateral negotiations result in a phasing in over several years of liberalization of industrial trade, together with new rules, procedures, and phasing to deal with industrial nontariff barriers, the same general approach in agriculture could be perceived as fully consistent. A combined agreement to move in a new, more rational direction, and agreement on concrete steps to get there, are what this, in essence, is all about.

---

*After this paper was written, world market price rises in food and feed grains, and meat began to create economic difficulties in many countries. Some unilateral, temporary liberalization of import restrictions took place as antiinflationary action. Elimination of export subsidies also took place. The measures initially taken were not orchestrated among capitals. It might well be worthwhile to contemplate, during the early phases of negotiation, to try to harmonize the antiinflationary trade measures of various countries and to seek to keep in effect the liberalization that takes place as a first step in the phased sequence of actions which might, in due course, result from the overall negotiations.

APPENDIX: GENERAL AGREEMENT ON TARIFFS AND TRADE, ARTICLE XI

General Elimination of Quantitative Restrictions

1. No prohibitions or restrictions other than duties, taxes or other charges, whether made effective through quotas, import or export licences or other measures, shall be instituted or maintained by any contracting party on the importation of any product of the territory of any other contracting party or on the exportation or sale for export of any product destined for the territory of any other contracting party.

2. The provisions of paragraph 1 of this article shall not extend to the following:

(a) Export prohibitions or restrictions temporarily applied to prevent or relieve critical shortages of foodstuffs or other products essential to the exporting contracting party;

(b) Import and export prohibitions or restrictions necessary to the application of standards or regulations for the classification, grading, or marketing of commodities in international trade;

(c) Import restrictions on any agricultural or fisheries product, imported in any form,* necessary to the enforcement of governmental measures which operate:

    (i) to restrict the quantities of the like domestic product permitted to be marketed or produced, or, if there is no substantial domestic production of the like product, of a domestic product for which the imported product can be directly substituted; or

    (ii) to remove a temporary surplus of the like domestic product, or, if there is no substantial domestic production of the like product, of a domestic product for which the imported product can be directly substituted, by making the surplus available to certain groups of domestic consumers free of charge or at prices below the current market level; or

    (iii) to restrict the quantities permitted to be produced of any animal product the production of which is directly dependent, wholly or mainly, on the imported commodity, if the domestic production of that commodity is relatively negligible.

Any contracting party applying restrictions on the importation of any product pursuant to subparagraph (c) of this paragraph shall give public notice of the total quantity or value of the product permitted to be imported during a specified future period and of any change in such quantity or value. Moreover, any restrictions applied under (i) above shall not be such as will reduce the total of imports relative to the total of domestic production, as compared with the proportion which might reasonably be expected to rule between the two in the absence of restrictions. In determining this proportion, the contracting party shall pay due regard to the proportion prevailing during a previous representative period and to any special factors* that may have affected or may be affecting the trade in the product concerned.

Ad Articles XI, XII, XIII, XIV, and XVIII

Throughout Articles XI, XII, XIII, XIV and XVIII, the terms "import restrictions" or "export restrictions" include restrictions made effective through state-trading operations.

Ad Article XI

Paragraph 2 (c)

The term "in any form" in this paragraph covers the same products when in an early stage of processing and still perishable, which compete directly with the fresh product and if freely imported would tend to make the restriction on the fresh product ineffective.

Paragraph 2, last subparagraph

The term "special factors" includes changes in relative productive efficiency as between domestic and foreign producers, or as between different foreign producers, but not changes artificially brought about by means not permitted under the agreement.

9

SUMMARY AND CONCLUSIONS:
POLICIES AND APPROACHES
FOR THE NEXT DECADE
D. Gale Johnson
John A. Schnittker

This chapter represents the basic conclusions and recommendations of the Agricultural Steering Committee of the Atlantic Council. It is based on a series of meetings held by the committee, as well as on the findings reported in the previous chapters, which served as working papers for the committee's discussions.

U.S. AGRICULTURE IN PERSPECTIVE

Four characteristics distinguish U.S. agriculture in the 1970s:

1. There is a growing concentration on the production of feed grains, oilseeds, and livestock products to support a high-income economy. These products now account for about 75 percent of all farm marketings.

2. There is greater attention to agricultural exports and an increasing tendency to dominate world markets for coarse grains and oilseeds for an extended time because of existing and latent productive capacity.

3. It shows retention of a predominant but changing family farm structure into the 1970s and probably for an indefinite time beyond. This pattern has continued even while agricultural marketings have become rather highly concentrated. United States agriculture has polarized into two segments in the past 20 years. One group is made up of roughly 1.1 million full-time farm families who marketed some 90 percent of all farm products grown in 1972. The other group is composed of about 1.8 million farm families who market few commodities, who look increasingly to the expanding industrial and service economies for income growth, and who have, with some exceptions, made rapid income gains. They retain their identity as farmers

through limited agricultural production and by virtue of a census definition that requires little farm output to be classified a farmer.

4. There is also rapidly rising labor productivity, now slowed somewhat, and a perennial excess capacity, which has appeared both as large stored surpluses and as massive idle acreages for about 20 years. High productivity and excess capacity developed partly out of incentives provided by federal price support and stabilization programs, but also from the skill, hard work, and adaptability of American farmers.

The U.S. output mix, both in terms of value and area of production, is clearly livestock based. Some 180 million acres out of 300 million acres harvested each year are devoted to feed grains and forage for livestock. About 60 percent of all cash receipts of farmers each year are from this broad sector. It is also the livestock sector that is least dependent upon federal farm stabilization and subsidies, although this independence from government is not so complete as is often claimed. Milk prices have long been supported by federal law. Further, output and prices in the feed grains sector have been stabilized by price supports and production controls that relied on federal payments ranging from $1 billion to nearly $2 billion per year over the past 12 years. Beef prices have been protected by import controls for nearly 10 years, and the livestock sector generally has benefitted from the extraordinarily stable supply of low-priced grains and from federal food distribution programs that utilized large quantities of meat whenever meat prices declined.

The strength of the U.S. family farm structure in a growing corporate economy is a continuing surprise to many people. Fears of a rapid corporate take-over of farming, especially in field crops, are premature. Corporate farms controlled only 2 to 3 percent of all farms in the United States and made only 10 percent of total farm marketings. Even so, corporate structure and large farming units under individual control are now dominant in cattle feeding and broiler production and are predominant, if not controlling, in eggs, fruits, and vegetables. Cotton production is more concentrated on large farms than other field crops, yet farms with more than 200 acres of cotton account for only 30 percent of U.S. cotton acreage.

The question of who controls and will control U.S. agriculture is important from the political and social standpoint, but is probably less important from the standpoint of economic efficiency. Maintenance of the agricultural exporting capability of the United States, which is based largely on products from family farms, does not depend on more rapid increases in farm size than has occurred in recent decades. Nor does it depend upon preservation of the present family farm system everywhere. Change in this area can neither be stopped nor greatly influenced by policy. Broilers moved into corporate production units 15 years ago and were a major export product until protective measures abroad stopped the flow. Large-scale family farms appear to be as efficient as giant corporate farms in most lines of production, and more efficient in some. The present family farm structure of American agriculture is probably protected far better against rapid deterioration by its efficiency and by more cooperation among farmers than it could be protected by law in the years just ahead.

The ability of U.S. farmers to expand production on short notice is not matched by farmers in any other country; no other country has had such a large share of its crop acreage set aside from production. Some 50 to 60 million acres, or 15 to 20 percent of total cultivated acreage, have been set aside each year for many years (with exceptions when carry-overs had to be replenished) in return for federal payments to farmers under the price support programs. This idle land is not the most productive, but it does represent an immediate capacity to produce 5 to 10 percent more grain and oilseeds in any year to meet U.S. and world requirements. Withholding this productive capacity is one of the most important contributions U.S. agricultural policy has made to world agricultural stability. Similarly, using this land periodically to meet expanded demand and to provide reserve stocks makes the world's food supply more secure. Thus U.S. policy has contributed importantly to the achievement of agricultural objectives all countries support. Tailoring farm production to requirements at remunerative prices stabilizes world markets both when land is idled and when it is again in use. Government funds spent to produce these results are not "farm subsidies" in any narrow sense; they do not add to the level of protection afforded U.S. farmers.

The U.S. agricultural sector has been an important element in world markets and a focal point of international negotiations for many years. Even so, U.S. agricultural policy has been tailored principally to domestic farm price and income objectives, not trade expansion. The early Agricultural Acts in 1933 and 1938, which firmly established an agricultural production and stabilization policy for the federal government, were enacted to help farmers cope with a worldwide depression at a time when international trade had stagnated; the emphasis on prices and incomes was essential. Trade considerations first became a factor in modern (post-1933) farm policy as a means of protecting farm prices by preventing interference by imports with price support programs after other nations had generated surpluses.

During World War II, U.S. price support guarantees were raised to encourage greater output. But the price expectations of farmers rose even higher on the strength of prices far above guaranteed levels as a result of postwar food shortages. For 15 years after the end of the war, Congress tried to maintain, as nearly as possible, the price levels that U.S. farmers had enjoyed during the world food crisis just after the war. Laws were amended, but no sustained and realistic efforts were made either to cope with rising agricultural output based on new technology, to adapt to a demand structure being generated by rising incomes and rapidly changing technology, or to address the income and structural issues arising out of a vastly altered and increasingly concentrated agricultural economy. Postwar policies and programs were characterized by high price supports and rather ineffective production controls. Together with the research-based technological revolution on American farms, they finally brought on massive commodity surpluses and unacceptable storage costs by the end of the 1950s. Major changes in agricultural policy objectives and in agricultural programs could no longer be postponed.

New programs adopted in the 1960s were designed to limit farm production to market requirements by means of acreage controls alone, except for tobacco where poundage limits were set on marketings. Farm prices continued to be supported and stabilized, but at or near world values. Farm incomes were supplemented by direct federal payments as market prices dropped. Technical change was unabated and progressed as rapidly as individual investment decisions and the development of new farming methods allowed. Surpluses of grains and cotton were reduced in the mid-1960s, and annual production began to be tailored roughly to annual demand, although this is not an exact science.

The principal tool of the new policy was a reduced price support guarantee supplemented by payments made to those farmers who reduced their crop acreages according to a program announced by the secretary of agriculture. By 1965 the revised programs had been applied to feed grains, wheat, and cotton, the crops harvested on about four-fifths of all the cropland acreage in the United States.

In shifting to effective supply adjustment policies from the previous surplus-oriented policy, little attention was given to the distribution of benefits from U.S. farm programs. The key objectives were to increase total net farm income and the average net incomes of all farm families, as well as to gear production to market demand. Neither the rapid polarization of U.S. family farms into two groups, nor the tendency of large farmers to receive most of the benefits from federal programs was altered by the new programs. In some cases, especially in the cotton belt, the new programs may have hastened the exodus of small farmers and accelerated the concentration of farm program benefits. Sharecroppers and laborers were especially hard hit in the mid-1960s by changes in the cotton program.

Farmers and farm organizations in the United States viewed with mixed feelings the farm program amendments made in the early 1960s and which were continued with some amendments in 1970. The support they attracted, largely from a coalition of several regional farm groups and commodity organizations, was attributable to the fact that federal payments guaranteed to farmers by law compensated for sharply reduced price supports. The prospect of some price improvement as a result of reduced surpluses was also a factor in farm support. The largest U.S. farm group, the American Farm Bureau Federation, was not a member of the supporting coalition, but opposed the changes in favor of a general withdrawal of government from agricultural stabilization and production control.

Farm groups did not support these measures on the grounds that they would increase exports. It was almost coincidental that the new programs of the 1960s were distinctly oriented toward trade expansion through a more efficient and responsive relationship to world markets. Making domestic policies more defensible in trade negotiations was not a principal objective of the government, the farm organizations, or the Congress.

As farm policy revisions were slowly adapting the machinery of U.S. farm price and income support more closely to the real and prospective conditions of world agriculture, U.S. farm organizations were also showing their first serious postwar interest in expansion of commercial agricultural trade. After World War II, U.S. farm organizations and political leaders had responded to massive surplus accumulations generated by ineffective farm programs by supporting enactment of the Agricultural Trade Development and Assistance Act of 1954, The Food for Peace program. Designed to provide food to needy nations and to dispose of surplus U.S. agricultural products on world markets as rapidly as possible, this effort served to rekindle the interest of U.S. farm groups in world agriculture. To a degree, it set the stage for the subsequent interest of farmers and farm leaders in trade expansion, since it initiated market development efforts, and, on concessional terms, tapped markets which later became commercial customers.

In 1962, in the midst of farm program revisions, U.S. farm organizations expanded their international activities and became a key political link in U.S. efforts to expand commercial trade. The issue was the Trade Expansion Act of 1962 and the role of agricultural products in future negotiations. Farm organizations deserve much credit for passage of that act and for the overall achievements of the Kennedy Round of negotiations, even though the agricultural strategy ultimately failed. That strategy was to lock agricultural products that had not benefitted materially from previous general trade negotiations into the new round of negotiations in the belief or hope that U.S. concessions on industrial products could be traded for concessions in agricultural products by other nations.

Altering the emerging Common Agricultural Policy (CAP) of the European Community (EC) to the advantage of the U.S. and other agricultural exporters was one principal negotiating objective. In retrospect, this effort appears to have been destined for failure from the start. The EC was held together in the late 1960s largely by an agreement to establish a CAP and by the emerging elements of the CAP. If that solidarity had been sacrificed to make major agricultural concessions to the United States and the rest of the world in the Kennedy Round, the very existence of the EC would have been threatened.

Since neither the United States nor the EC was prepared to make meaningful concessions on farm products in the Kennedy Round, the U.S. objective of substantial trade liberalization in agricultural as well as industrial products had to be abandoned, although small gains were salvaged. The Kennedy Round almost failed because U.S. agricultural objectives were unrealistic and because Europe was inflexible on the same agricultural questions that the United States chose to make important issues in the negotiation.

Fortunately, world agricultural trade and U.S. exports continued to expand despite the acknowledged shortcomings (from a trade standpoint) of the various national farm policies in major countries and the lack of progress toward reducing or eliminating barriers to agricultural trade. Paradoxically, one of the most difficult problems that faces groups interested in maximum trade expansion is the likelihood that agricultural trade will expand again in the 1970s without regard to the success of international negotiations. The role of the USSR and China as grain importers, the capacity of Europe to expand output and reduce its grain and meat imports, and the success of developing countries in expanding agricultural production are the key elements that will determine the level of trade a decade from now.

It is hoped that nations interested in the gains from trade will not be deterred by the present prospect that trade will expand from striving for even more rapid progress through international rationalization of agricultural policies, as well as conventional trade negotiations. Clearly, the rate at which trade expands will be determined by the success or failure of forthcoming trade liberalization efforts. In pursuing the objectives of expanded trade, the United States and other nations with a large stake in growing agricultural trade should keep in mind the fact that other nations have other objectives and that trade is an instrument, not an end in itself.

EVALUATION OF U.S. FARM PROGRAMS

All governmental programs that involve substantial expenditures on the part of taxpayers and consumers should be subjected to periodic evaluation and review. Such evaluation is particularly appropriate when conditions have changed as much as they have in U.S. agriculture over the past decade. Farm family incomes have risen substantially in real terms. Farming has become increasingly dependent upon goods and services purchased from the rest of the economy. Farm employment has decreased to less than 5 percent of national employment. To an increasing degree, the economic welfare of U.S. agriculture has become dependent upon commercial exports.

Federal farm programs have adapted to this pattern of change, although slowly and with great difficulty. If U.S. agriculture is to participate effectively in a progressive liberalization of trade, some farming sectors will have to make significant further adjustment as barriers to trade are lowered. Thus an objective evaluation of past farm programs is especially timely, both from the standpoint of domestic objectives and trade.

Objectives of Farm Programs

Five major objectives have been important for U.S. farm programs for the past decade. These are
1. to raise the average level of farm incomes to a more satisfactory level,
2. to achieve a reasonable degree of stability for farm prices and incomes,
3. to provide an adequate and stable supply of food and fiber for U.S. consumers at reasonable prices,
4. to manage the supply of key farm products so that the first two objectives can be achieved without acquiring unacceptably high surpluses and imposing heavy costs upon taxpayers,
5. to improve the capability of American agriculture to expand exports, while protecting it carefully but not completely from imports of competitive agricultural products.

These objectives have been achieved to a substantial degree, especially since 1960, but also during the recovery from general and agricultural depression in the 1930s and in the 1950s. Average farm prices and incomes in years of surplus production have been higher than they would have been if the farm programs had not been in operation. Certainly farm prices have been stabilized, both because federal supports prevented disastrous declines when crops were big and because stored surpluses could be marketed to keep prices from rising sharply when crops were relatively short.

Efficient organization of farms, favorable geographic conditions, rapid adjustments to changing conditions, and generous supplies of highly productive farm inputs as well as efficient markets for farm products have given the United States important advantages in world markets. The United States is a low-cost producer of feed grains,

soybeans, wheat, poultry, and tobacco, and is reasonably competitive
with other countries in producing cotton, pork, and grain-fed beef.

United States farm programs have also made more than a negli-
gible contribution to price stability in world markets through the
maintenance of reserves to meet emergencies or unexpected demands.
As noted earlier, the United States has acted to withdraw land from
cultivation when surpluses threatened, and to return land to production
when reserve stocks had declined and prices had increased. By holding relatively large stocks of wheat, feed grains, and cotton as a matter
of policy, the United States has been able to minimize year-to-year
variability in world prices. The record rise in world grain and oilseed prices in 1972 and 1973 is the one recent exception to this rule,
but the circumstances causing the exception were truly extraordinary.

Certain other rhetorical objectives beyond the objectives cited
above have been stated in farm laws; parity prices and parity incomes
are the principal example. These goals were seldom pursued directly.
If farm programs were evaluated in terms of those stated objectives,
they would have to be judged as falling somewhat short of their
targets; prices in relation to the parity standard have long been declining (until 1972-73), and farmers' average returns have usually
not been up to the income standards. However, the 1 million farmers
who received most of the income benefits from farm programs have
had family incomes significantly above the national average.

Other questions need to be raised in any general evaluation of
the past farm policies:

1. Have the income benefits of the farm program been distributed among farm families and the owners of the various farm resources in a generally acceptable manner?

2. Have adjustments in the use of land and labor that are called
for by changing demands, new methods of production, and the comparative advantage position of U.S. agriculture been impeded by the
farm programs, either generally or by particular features?

3. Have the programs designed to meet certain special objectives such as price stabilization and supply management been effective in reaching those objectives at reasonable costs to taxpayers
and with the minimum interference with resource use?

4. Have the various programs been a part of an effort that
recognized the interests of other countries, including other exporting
nations and developing countries, which wish to expand the volume
and the value of their exports?

Effects of Farm Programs on the Level and
Distribution of Farm Income

Farm income issues are important to trade policy. It has been
the pursuit of farm income objectives in many countries that has led

to programs providing high levels of protection for farm products. However, if one objective of farm policy is to improve the circumstances of low-income and disadvantaged segments of the farm population, there are other more direct means of meeting their needs that would involve much less interference with trade than farm price supports or payment programs directly related to farm output. Payments geared to need or to farm size, family assistance, early retirement, and education to increase mobility are all in this category.

Understanding the effects of farm programs on the level and distribution of farm income is of critical importance. In the United States, Japan, and the EC, as well as in most other industrial countries, farm policies impose substantial costs upon consumers and taxpayers. It is only reasonable to try to determine whether such costs have effects that are generally accepted as desirable or worthwhile. If we are to act responsibly in changing farm programs, we need to know how much farm incomes have been increased, what types of farm income have gained, and whether the major income benefits have accrued primarily to relatively low-income people. Raising the aggregate and the average levels of farm incomes has been a major objective of U.S. commodity programs. Yet there has never been general agreement on what constitutes a fair or reasonable level of farm income. Put in another way, the income objective has never been defined in terms clear enough so that Congress, the administration, and the public would know whether the objective had actually been met or approached to some reasonable degree.

This is a failing not only of U.S. policies, but for all countries that give significant weight to a farm income objective. Either the income objectives are stated so broadly that they are not a good policy guide or they leave out so many important considerations that the objective could never be achieved so long as individual farmers are relatively free to determine how many resources they wish to devote to agriculture.

Several years ago, at the direction of Congress, the U.S. Department of Agriculture (USDA) and a committee of independent agricultural economists studied returns from agricultural resources in the United States to determine if comparable resources were receiving the same returns in agriculture as in the rest of the economy.[1] While the methods used to estimate comparable resources and returns can be criticized and improved, the results indicated that returns to resources on the larger farms (representing about 70 percent of all farm products marketed in the United States) were as high or higher than earnings of comparable resources in the rest of the economy. For agriculture as a whole, however, returns were less than the same collection of farm resources would have earned in other uses. Average returns for all farms were reduced by low returns on farms that received little income from farming and had little effect upon farm output. Nevertheless, emphasis has continued to be placed on higher prices, payments proportional to production, and greater aggregate net farm income. Perhaps the study was of some help in initiating the imposition of a token ceiling on payments per farm under each of the three major farm commodity programs, but for the most part it was simply ignored. Unfortunately, that study has not been brought up to date to show how commercial farms fared in 1971 and 1972.

An income comparison that has long been popular in the Department of Agriculture is a comparison of national per capita disposable income from all sources with per capita incomes of farm people. In 1972 farm per capita income was 82 percent of nonfarm, a sharp increase from about 50 percent in 1960. Unfortunately, this comparison neglects important differences between the farm and nonfarm populations—dependency ratios, age distribution of the labor forces, and differences in assets owned. Farm operators not living on their farms are excluded, but farm hired workers who live on farms are included. Most important, the inclusion of some 2 million low-income farmers in the averages distorts the position of larger farmers. This kind of comparison is a faulty guide either for assessing the effectiveness of farm programs in increasing farm incomes, or as a measure of income position of farmers relative to the nonfarm population.

There can be no doubt that the farm programs have increased net farm income. It is also quite apparent that the programs have increased the returns to agricultural land and, in turn, the price or value of that land. For three major farm crops—corn, cotton, and wheat—as well as for peanuts and tobacco, payments or price support benefits have been directly related to the acreage of a particular crop or group of crops on the farm. A substantial part of the payments or the price support has been capitalized into the value of land or, especially in the case of cotton, tobacco, and rice, into the value of acreage allotments when allotments are transferred from farm to farm.

That a large part of the income benefits from the farm programs has been capitalized into the value of farmland is shown by the relationship between total net farm operator income and the value of farmland. In the period between the two world wars, net farm operator income varied from about 10.5 percent to 13 percent of the value of farmland; in 1960 it was 9.2 percent of the value of farmland, and in 1970 only 7.9 percent. Thus the claim of farm real estate on farm net income has risen significantly during the past two decades of farm programs. These results are consistent with numerous studies of the cash value of acreage allotments for various crops.

What has been the effect of the farm programs on the returns to other resources engaged in agriculture? Here the evidence is less clear. The few studies that have addressed themselves to this issue have found no significant long-run program effects upon returns to farm labor. Given the persistent movement of labor out of agriculture, it would be surprising if either higher prices or direct payments had any permanent effect on the average or marginal return to farm labor.

How much would net farm income decline if the major farm program and price supports were eliminated? Over the past several years, a number of efforts have been made to provide a quantitative answer to this question. The most recent projection of this kind (by Mayer, Heady, and Madsen of Iowa State University) indicated that after adjustments to the new conditions were completed, aggregate net income of farm operators would be about 25 percent lower than the average level of 1965 and 1967. The projected decline in income was approximately $3.4 billion, while the decline in government payments (as of 1967) associated with the end of programs was $2.7 billion. Earlier projections had indicated approximately the same percentage decline in net farm income. It is of interest to note that all of the decline in net farm income in the Iowa State study was attributed to resources other than labor. The return to family and hired labor in these estimates (without farm programs) was more than 10 percent above the return in 1967.

Effects on Income Distribution

The farm programs have probably increased the inequality in the distribution of incomes of farm people rather substantially, although the evidence of this is largely inferential rather than direct. The distribution of direct government payments to farmers is about the same as the distribution of net farm income by farm sales groups, except that on the largest farms (40,000 receipts and over) direct government payments are only 34.5 percent of net farm income compared with 43 percent for all farms. However, if the total income of farm families is considered, the highest-income group received 25 percent of that total in 1971 and, as indicated, 34.5 percent of government payments. Farm operators on farms with sales from $2500 to $4999 had the lowest average total family income and received 9.0 percent of the income of all farm families but only 6.5 percent of the direct government payments.

The heavy concentration of direct government payments paid to a relatively few high-income farmers is further indicated by the distribution of 1971 payments. Almost 60 percent went to slightly more than 600,000 operators who constituted only 21 percent of all farm operators. The average payment per farm for this group of farms was $3020 compared to an average payment of $499 for farms with sales of $2500 to $4999. The concentration of payments was both a cause and effect of changes in the structure of agriculture, since such payments permitted the larger farmers to bid strongly for the land held by small farmers.

In evaluating the effects of farm programs on the level of farm incomes, it should be borne in mind that between 1960 and 1970 the increase in off-farm income of farm operator families was substantially larger than the increase in farm net income (net operator income, farm wages and rent to nonfarm landlords). The latter increased by $5.8 billion, while off-farm income increased by $8.8 billion. Farm programs contributed nothing directly to the increase in off-farm income. But a relatively full employment economy substantially increased the incomes of farm families, probably more effectively than did government payments and other aspects of the farm programs.

Effects on Stability of Farm Prices and Incomes

There is considerable evidence that farm prices and incomes have been more stable during the past two decades than during earlier times. Some of the increase in stability can be attributed to improved general management of the economy and the prevention of large-scale and extended depressions. But some must also be attributed to the farm programs, including price supports and government management of stocks of major farm products. Greater price stability has been achieved for the major crops and dairy products than for beef cattle and pork, since government programs have not attempted to stabilize directly the prices of meat-producing animals. In terms of meeting this particular objective, the U.S. farm programs have functioned with a considerable degree of effectiveness, especially during the past decade. Not all price instability has been removed, nor can it be. To remove a significantly larger degree of price instability would require greater intervention by the government in markets than appears to be acceptable.

Managing Supplies at Acceptable Costs

There are two key questions here. How much is farm production being reduced by acreage controls? Could the required degree of supply management be achieved at significantly lower costs?

We do not know with any degree of exactness how much production would increase if acreages were not limited. It is probable that farm programs are currently having less impact upon the output of wheat, cotton, and the feed grains than they did during the 1960s. This is not said in criticism of the current programs because whatever degree of supply management that is now being achieved is consistent with relatively high levels of farm income. Whether this is due to good luck or good planning is, to some degree, beside the point.

Clearly, the magnitude of the set-aside or diverted acreage relative to total cropland harvested is not an accurate measure of the reduction in acreage of land devoted to the major farm crops. A direct comparison would imply that production has been reduced by about one-fifth from the potential level. Recent experience with changes in diverted acres (now called set-aside) indicates that planted area of wheat and feed grains changes relative to the diverted area in the ratio of approximately one to three. In other words, when the diverted area changes by 3 million acres, the planted area changes by about 1 million acres. Part of the "slippage" is due to the inclusion of much of the 37 million acres of summer fallow in the diverted area. The Mayer, Heady, and Madsen estimates of a free market in agriculture project only a 10-million-acre increase in the acreage of wheat, feed grains, soybeans, and cotton from a land base including a diverted area of 52 million acres. This implies an impact that is less than one to three terms in of the effectiveness of the diverted acres.

In the case of cotton, the federal programs since 1967 have had little effect on output. Thus the payments made under the cotton program now have to be considered almost entirely as income transfers and cannot be justified on the basis of any need to limit cotton production. Whether or not federal subsidies can be justified to expand cotton production is highly questionable.

For wheat and feed grains, some output restraint has apparently been imposed by recent programs. The Mayer, Heady, and Madsen study projected an increase in wheat and feed grain output of about 9 percent over 1966 and 1967 if the farm programs and payments were eliminated. But it significantly underestimated the growth in demand for soybeans. If there were no farm programs, the area that could be profitably devoted to soybeans in 1973-75 would be significantly higher than the 39.5 million acres they projected as the long-run equilibrium level. By 1972 the soybean acreage had increased to 47 million acres planted. We shall actually need some 55 to 60 million acres planted in soybeans to stabilize prices in 1973-75 midway between 1969 and 1973 levels. In fact, the 1972 feed grain and wheat programs have restricted the expansion of soybeans by providing a level of payments for voluntary acreage diversion so attractive as to impede expansion in soybean production. When more acreage was made available in 1971, most of it was planted to corn.

The degree of supply management being achieved on U.S. farms could be achieved at significantly lower cost, probably at about half the level of recent years. This would be done by limiting farm payments strictly to levels needed to get targeted acreage reductions. It would be desirable to modify the programs both administratively and by law in order to lower costs for two important reasons. The present high and visible level of costs and the large percentage of the payments that go to a relatively few farmers make the programs vulnerable to political criticism. The programs do help farmers, but unless costs are reduced, there is a high probability that they cannot gain necessary legislative approval indefinitely.

A further reason for lowering farm program costs by maintaining payments close to the levels absolutely required for supply management is to improve our bargaining position in future trade negotiations. Present payment levels are high enough to convince those with whom we shall negotiate that we are looking for expanded export outlets for highly subsidized farm products; our claim that we are seeking more favorable terms of access for low-cost farm products carries little weight under such circumstances.

Effects of Farm Programs on Resource Adjustment

Every line of work faces the need to adjust to changing conditions. The costs of adjusting are often high, but the costs of not adjusting are often greater. Farm people want to share in the general increase in incomes and living standards. With a relatively slow rate of growth in demand for farm products, this is possible only by continuous adjustments in the resources used in agriculture. If farm people are to match the relatively stable growth of returns to labor in the rest of the economy, the number of persons employed in agriculture will have to decline, both relative to employment in the rest of the economy and in absolute numbers. Those who remain in agriculture can increase their incomes only if they change methods of production, invest in resources that make farm labor more productive, and purchase current inputs that will increase the effectiveness of each hour of farm labor. It is not enough for the farm labor force to decline; a continuous reorganization of agriculture in terms of farm size, machinery, and other inputs is also essential.

There is a legitimate concern in all industrial economies that farm programs have helped keep too many resources in agriculture. It is not that the farm programs have brought new people into agriculture, or kept farmers from attractive occupations in other sectors. In all the industrial countries, the reduction in the number of farm

211

workers since the end of World War II has been so large that it is difficult to imagine that it could have been much greater. The U.S. farm labor force declined by more than 50 percent between 1950 and 1970. Farm programs have influenced the amounts of other resources engaged in agriculture—machinery, fertilizer, insecticides, and land and buildings—thus putting downward pressure on the labor force.

Evaluation of the effects of the U.S. farm programs on resource adjustments is largely impressionistic. The studies that would be required to provide reasonably precise answers do not exist. We do not believe that the major farm programs (wheat, feed grains, and cotton) have interfered to any significant degree with the required adjustments in the farm labor force. Some economists argue that this conclusion follows from the presumption that these programs have not substantially increased the return to labor engaged in producing these particular crops, thus leaving labor free to be attracted to other sectors.

In other cases, because farm output has been increased by a program above the level that would have prevailed in the absence of the program, farm employment has been maintained at a higher level, impeding to some degree adjustment in the labor force. But in such cases—manufactured dairy products, sugar, and peanuts—the farm programs do not appear to have influenced the rate at which the labor input per unit of output has declined over the past two decades. For example, the number of hours required to produce a hundredweight of milk declined by almost 70 percent between 1945-49 and 1966-70, and the hours required for a ton of sugar beets by slightly more. The time requirements for corn and grain sorghums also declined somewhat more than 70 percent, but the percentage decline for wheat was the same as for milk and sugar beets and, for beef and soybeans, rather less.

Where the acreage limitation programs have been effective, the farmer response has been to increase his use of inputs that are effective substitutes for land. If the area to be devoted to a crop is limited, farmers seek other means of increasing output. Under these circumstances more fertilizer, insecticides, and herbicides are used than if no restraint were placed upon the amount of land to be used. It is difficult to quantify the importance of this response by farmers.

For cotton, wheat, and the feed grains, the incentive to use more nonland inputs was reduced somewhat when price supports were lowered in the 1960s, and subsidy payments applied to only a part of the crop. For these crops some incentive may remain to use more inputs than would be profitable at market prices, in order to increase the claim to increased payments under the government program. Current yields have some effect upon future payment levels. But under the peanut, rice, and sugar programs, the incentive of high-price guarantees continues to induce greater use of yield-increasing inputs. The tobacco programs have been modified to some degree by the introduction of acreage-poundage quotas for flue-cured tobacco and poundage quotas for burley tobacco. The major reason for the change to poundage quotas was that continuing and rapid yield increases were requiring further reductions in the already small average size of tobacco acreage allotments.

While the result may have been unplanned, the nearly completed adjustments required in resources devoted to cotton have probably caused the least possible economic and social distress, at least for the period since World War II. In the late 1920s, about 20 percent of all the direct labor used in agriculture was in cotton; in the late 1960s, only 4 percent of direct farm labor was used for cotton production. There has been a substantial shift in cotton production from high-cost to low-cost areas. Total cotton output is not now much larger than it would be in the absence of the cotton program, although land devoted to cotton is more costly. It could be argued that a program designed specifically to facilitate resource adjustments in cotton production could have completed the task sooner, at lower cost to taxpayers and with a more equitable distribution of the burden of adjustment, which has fallen most heavily on hundreds of thousands of poorly educated croppers and hired farm workers, who were literally forced off the land without compensation. And there remain the problems of the capitalized value of the cotton allotments and how the impact of the possible elimination of the cotton payments on the capital structure of agriculture in cotton-producing areas could be minimized.

There are now relatively limited excess resources in the wheat- and feed-grain-producing sectors, even though some 50 to 60 million acres are diverted for federal payments to grain farmers. In part this is due to developments that are external to the government programs, namely, the continuing growth in demand for soybeans and beef. In addition, developments in foreign markets for feed grains and wheat since 1960 have reduced the extent of excess resources. Excess resources in the wheat and feed grain areas, even in normal times, are certainly less than implied by the acreage restraints that have been imposed under the federal programs until 1973. The acreage set aside in 1972 was more than one-third as large as the acreage harvested from wheat and feed grains. Yet, in 1973, when little land has been set aside, grain production will probably increase by no more than 10 percent and perhaps not that much if soybean acreage and production expand as rapidly as demand. Cattle production will also be increased somewhat on land diverted from crops under program features in effect in 1973.

Prior to 1973, certain features of the wheat and feed grain programs restricted the use of resources for beef and soybeans. Beef production has been restrained by the limitation on the pasturing of diverted land during the five principal months of the growing season. The secretary of agriculture has the authority to modify this provision, but only if he can determine that such grazing "will not adversely affect farm income." This has now been done for 1973.

If soybean output continues to lag behind demand growth in the years ahead, output of competing crops will increase, and the search for substitute sources of protein will become more extensive. There is danger that past efforts to achieve short-run income gains for beef and soybean producers will result in long-run income losses and will contribute to higher operational costs of the feed grain and wheat programs.

Except in quite abnormal circumstances, it is always difficult to relax restrictions or to modify them in a governmental program when one or several groups of farmers might gain, and when actual or potential losses may be imposed upon other groups not now benefitting from the program. Ranchers who specialize in calf production are generally opposed to permitting farmers in the wheat and feed grain programs to pasture diverted acres during the main growing season, since this would have some adverse effect upon calf prices over time. But if efficient and relatively full use is to be made of our agricultural resources, and if unnecessary federal costs are to be avoided, such conflicts must be and should be resolved when market conditions are as favorable as they are in the 1970s. The administrative actions taken early in 1973 to expand beef and soybean production are encouraging in this respect.

Improving the Export Capability of U.S. Agriculture

It is possible to improve the export capability of agriculture in two direct ways:

1. to provide the setting for the organization of a more efficient agriculture through research and education, minimum interference with the allocation of resources by farmers, maintenance of competition and efficiency in the provision of inputs produced in the rest of the economy, and by providing the institutional setting for the efficient marketing of farm products to both domestic and foreign consumers;

2. to provide from public funds, or through multiple pricing systems, the means to meet competing prices in international markets.

The United States has followed both approaches in varying degrees over the past two decades. During the 1950s substantial emphasis was given to concessional sales of farm products. Grains and cotton moved into commercial exports only because export subsidies were available to bridge the gap between domestic market prices and export prices. With the important changes made in the farm programs during the 1960s, when price supports were reduced to levels that were expected to permit unsubsidized sales for export, the costs of export subsidies declined significantly. But some export subsidy programs remain (although subsidy quotations were suspended in 1973) when there appears to be little or no justification for their continuation. The export subsidy on wheat has been difficult to justify for several years, since the price support has been at levels that would have permitted exports without subsidy. The payment levels under the wheat program appear adequate to meet a reasonable income level for wheat producers without the price escalation sometimes due directly to unwise use of export subsidies. The main effect of the wheat export subsidy has been to increase the domestic market price of wheat, though some would argue that the subsidies have also been required to compete with the monopoly systems of other major exporters.

The rapid and substantial increase in the size of per bushel wheat export subsidies during mid-1972 surely served no useful purpose. Based upon errors in assessing world demand for wheat, it provided the wrong signals to both producers and buyers. If the supply of wheat were inadequate to meet demand at existing prices, the price of export wheat should have been permitted to increase to reflect this fact. If the supply of wheat were adequate to meet demand at existing prices, the speculative fever in the domestic market should not have been aided and abetted by increasing the export subsidy to make up any difference between domestic and export prices.

It is a continuing anomaly that while export subsidies were abandoned for cotton after 1965, and essentially so for the feed grains after 1962, exports of wheat have been subsidized in every year since that time. In some years all wheat exports were subsidized. The average size of the subsidy has been reduced significantly, though in both 1966 and 1972 the size of the subsidy became substantial at the same time that export demand was relatively strong. The increasing market orientation of U.S. farm programs makes it possible to terminate the wheat subsidy permanently in 1973. Recent actions suspending export subsidies for rice, tobacco, poultry, and lard may help to hold the line against reinstating the wheat subsidy in 1973 or 1974.

Alternatively, the United States could follow a much more aggressive policy of export subsidization than it has, but this would be most unfortunate. The United States, or any other industrial country, should go beyond minimizing or eliminating her use of subsidies on exports. The general trend toward a less aggressive export subsidy policy that has occurred in recent years can be commended, but it has not been accompanied by the liberalization of imports of agricultural products. There were a small number of meaningful reductions in tariff duties on farm products during the Kennedy Round, but there have been no general reductions on import quotas on manufactured dairy products, peanuts, or sugar. And the imposition of U.S. meat import quotas during the Kennedy Round was hardly helpful in buttressing efforts to achieve a reduction of trade barriers for farm products.

There are a number of positive elements in U.S. agricultural policy in relation to world trade. Stabilization of prices and supplies of several important farm commodities and a general, though not universal, willingness to explore the possibilities of accepting increased imports when such imports would compete effectively with domestic production are constructive aspects. As we shall argue later, a negotiating effort cannot be built entirely upon increasing exports; there must also be a willingness to provide reasonable access to imports. The agricultural policies of the United States must take account of the legitimate interests of other countries as well as our own.

AGRICULTURE IN A GENERAL TRADE NEGOTIATION

The basic problems of world agriculture obviously are much deeper than conflicts in trade policies. Governments in all major trading countries and many of the developing countries intervene in agricultural markets, technological innovation, land utilization, incomes of farmers, and other aspects of farming. These policies are aimed at not only technical and economic objectives, they are aimed also toward social and political objectives. Among the social and political considerations to which governments often give heavy weight are the balance between rural and urban income levels, the employment opportunities available as alternatives to farming, the conservation of land, the rural environment, a stable supply of food for national populations including insurance against shortages generated in other parts of the world, and the basic political balance between rural and urban areas. These are critical determinants of policies, and trade measures are often only instruments or residuals of more basic domestic policies. Proposals for trade policy changes must also recognize that balancing world production with world demand and ensuring that the global food supply is distributed equitably among the world's people are essential objectives.

The interaction of measures taken by one country with the measures taken by other countries compounds the problems in trade.

Lacking generally accepted rules to guide national farm policies, and often able to lay blame on the policies of other nations, governments have been encouraged to solve their agricultural problems without regard to external implications—and indeed to solve them by pushing some of the required adjustments on to farmers and traders in other nations. These are not theoretical charges. United States cotton subsidies and the levy on grain imports by the EC fit this pattern exactly, as to other policies on all sides. Conflicts over their respective national farm policies cause continuing difficulties among nations. Political tensions mount, and costly defensive measures are taken, as in the late "Chicken War."

National farm policies are economically inefficient in a variety of ways. They often discourage needed adjustments in the mix of products grown, in land use, and in labor. When farm policies in major producing countries generate surpluses of products that had been important in trade by encouraging additional production and discouraging consumption through high price supports, they distort farm economies abroad as well. Stimulating production and reducing consumption in one country results at first in reduced imports. This may be followed by a transition from importing to exporting, usually with the aid of export subsidies—further intensifying the adjustment difficulties of other nations. This, in turn, causes the affected nations to erect protective mechanisms to insulate their own markets from the depressed world prices generated by the price support system of the first country. Or the nations react by introducing export aids of their own, and world prices tumble further.

While agricultural policies are aimed at domestic objectives, they affect social and political conditions in other countries. These political interactions among nations have lately caused considerable diplomatic friction, brought about a deterioration of the atmosphere of international economic cooperation, and have intensified dangerous political schisms. Moreover, it has been made clear that for some governments, further efforts to improve general trade relations and to liberalize other sectors of world trade depend politically on substantial improvement in agricultural trade conditions. Even more disquieting is the growing awareness that failure to improve the conditions of agricultural trade may well result in intensification of protectionist sentiment on world trade generally.

Farmers in all countries have a number of basic interests, including,
1. an adequate level of income for their effort and invested capital,
2. reasonably assured market outlets,
3. reasonably stable prices as safeguards against the inevitable risks of farm production, and
4. a way of life at least as satisfactory as that of other groups.

The problem is how to advance the common interests of farm people, not that of one group of farmers at the expense of other farmers. Governments should give more attention to increasing the real value and volume of agricultural production for the world as a whole, rather than attempting to restrict markets by barriers and high consumer prices. Since conflicting national agricultural policies are deeply rooted in domestic affairs and politics, identifying and dealing with the common national interests will inevitably be a long and arduous process. But it is the essential first step.

Improving the climate for world agricultural production and trade must involve recommendations and actions that take into account the basic social and political limitations governments face. Few governments could accept measures that would reduce most family incomes in agricultural areas, and none has yet found the means of helping small farmers without helping large farmers more. Most governments believe it essential to pursue the long-run objective of raising farmers' incomes, so that average pay for farm work and for comparable work in industry or services is more nearly equal. It is usually recognized that improving farmers' incomes requires a decline in the number of people engaged in farm production and, in the future, direct employment capacity of the agricultural sector.

Liberalization of trade in recent decades has not covered trade in agricultural products to any significant degree. There is continued widespread use of quantitative restrictions, export subsidies, special protective levies, and nontariff restrictions of other types. The international rules governing trade in agricultural products are less comprehensive, more ambiguous, and less strict than those governing industrial trade. Where there are rules, they are often ignored.

The General Agreement on Tariffs and Trade (GATT) prohibits special protective measures for agriculture, except where domestic production restraint measures are applied. The idea behind the GATT exception is simply that a price support program backed up by production controls is less likely to interfere with trade than a support program without production restraint. If domestic production is limited, imports should not be allowed a "free ride" into the market that has a limitation on domestic supply. The GATT exception was written at least in part to make allowance for U.S. farm policies in the late 1940s. The United States, unfortunately, thought this exception was not sufficient for her own needs and in the 1950s achieved adoption of a waiver of her agricultural obligations under GATT. The waiver continues to exist and is pointed to by many countries as one of the most serious flaws in the GATT structure and is noted when the United States argues for greater adherence to international rules.

Some believe that the results of trade liberalization are in themselves desirable, though liberalization is not the only important policy objective. Others doubt that liberalization in itself will necessarily bring about socially desirable ends and could even impede the achievement of these ends. Further, it is thought by proponents of this latter view that a degree of organization of markets will always be necessary in the agricultural sector. Nonetheless, it is widely agreed that the existence of differences regarding basic trade liberalization philosophy should not impede the search for practical solutions at this time. Even with the differences in basic positions and outlook, it is necessary that the various points of view be brought into harmony in respect to particular pragmatic suggestions. Certain possibilities for common action and agreement on common objectives do emerge from discussions of the trade problem.

Moreover, trade and production problems do vary from one commodity to another, and from one country to another. Forms of protection vary, as do aids to farmers or traders. Problems of seasonal trade in fruits and vegetables differ from problems of long-run cereals production and trade. Given the great complexity of farm policies and the fact that strongly held domestic national policies are involved, a degree of pragmatism and particularly of approach is essential. On the other hand, particular solutions are difficult to reach in the absence of some general guidelines or agreed objectives.

Approaches to Negotiations

An approach at this time that is not successful in making significant progress toward achieving worthwhile objectives will be counterproductive. The industrial nations should commit themselves to the ambitious objective of substantially lowering the levels of protection for farm products over a designated period of years, in order to considerably expand trade and improve consumer welfare. The objectives must be long run because of the need to provide time for farmers to adjust to changing conditions, and to allow governments to devise programs to prevent significant declines in farm incomes where changes in policy might lead to such declines. Because of the many changes that must be made in domestic farm policies of the industrial countries for trade, income, and budgetary reasons, achieving the long-run objective of a substantial reduction in the level of protection for agricultural products might well require longer than the remainder of this decade. But it should begin now.

Unless there is agreement on the desired direction of change, it is unlikely that a round of negotiations in the next year or two would lead to anything but frustration and acrimony. The new round of negotiations will be conducted during the early stages of the transition established for the enlargement of the EC from 1973 to 1975. Because of the complexities involved in integrating the farm policies of the three new participants in the CAP, radical changes in that policy should not be expected in the short run. It is reasonable, however, for other trading nations to expect that some of the trade restricting and diverting effects of EC enlargement be given attention over the next two or three years. And in fact in the EC there are already indications of reconsideration of certain aspects of the CAP as it applies to a larger Community. The issues raised by enlargement are noted primarily to indicate that negotiations will have to deal quite pragmatically with what is feasible in the short term as well as with agreement on long-term objectives and eventual means of achieving them.

There must be a beginning if there is to be an ending. The beginning, in our view, should be an effort to agree upon a number of rather broad general principles or objectives and the ground rules under which the negotiations should take place. The remainder of this chapter will discuss these codes of conduct as well as two alternative methods of approaching the trade negotiations. The two alternatives presented are both consistent with the more general objectives and ground rules discussed first. One alternative, however, accepts agricultural trade liberalization as a major objective that should be approached as rapidly as possible, given the many policy and resource adjustments that are required. The other, which can be said to represent the views of our European colleagues who worked on this study, emphasizes market organization and gradual trade expansion, but requires no international commitment to the eventual elimination of protection for agricultural products.

Basic Objectives and Codes of Conduct

We believe that agreement on certain basic objectives and codes of conduct before negotiations start would provide the basis for a fruitful exchange of ideas and lead to graduated reductions in trade distortions over an extended time span. The purpose would be to avoid the kind of unproductive confrontation that occurred during the Kennedy Round, when much of the discussion consisted of little more than the various governments describing their own agricultural policies, and articulating the reasons why they believed they were already doing the right thing.

There is a need for continuing discussion and consultation on trade problems. This could occur in one or more international organizations as well as bilaterally. The purpose of such discussions would be to consider principles of conduct for and common objectives between the trading nations and to clearly outline the interrelation of those principles and objectives with the actions of individual governments. While such discussions should precede or be the first step in the new round of negotiations, it is envisaged that machinery might be devised that would function over a long period of time, since few, if any, of the major issues in agricultural policy and trade are going to be fully resolved at any one time.

As one of the first steps, it would be useful to devise a behavioral principle that might channel government actions and provide a basis for meaningful consultations. The suggested principle is: It should be agreed that agricultural measures taken should not involve a transfer of costs of adjustments to farmers and traders of other nations, except on an agreed basis.

As regards the policies and measures themselves in relation to the apparent social objectives of governments, some principles might be agreed internationally that would help governments domestically. One such principle could be: Structural adjustment in agriculture should continue and should be accelerated wherever possible. If this were explicitly agreed, it would provide a basis for international discussions of the nature and effectiveness of alternative structural adjustment measures. For example, is a proposed measure likely to significantly increase the production of a commodity already in surplus? Or would the measure assist in transferring productive resources to products with a growing demand? As matters now stand, examination of the structural programs of another nation is considered in many quarters to be illegitimate interference in the internal policies of that nation.

With structural adjustment proceeding satisfactorily, it could be generally agreed that: Support measures in each country or region should be such as to ensure a measure of stability of prices at levels designed to provide reasonably efficient farmers with a return for their labor, management, and investment comparable with that achieved in other sectors of the economy.

Efforts should be made to devise social and economic measures that have minimal adverse effects on other nations. In this direction, it might be further agreed in principle that: Measures of support should be tailored more precisely to social objectives (that is, income distribution) and that an effort should be made to alter the form of support in order that production and sale may become more market oriented and compatible with expanding consumption.

This would be an important principle, because it would result in changing some methods of support—but not necessarily in the case of every product nor of every country. It would involve, for example, tailoring support measures to benefit the relatively disadvantaged farmers or relatively disadvantaged regions, without windfalls and undesirable excessive incentives to stimulate production by high-income and large-scale farmers.

The particular support measures that have been developed in many industrial countries have failed to recognize that the cost and quality of food is important to any sound national social policy, as well as to sound national economic policies. There has been a distinct tendency to distort the relative incentives as between higher-protein foods (especially meats) and the more traditional basic commodities. Production is stimulated in products for which demand is growing relatively slowly, if at all, while products for which the demand prospects are much better—indeed, very promising—are subject to disincentives and trade restrictions. For example, current meat shortages in restricted markets make little economic or social sense, and an effort to alter the balance of incentives as between cereals and meat would benefit all countries. An effort should be made to reach agreement on the principle that: A better balance should be developed between the measures used to aid individual commodities, so that products for which there is relatively high prospect for increased demand are given greater encouragement, while those that appear to be in surplus in the light of world market conditions and prospects are subject to gradually reduced absolute and relative incentives.

Going beyond statements of general principles, there should be an effort to reach agreement on the objectives and scope of the negotiations. It might be agreed that it is important to develop a yardstick to be used as a guide for determining the degree of protection, especially in the most protected sectors and then to set the pace at which protection would be reduced. A considerable part of the inefficiency in the use of agricultural resources is due to some products being accorded very high rates of effective protection relative to the average for that country. What is sought here is that the discussions should give emphasis first to those farm products with relatively high rates of protection and where high-cost production situations prevail.

The approach to reducing protection where it is the highest could be elaborated in the form of explicit rules obliging nations to move further in the desired directions at regular intervals and in measured steps. Such rules might also be linked to the degree of self-sufficiency. Thus, where there is an increase in the self-sufficiency ratio in the case of products subject to reductions in relative protection, the rate of reduction of the support level might be accelerated. An increase in self-sufficiency in such instances would indicate that trade was being harmed by a perverse development in domestic production.

An effort should be made to devise operationally meaningful rules for the regulation of export subsidies and other aids to exports. Where export aids are determined on the basis of competitive offer prices, as has been the occasional or general procedure of the United States and the European Economic Community (EEC), there is no real control on the extent of subsidization. Perhaps it would be possible to introduce collective discipline among the major trading nations, with respect to export subsidies and other aids and on stockholding. While different forms of price support rely in varying degrees upon export aids to dispose of excess output, there is clearly a common desire not only among the major industrial nations but also among the developing countries to halt predatory and trade-disrupting use of export aids. Yet it must be kept in mind that the establishment of export subsidies generally occurs when internal supports raise prices above world levels. Export subsidies will not be needed when price supports are lower.

Other extensions of this pragmatic approach to increasing trade in farm products and minimizing irritations among nations would include efforts to reduce or eliminate quantitative restrictions, wide and uncertain fluctuations in border charges, erratic behavior by state-trading organizations, and health and sanitary regulations designed primarily to restrict trade. There should be discussion and clarification of criteria for valuation, classification, quality requirements, and other conditions of entry, and such rules and regulations as do exist should be in such a form as to be publicly explainable. Changes in such regulations should only be made after adequate public notice, with full opportunity to explore the trade effects, is made.

These are some of the undertakings that might both lay the groundwork for successful negotiations and provide a forum in which a wide variety of issues affecting agricultural trade could be fruitfully discussed and the basis for further negotiations created.

In any event, it seems wise to conclude at this stage in international relations that gradual movement in the direction of more efficient use of world resources is better than movement in other directions, that control of political conflicts and moderation of mercantilistic tendencies is better than a vicious cycle of protectionist actions and counteractions, and that aiming social policies at those who need help is better than wasting scarce economic resources through vaguely defined policies that provide most of their benefits to those who need them least. This approach recognizes the fact that change will come slowly, but the stipulation of general long-term objectives, together with a series of small but concrete steps in the direction of those objectives, might be the best way to get moving.

We turn now to two alternative approaches to trade negotiations. As will become clear, the alternatives would result in quite different modes of conduct of international trade in farm products. The first presents a plan for organizing and stabilizing the international markets through a series of agreements with respect to the international prices of the major temperate zone farm products. But consistent with the principles and objectives outlined above, the first alternative provides for continuous consultations and the acceptance of responsibility by governments to modify domestic programs when stocks grow to undesirable levels. The second alternative accepts trade liberalization as a major, albeit long-run, objective and presents methods that are designed to permit the achievement of appropriate social objectives and income for farm people as well as to minimize costs for consumers and taxpayers.

Organization of International Markets

The first alternative is a plan designed to serve as a basis for agricultural cooperation. The principles underlying the plan and the implications of the plan for exporters, importers, and developing countries are presented first; then the basic elements of the plan are discussed.

If any solution to the world agricultural problems is to result from the forthcoming world trade negotiations, it must respect a number of principles. First, the solution must not be biased in favor of any particular group of countries. Second, it must provide reciprocal benefits as well as reciprocal obligations. Third, nations and regional groupings must retain their freedom to determine their agricultural policies subject to constraints that are freely undertaken in accordance with international agreements. Fourth, these constraints must be such as are likely to be respected by national executives and legislatures. Fifth, the solution must have regard for the interests of developing as well as to those of developed countries. Sixth, while recognizing that consumers desire to buy their food as cheaply as possible, the policy must have consideration for the basic need of home producers of a fair return for their efforts and capital investment. Finally, considering that resource adjustment in agriculture is a relatively slow process and that there are inelasticities on the part of both supply and demand, and allowing also for the varying economic and social contexts in which agriculture operates in different countries, the solution must recognize that the laws of economics and, in particular, the principle of comparative advantage do not work smoothly in agriculture.

Implications for Exporters, Importers, and Developing Countries

In order to have any chance of acceptance, the plan must endeavor to fulfill the following aspirations of exporting countries:

1. It must provide them with some assurance of continued access to their traditional markets.

2. It must provide some safeguard for their exports against competitive dumping in third markets.
3. It must give them some knowledge of the future potential for their exports, thereby enabling them to adapt their domestic production policies to the prospective total of domestic and export demand. A sharing of this production adjustment burden is also important.

For importing countries, any acceptable plan must fulfill the following:
1. Put an end to competition at arbitrarily low and uneconomic prices, which result in great difficulties for domestic producers and national exchequers.
2. Enable such countries to establish farm prices at levels that take proper account of the income needs of their producers.
3. Have regard to the fact that accumulation of stocks may lead the national or regional authorities concerned to institute limiting measures.
4. Place limits on the extent of export subsidies (restitutions).

To be acceptable to developing countries, certain criteria must also be fulfilled. To the extent that such countries wish to increase their earnings for primary commodities, international price stability must be provided. Second, the developing countries must have some assurance from the industrial countries that their policies will ensure a degree of access for products of the former. Third, developing countries still dependent upon imports of food will require assurances that such imports do not disturb their own efforts to increase their agricultural production.

The plan set out below is designed initially to be applied, according to the particular circumstances of the commodity, to a limited number of temperate zone products. Some of these would naturally be of direct interest also to the developing countries. The commodities for which agreements are contemplated are grains, dairy products, certain oilseeds, sugar, and meat, though for the present the last commodity is not a priority sector. The principles of this arrangement could be extended, however, to include agricultural products of the tropical zone.

Elements of the Plan

An international reference price would be agreed for ordinary commercial transactions for, say, a three-year period. This price would be for an appropriate grade or quality of the product at a base point or a series of base points.

The trading price would be fixed somewhere between the lowest existing export price in a main exporting country and the highest

225

producer price, also in an important producing area. For example, in the case of wheat, the price could be fixed somewhere between the U.S. price and the producer price in the EC. In order to narrow the debate as to where the price should be fixed, it might be agreed in advance of the negotiation that the point should lie in the range of one-third to two-thirds of the existing gap between the highest and lowest prices, but this would have to be related to the ability of exporting countries to meet the reference price.

In assessing the level of existing prices, account would be taken of any direct grants or subsidies that could be measurably attributed to the commodity. Grants of a general or structural character would not, however, be taken into account.

A lower, second-tier international reference price would be determined to apply to noncommercial transactions. Entitlement to supplies at this price would be governed by strict rules.

Within the limits of the criteria set out below, the agricultural support policies for participating countries or areas would still be determined by the governments and/or authorities responsible for these countries and areas. However, the reconciliation between these policies and the needs of the international community would be sought by adhering to the following criteria:

1. Each contracting nation or region would be free to vary the level of its price guarantees or other commodity commitments to allow for changes in the level of farm incomes in the area as a whole, changes in the particular commodity sector, and changes in production costs and other relevant factors.

2. Exporting countries would undertake to sell their product abroad at no less than the agreed international reference prices for commercial transactions (subject to point 5 below).

3. Self-sufficient countries or areas and net importing countries that occasionally produce more than their domestic needs would also agree to abide by the international reference price for their exports on world markets.

4. A generalized agreement would be made by all participating countries to pursue trading policies that would, as far as possible, assure an orderly expansion of trade within the boundaries set by the agreed international reference prices.

5. The lower-tier reference price would apply to purchases by developing countries that undertake to observe the conditions of participation in the plan. Such countries would, for example, have to accept supervision by the appropriate international commodity council to ensure that such purchases were not being made for resale on the world market at the higher reference commerical price. Care would also have to be taken that the developing country did not use lower-priced imports as substitutes for its own home production, which

would then be reexported at the higher commercial price. The financing of noncommercial transactions would be a matter primarily for the international lending or aid agencies concerned (World Food Program, special loans or grants).

6. In order to respect the international reference prices, participating countries would agree to hold additional stocks as and when this became necessary (see below).

Although agreements would, in principle, be negotiated for three-year periods, participating governments, through the medium of an international commodity council, would undertake an annual review of the operation of each arrangement. These governments should be free to make variations in reference prices should the need arise as a result of production and trade developments that occurred in the course of the preceding year.

The critical elements in this plan are the acceptance of the obligations to acquire and hold stocks of any commodity for which supply exceeds the demand at the reference price and to adhere to the international reference price in all exports and imports. Those who support this alternative do not believe that the main agricultural trading nations of the world are ready to accept the principle of direct international supervision of their national agricultural policies. There is, however, an increasing awareness of the fact that something more must be done than in the past to ensure that national policies, or policies for regional groupings such as the EEC, have greater regard for world production and trade considerations. When prices fell or threatened to fall to the international reference price, governments would be required to intervene in the market by acquiring stocks.

Operationally, an international council would determine how much of a product would be taken off the market and added to stocks. The responsibility of each government would be determined by a formula agreed upon in advance. One formula would measure the obligation by the degree to which current production of the commodity in the participating country or regional grouping exceeded output in an agreed base period. An alternative would be for an international council to establish the quantities to be stocked by each country on the basis of various negotiated criteria, for example, self-sufficiency rate over a reference period, existing stocks over a reference period, exports of principal countries concerned, and so on. If excess stocks were accumulated because output was expanding more than demand, governments would be obligated, largely for budgetary reasons, to modify support policies so that their country did not contribute further to the accumulation of stocks.

This plan is designed to add stability to international markets, with respect to both prices and quantities. It is also designed to impose costs upon governments of countries that follow policies that

227

expand the output of farm products when world supply exceeds demand at the agreed reference price. Thus, while governments would be left free to determine the level of support for agriculture, there would be discipline over their actions due to their acceptance of the obligation to add to stocks when required in order to protect the reference price. Those who support this plan believe that it would result in a significant and orderly expansion of international trade in farm products.

Phased Trade Liberalization

A second alternative was advanced by those who felt that it was appropriate in the forthcoming round of negotiations for governments to commit themselves to achieving the same degree of trade liberalization for farm products as for industrial products. This alternative rests on the assumption that governments, given both a firm commitment and adequate time, can devise policies and programs that will achieve their economic, social, and political objectives for farm people and rural life without requiring significant interferences with trade and thus not imposing significant costs upon the farmers of other nations. This is clearly an approach for the long run, but it is an approach that assumes gradual but consistent progress toward a goal of trade liberalization for farm products.

This alternative rests on the explicit assumption that in the long run there are the same advantages to be derived from specialization in the production of agricultural products as in industrial products. The view, often expressed in Western Europe, that highly developed and industrial countries such as the United States and the EC should not have a surplus of basic agricultural products such as grains and that trade in farm products should be restricted to quality products requiring highly specialized farming is clearly inconsistent with this alternative. Such a view is a negation of the advantages of trade, since it follows from this view that highly developed and industrial countries should not have an export surplus of such basic and mass-produced items as automobiles, radios, television, desk calculators, steel, and aluminum. These items, or reasonable substitutes for them, can be produced in most industrial countries at cost disadvantages far smaller than those that now prevail for many basic agricultural products.

It is not implied that the social, economic, and political concerns of farm people are to be neglected. Quite the contrary. This alternative requires that, perhaps for the first time, the industrial nations consider in detail and with compassion what the effects of current farm policies have upon the low-income and relatively disadvantaged groups in agriculture, and actively search for different ways of meeting the most important problems of farm people. Continuing to rely upon higher price supports or higher payments mostly to prosperous farmers will not do.

This alternative requires a search for farm programs to facilitate adjustment while achieving social objectives rather than impede adjustments while ignoring social and economic objectives (including the level and distribution of income) and further polarizing income distribution among farmers.

A Suitable Environment for Negotiations

The prospects for successful negotiations would improve if it were possible to move away from the traditional and narrow export-oriented motivations such as have guided previous negotiations. Nations must move toward acceptance of objectives that give full weight to the mutual benefits of economic interdependence in terms of economic efficiency and growth, consumer welfare, and good international relationships. While major reforms of the ways in which industrial countries manage their agricultures are required, the negotiations must recognize the validity of the basic objectives of present farm policies. The negotiations should be the vehicle by which agreement is reached concerning alternative means for achieving the goals of domestic farm programs in ways that do not artificially stimulate production, restrict consumption, or impose heavy financial burdens upon consumers, taxpayers, and other countries. The negotiations should recognize that farm people everywhere face difficult adjustments and that governments cannot afford, either morally or politically, to abandon efforts to provide opportunities for farm people equivalent to those enjoyed by other members of their economy with respect to education, health, social security, culture, economic stability, general income maintenance, and assistance in meeting changing conditions.

Perhaps the most important barriers to thoughtful consideration of the liberalization of agricultural trade is uncertainty—uncertainty on the part of farmers and policy makers about the effects of freer trade in farm products. Very little has been done to understand what adjustments would be required of farmers in the United States and the EC if the current programs were modified or phased out as a result of a multilateral agreement to do so.

As an example, it is generally recognized that if feed costs were lower in Western Europe, there would be a substantial expansion in the demand for and production of livestock products. What is not known is how much the increase in production of livestock products would increase the demand for farm resources and how the magnitude of this increase would compare with the loss in demand for resources used in the production of wheat and other grains. Some very rough estimates, based on labor requirements for grain and livestock in the United States, indicate that if there were a 10-percent increase in the production of meat and milk in the EC as a result of lower grain prices, the increase in labor requirements would more than offset a reduction of one-fourth in total cereals production. And this estimate did not take into account the additional labor required for the added production of hay and roughage required for the larger output of livestock products. There could be no certainty, of course, that the particular farm workers released from cereals production would find employment in livestock production. The 10-percent increase in consumption is based on the Food and Agricultural Organization (FAO) estimate of the decrease in consumption of milk and meat that is expected to occur in the United Kingdom (UK) as a result of entry into the EC. Since there is evidence that farmers in the EC have a comparative advantage in the production of most livestock products, the fear that reducing the protection on grain in the EC would force a large net exodus of labor from the farms may be a fear without foundation. We do not claim that our rough estimates are sufficient to arrive at a conclusion on this matter, but to the best of our knowledge, no systematic study of this sort has been undertaken. It is possible that if such a study were made, it would change opinions of both farmers and policy makers concerning the effects of freer trade on the agriculture of Western Europe.

Those who submit this alternative believe that it is the responsibility of governments and farm organizations, prior to the completion of negotiations, to provide their farmers and other citizens with relevant analyses of the effects of their current farm programs, of what the anticipated future effects would be if the programs are unchanged for several years, and of the effects on their agriculture of a gradual move to free trade or a limited degree of protection of agriculture. Studies should be undertaken by farm groups and individual governments, as well as by a special study group brought together by an international organization such as FAO or the Organization for Economic Cooperation and Development (OECD), to determine as objectively as possible

1. the degree of protection provided for agriculture,
2. the effects of the protection upon output, consumption, and trade for a recent period,
3. the long-run effects of current policies on farm employment and the returns to labor and other resources engaged in agriculture,
4. the importance of nonfarm sources of income to the farm population and possible future developments in the amount of such income,
5. the likely effects of freer trade on production, consumption, trade, farm employment, and incomes, and

6. the present and anticipated costs of alternative farm programs, with emphasis on the expected costs of current programs compared to programs that would assist farmers in adjusting to freer trade.

Admittedly, it is not possible to obtain precise results in each of these areas, but we do not think that this justifies failure to either support or undertake studies that would provide the best results that current information and methods of analysis permit.

We have a basic faith in the rationality and reasonableness of farm and urban people; we believe that if both groups are provided with the information that is necessary for making a decision, one can have confidence in that decision. This does not mean that if farmers had all the relevant information, their views of appropriate policy measures might not conflict with the interests of other members of the population. But democratic governments should make every reasonable effort to provide information and analyses that will help their citizens to make informed public decisions. By and large, governments have been unwilling to engage in systematic evaluation of their farm programs and to consider a variety of alternatives to them—or if they have, they have kept such evaluations secret. Some agricultural adjustment problems arise because of unrealistic expectations of farmers created by political promises or programs that cannot achieve their objectives.

Perhaps the most important requirements for a suitable environment for negotiations is the recognition of governments and farm people that it is necessary at this time to explore and consider new and different means of meeting the needs of farm people for a satisfactory level of income, a reasonable degree of stability and security, access to adequate education for their children, and a satisfactory social and cultural setting for rural life. So much of the resources of government have gone into maintaining prices or payments at high levels that too little emphasis has been given to other aspects of rural life, including providing rural young people with the education that would permit them to compete effectively with urban youth in job markets or in competition for places in colleges and universities.

What Should Be Negotiated?

Negotiations designed to achieve a substantial liberalization of trade in farm products should be concerned with two major objectives:
1. achieving an agreement on the procedures for achieving gradual and staged reductions in the degree of protection, and
2. achieving agreement on appropriate measures for meeting the legitimate economic, social, and political objectives of farm

231

people that would have acceptable and minimal impacts upon production, consumption, and trade.

The primary emphasis in the negotiations for reducing protection should be on the amount of protection rather than the form of protection. Too much time and emotion have been wasted in criticizing and justifying variable levies or Section 22 import quotas. The basic problem is not primarily that the levies are variable or that the import quotas have negated tariff reductions or standstills. The basic problem is that the levies or quotas have been a part of farm programs that resulted in high prices and restriction of trade.

This view suggests that energy should be devoted to developing a common yardstick for measuring protection. One of the important aspects of the studies referred to above was to undertake the measurement of protection, not for the purpose of proving which country provided the most or least protection, but to serve as an information base for conducting negotiations and, equally important, to indicate to farm people, farm organizations, and legislators where the greatest adjustments would be required if trade were liberalized.

Due to the complexity of programs used to protect agriculture and the numerous economic interrelationships in production of farm products, it is difficult to devise a simple measure of the degree of protection. If the only means of protection were higher prices, the task would be less difficult, though it would be by no means easy to devise a meaningful measure in this case. One yardstick, suggested during the Kennedy Round, became known as the montant de soutien (MDS). The idea was to measure the difference between the price that a farmer in a given country receives and the world market price. Where the world market price may be lower than what might be reasonably felt to be the cost of efficient producers, because of distortions resulting from government policies, a negotiated "reference price" could be developed. Except for the introduction of the reference price, the MDS is the same as that which the economists call nominal protection—the percentage excess of domestic prices over import or export prices.

A major difficulty with the use of nominal protection, especially if it is to serve as a guide to farmers as well as to negotiators, is that it may indicate a substantial degree of protection, where in fact little or none exists. For example, the nominal protection for pork production in the EC was estimated to be about 50 percent in 1968. Yet when one takes into account the higher feed prices that must be paid by pork producers in the EC, the real or effective protection of pork production and the transformation of feed and other inputs into pork may be zero or very nearly so. Thus if it were felt that because pork production in the EC is very efficient, which it appears to be, the nominal protection of pork could be reduced at a faster rate than the nominal protection for grain, this would be a mistake. And if the emphasis were put upon nominal protection, this could mislead pork producers in the EC because they might interpret the measure as an indication that as trade liberalization occurred, it would be necessary for them to reduce pork production. In fact, under free trade or more liberal trade in farm products, pork production would increase in the EC to meet the increase in demand due to the lower prices to consumers.

A more complicated but more meaningful concept of protection is effective protection. This is a measure of the protection of the value added to a given sector. It requires a measurement of the value added at domestic and world prices and a comparison of the former with the latter. Using pork as an example, the value added by pork production is the difference between the price received and the current inputs purchased from the rest of the economy or transferred from the rest of agriculture. In other words, it is the gross return to labor and capital used in production of pork and excludes the cost of feed (whether purchased or not), medicines, and any other current input purchases. One estimate would be made at domestic prices and the other at world prices for both the output (pork) and the principal inputs (various kinds of feed). Where the nominal rates of protection differ by so much, as they do for feed and pork in the EC, it may turn out that while the nominal rate of protection is fairly high for pork, the effective protection may be near zero, or it could be negative. If it were negative, it would mean that the higher pork price in the EC did not fully compensate for the higher feed or grain prices.

An advantage of the effective protection concept compared to nominal protection is that it permits an easier means of including direct payments such as used in the cotton, feed grain, and wheat programs in the United States. It is not impossible to include such payments in the concept of nominal protection, by determining the average payment per unit of output, but this may give a misleading indication because it ignores the costs of cultivating diverted land as well as what the diverted land would have contributed to value added if it had been used in production.

Objections can be raised about either concept of protection and especially about the difficulties of reasonably exact measurement. Prices vary from day to day, and there is no exact relationship among prices for different qualities of the same product; reasonably exact data on input requirements that are needed for the measurement of effective protection do not exist for most countries. But assuming that a relatively long transition period is accepted during which there would be gradual and definite reductions in the degree of protection, such objections are relatively unimportant at least for the early years. The present degrees of protection are sufficiently great in numerous cases that any reasonable measure of protection will indicate with sufficient accuracy where the major reductions in protection must be made if trade is to be liberalized. In fact, during the early years, protection could be measured by the average prices of the past two or three years or by the negotiated reference prices for the international prices of outputs and inputs.

The negotiations, then, should deal with the defining of an acceptable measure of protection and the rate at which the degree of protection should be reduced over time. The negotiations concerning the reduction in the degree of protection could take several alternative routes.

1. The governments would agree to the rate at which existing average degree of protection would be reduced, such as 5 percent annually, with each government free to decide how it was to reduce the degree of protection, both in terms of different farm products and changes in domestic programs.

2. The governments would agree not only on the rate at which the average degree of protection for agriculture would be reduced, but would make specific commitments concerning major sectors such as grains, feeds, and livestock or specific commodities, such as wheat, sugar, dairy products, and barley.

3. The governments would agree to timed changes in specific policy variables for specific commodities, such as variable levies, import quotas, export subsidies, price support payments, support prices, and intervention prices.

There are other approaches which the negotiations could consider, but these three illustrate the general range of possibilities. If the commitment to reduce the degree of protection is a serious commitment, the first alternative has the advantage that it would permit governments the flexibility to meet particular and difficult domestic problems by varying the rate at which protection was reduced. This would allow for situations in which adjustment difficulties were severe; these might arise if production of a particular product were heavily concentrated in a depressed region where few alternative sources of employment existed.

But the negotiations should consider a broader range of issues than reducing the degree of protection. If this is the sole objective of the negotiations, they would almost certainly be doomed to failure from the beginning. The negotiations must also concern themselves with reaching agreement on measures designed to meet the legitimate income objectives of the farm population and to provide a reasonable degree of price stability. It is not only that such considerations are of great importance in themselves, but that serious attention to them might well hasten the rate of which protection would be reduced to a more reasonable level.

Sole emphasis upon reducing the degree of protection is not enough. The objective is to reduce the effect of domestic farm programs upon the levels of production and consumption and thus upon trade. There are policy measures that would transfer significant income to farmers and which might include a degree of protection. Such measures might be fully consistent, however, with reducing production and consumption impacts and thus increasing the flow of trade.

These points can be illustrated by the proposal made in A Future for European Agriculture for minimizing the impact of lower market prices for farm products in the EC. The proposal was to reduce the market prices for farm products toward world market levels; payments would be made "to maintain the income of farmers as prices are lowered."

> The method proposed here would combine four essential rules. The first of these would compensate for lower prices on the basis of average yield in the Community. The second would fix payments depending upon the area under cultivation in the years preceding the decision to lower prices. The third would involve minimum and maximum time periods and would limit the subsidy to the life of the farm operator so that it could not be passed on to his successors. The fourth would make it vary inversely with the size of the farm.[2]

Even though net farm income would remain unchanged if prices were lowered and the program described above were put into effect, there would be marked and desirable effects upon production and consumption and also upon international trade. Farmers would not be encouraged to seek high yields to receive the benefits of high market prices, and they might be encouraged to transfer grain land to less intensive uses. Consumption would increase because of the lower prices of livestock products, and the profitability of livestock production would increase to induce the expansion of output. Assume for the moment that the level of payments exactly equaled the decline in gross farm income, by the usual measures of protection (adding the payments per unit of output to the market price), there would have been no reduction in protection. But since the income supplement plan would have minimum impact upon the level of production, which would be guided primarily by the lower market prices, the plan would be quite consistent with the objectives of freer trade or, in fact, with free trade if market prices were reduced to world market levels.

An important part of the negotiations should be concerned with establishing criteria for farm policy measures that would not be included in the measurement of protection or, put positively, farm policy measures that are consistent with the objective of freer trade. There are numerous measures that would have minimal distorting effects upon production, consumption, and trade, and their adoption should be encouraged.

A number of rules could be agreed upon, namely, that payments based on past levels of output, crop area, or livestock numbers, payments to the elderly or low-income families not associated with current levels of output, payments for training for nonfarm skills or subsidies for the improvement of rural housing would be accepted as having minimal effects upon trade. In addition, expenditures that were required for supply management might be excluded from measures of protection. It would probably be desirable to establish a procedure by which advance approval could be obtained from GATT or another acceptable international organization for a program that was consistent with the agreed-upon reduction in protection.

Another important problem should also be covered in the negotiations, namely, the problem of price stability. In the transition period during which the degree of protection is being reduced, the kinds of price support policies that now exist would be acceptable if the degree of protection were measured in terms of the average of recent prices in the international markets. Thus if prices in international markets fell, a government that met its price support commitments would not be considered to be in violation of its agreement to reduce effective protection by a given amount during the year. Even under free trade, it would be possible to assure farmers of a minimum level of returns without unduly affecting international trade. This could be done by agreeing that price support or guarantee levels could be set at some percentage, such as 90 percent, of the average level of the past two or three years. If farm prices fell below that level, payments would be permitted to bring average returns to the guaranteed level. It would be best if the payments were based on past output in much the way suggested in A Future for European Agriculture. Even if they were based on current marketings, the production effects would be minimal and could probably be ignored. As has been shown by the U.S. experience, the price support level need not determine the actual level of prices received by farmers. Only when price supports are used to increase prices above normal and reasonable levels does it follow that reducing price support levels results in lower farm prices.

It is important to reemphasize that the objective of the negotiations should not be solely that of reducing the barriers of trade, important as that objective is. The emphasis needs to be much broader and to fully reflect the legitimate concerns and objectives of farm people. Governments should be both permitted and encouraged to assist farm people in achieving a satisfactory level of income, to assist in the difficult adjustment problems that farmers will face because of a transition to freer trade, and which economic growth imposes upon farmers, as well as to provide farm people with equality of access to a variety of educational, social, and cultural institutions that are taken for granted by urban populations. It is also possible and desirable to reduce some of the major uncertainties that farmers must meet, including limiting price or returns variability.

The Negotiations and the Developing Countries

The discussion of negotiations has been primarily concerned with the industrial countries and not with the relations between the developing countries and the industrial countries. If freer trade is achieved for the major agricultural products and if most-favored-nation treatment is either maintained or strengthened, several of the developing countries would clearly gain from the opening of markets at generally improved prices. The expansion of trade in grains that would be likely to result from a significant reduction in protection of grains would provide an outlet for the relatively modest grain export surpluses that may exist in the developing countries over the next decade. The gradual reduction of export subsidies on the part of the industrial countries would clearly add stability to prices in some instances. Better management of grain stocks would permit a broader response when hunger threatened anywhere. A number of developing countries would also gain from the probable increase in world trade in beef.

In addition to grains and beef, the major areas of competition between the United States and other industrial countries, on the one hand, and the developing countries, on the other hand, are in sugar, cotton, tobacco, and the oilseeds. A move toward freer trade by the industrial nations would have relatively little effect upon cotton, though the effect on oilseeds might be negative if freer trade resulted in lower prices of feed grains relative to oilmeals in major consuming markets. At the present time, the cotton program in the United States does not appear to be essential to continuing U.S. cotton production, especially if the price of cotton were to remain above 25 cents per pound at the farm level, and if the U.S. cotton industry had a few years to adjust to the new situation.

It is not clear what effect freer trade in tobacco would have on the export opportunities of the developing countries. Tobacco production would decline in some industrial countries, but would almost certainly increase in the United States in the absence of the tobacco program.

Virtually all of the temperate zone industrial countries subsidize the production of sugar and do so at high cost. The United

States imports less than half of her sugar; the EC actually produces a small export surplus, but the UK imports about two-thirds of her requirements. Australia is an important exporter of sugar (10 percent of the world export total in 1970), with its production based on preferential access to other Commonwealth markets and a modest size quota for the U.S. market. If the protection of sugar were reduced significantly, there would be a substantial expansion in imports by North America and Western Europe. The gains in employment opportunities in the developing countries would be important, though the gain in foreign-exchange earnings from sales to the United States would be smaller than the increase in our imports because quota holders now receive a price that is fairly close to the domestic price.

An important matter that should be considered in the negotiations is food aid. The developed countries should consider the proper role of food aid and its relationship to reserve carry-overs and export subsidies in the years ahead. The last time this topic was seriously considered at a multilateral level was at the end of the Kennedy Round as a part of the ill-fated International Grains Arrangement. Circumstances have changed considerably since that time. The expansion of grain production in a number of developing countries has significantly reduced their need for food aid in the longer run. India, which was the largest recipient of food aid during the 1960s, is now approximately self-sufficient in grains and, barring adverse weather, is likely to retain that status on the average during the current decade. (India is currently some 10 to 12 million tons short for 1972-73.)

The U.S. Food for Peace Act of 1966 called for a significant hardening of the terms under which a large part of the U.S. food aid was to be provided, and most of the commitments under PL 480 for 1972 involved repayment in dollars or convertible currencies, albeit at rather low interest rates.

The developing countries have dual and at times conflicting interests with respect to food aid, and it is the responsibility of the developed countries to attempt to minimize the adverse effects of food aid on the developing countries. There is clearly a desirable, humanitarian role for food aid to meet emergency conditions due to typhoons, floods, earthquakes, and droughts. Since it may be easier, quicker, and cheaper to move food supplies from one of the industrial countries than from another part of the afflicted country or from a nearby developing country, the developed countries can play a useful role in preventing human suffering. There may also be useful roles for food aid associated with particular development projects, such as those undertaken by the World Food Program, or under some bilateral arrangements. The social gains from particular programs such as school lunch or feeding programs for pregnant women and infants may be greater than the adverse effects upon local prices.

But the role of large-scale and relatively long-term donations, such as were provided under Title I or PL 480 until the late 1960s, should be reviewed and some agreement reached concerning the terms and conditions under which such donations or sales for local currencies represent acceptable actions. There should also be consideration, at a multilateral level, of the sale of such commodities under highly subsidized long-term loans. Developing countries that might have the capacity to export to other developing countries simply cannot compete with the United States or other industrial countries that provide 40-year loans at 2-percent interest. While the transition from sale for local currencies to long-term loans, at low interest rates that came as a result of the Food for Peace Act of 1966, was a desirable change, it is clearly time to determine if the current operations are in the best interests of the developing countries.

Perhaps the greatest opportunities for employment gains and increased foreign-exchange earnings in the developing countries would be achieved not through freer trade for farm products, but in reducing the barriers to trade in the products processed from farm products. The trade policies of industrial countries generally provide greater nominal protection for the processing of raw materials and finished manufacturing than they do for the raw products themselves. In numerous cases, there may be no tariff or other barrier against the importation of a raw farm product, such as an oilseed, but the processing of the oilseed into its components will be subjected to a low nominal tariff that may result in effective protection rates of 50 to 100 percent for the processing activity. Oilseeds are used only as an illustration; numerous other examples could be given—cotton, tobacco, jute. Most countries that import raw sugar, including the United States, virtually prohibit the importation of refined sugar. A significant component of the negotiations should be the reduction of the protection provided by the industrial countries for the processing of raw farm products. The possible gains to the developing countries would be substantial if such reductions could be achieved.

Summary of Alternative Approaches to Negotiations

A number of general principles that should be fully explored before detailed negotiations begin have been presented. These principles emphasize that one nation's agricultural support measures should not impose costs of adjustments upon other nations, that structural adjustment should continue and be accelerated wherever possible, that measures of support should be tailored more precisely to meet social objectives, that an effort should be made to alter the form of support measures to make production and sales more market oriented, and that a better balance should be developed between the measures used to aid individual commodities. Those products for which demand prospects are favorable should be given greater encouragement, and those products in surplus could be subject to gradually reduced absolute and relative production incentives.

There was further emphasis upon developing a yardstick for reducing the degree of protection in the most protected sectors, the need to develop operationally meaningful rules for the regulation of export subsidies and other aids to exports, and the need to consider greatly reducing or eliminating quantitative restrictions as well as certain arbitrary interferences at the border. There should be ongoing discussions of the impact of a nation's policies upon others, thus creating the basis for further negotiations.

The two alternatives discussed in this paper for carrying forward the negotiations, while differing in detail and in the desired degree of trade expansion and liberalization, do have important common elements:

1. Both emphasize the need for consideration of the interests of others in the operation of domestic farm policies and trade interferences.
2. Both recognize the need for and desirability of trade expansion, and both recognize that the responsibility of adjustment rests with both importing and exporting countries.
3. Both alternatives emphasize the need to limit the use of export subsidies as a means of obtaining unfair competitive advantages in international markets.
4. Both alternatives view price stability as an important objective, but differ with respect to methods and procedures.

The major difference between the two alternatives is that the first gives major emphasis to the negotiation of international arrangements as a means of stabilizing and expanding trade in farm products, while the second emphasizes trade liberalization and the elimination of restraints on consumption and government-financed incentives to production as the guiding principles for organizing trade in farm products.

A related difference is one of tactics. The market organization proposal is based on the premise that nations must be left largely (though not entirely) free to determine their own support policies, while the second alternative assumes that it is possible to have meaningful negotiations on all measures that affect international trade in farm products and that such negotiations are necessary before significant trade liberalization can occur. The first alternative does envisage that nations would make commitments that might significantly reduce their freedom of action, particularly the commitment to hold additional stocks when supply exceeded demand at the reference price, and to adhere to the reference price in all international transactions. When supply exceeded demand at the reference price, and if there were agreement on the equitable sharing of the costs of holding stocks, as is envisaged, it is anticipated that budgetary reasons would induce governments to modify support policies so that their country did not contribute to further accumulation of stocks.

The second alternative emphasizes the gains that can result from general trade liberalization by achieving a more efficient use of the world's agricultural resources. It is argued that there are social and economic programs that can more economically and effectively meet the social and economic objectives of rural people than do the current farm programs of the industrial countries. Present programs are primarily for the benefit of the relatively prosperous in the farm population, and do little to benefit those of average or lower than average incomes. This alternative is also based on the view that much of the disarray in international markets for farm products results from price levels that serve to restrict consumption and high price supports and subsidies that result in uneconomic production.

We believe that each of the alternatives merits study and consideration, in terms both of feasibility for the near term and the longer run. It is quite probable that any accord arising out of the trade negotiations will include features of each. Trade will expand more rapidly, and farm production will be carried on more efficiently, however, under the second proposal. Market organization addresses itself largely to stabilization of world markets and production patterns, while liberalization aims for adjustment and growth. Thus the world's consumers have an important stake in the outcome.

Finally, any revision of the rules for trade in agricultural products should consider carefully the need to create a system wherein the developing nations can operate freely and benefit from an open and stable market. Current high protective rates on certain agricultural products are more harmful to these nations than to industrialized trading partners, and high effective protection rates on the secondary processing of farm products impede the growth of potentially important industries and possible considerable foreign-exchange earnings. All these considerations must be brought into the context of the broader agricultural negotiations.

CHANGING U.S. AGRICULTURAL POLICIES: THE RELATIONSHIP TO TRADE NEGOTIATIONS

The United States has had two separate positions on trade in agricultural products, following roughly the degree of comparative advantage held by U.S. farmers in the production of particular agricultural products. Distinctly different agricultural policies for export and import commodities have followed the same pattern. On the one hand, commodities that the United States produces efficiently and exports in large volume have had relatively low price support guarantees, sometimes supplemented by federal payments to farmers, thus making them generally competitive in world markets. Grains and oilseeds are the principal examples.

On the other hand, U.S. price support policies and programs for products where our efficiency is low and our vulnerability to imports high have included price guarantees substantially above world trading levels and fairly strict import controls. Dairy products, sugar, rice, and peanuts are in this group. Except for milk, which has never been subject to production restraint, relatively effective limitations on output have been applied to these commodities in the United States, thus limiting exportable supplies or insuring some role for imports, as in the case of sugar.

This dichotomy of policy is understandable at home, for it pursues economic objectives that American farmers support. But it is increasingly difficult for us to make our domestic policies with respect to dairy products, for example, acceptable abroad, when at the same time we press for trade advantages for commodities that we produce more efficiently. Europe, Australia, and New Zealand look at U.S. policies on dairy products in much the same way as U.S. farmers look at Europe's CAP.

The question will surely arise in the context of the trade negotiations in the GATT as to how the United States is willing to modify her agricultural policies, change her price support and stabilization methods, or otherwise reduce her levels of protection for agricultural products in the 1970s. These questions were taken up in a preliminary way in 1973 as preparations were made for the trade negotiations. At the same time, new or amended price support laws were considered by Congress. The "level of protection" for U.S. agriculture, as viewed by our negotiating partners in the GATT, is tied closely to the level of federal expenditures for farm payments, or subsidies, under our agricultural programs.

Our negotiating partners are right on this score for the most part. There are important exceptions, however, to the rule that the level of protection afforded U.S. farmers, or the degree of subsidization of production, is directly related to the level of federal expenditures for U.S. farm programs. These exceptions arise out of the fact that for feed grains and wheat, federal payment formulas were originally designed principally to provide the incentive for farmers to limit production. As noted earlier, limiting production in the United States makes an important, even decisive, contribution to world agricultural stability. Limiting U.S. production stabilizes and supports U.S. prices and world prices at the same time, and this represents an important service to all nations that export grains and related products. Thus to the extent payments are geared to production restraint, they should not be viewed as subsidies or as an element of protection.

About two-thirds of annual expenditures under the U.S. feed grain program until 1971 and one-half the expenditures under the wheat program can be classified functionally as "stabilization costs," not production subsidies. Stated another way, payments to producers could have been reduced by about one-third for feed grains and one-half for wheat, with approximately the same production and price results. In 1971 and 1972, however, only about one-half of feed grain spending could be classified as contributing to stabilization of supplies and price, as political factors led to an increase in feed grain subsidies. In 1973 budget limitations and a need to expand output again limited the element of production subsidy in feed grain payments.

One other element of farm program expenditures must be considered as distinct from production subsidization. Annual costs to the United States of maintaining substantial reserves of grains and other storable commodities are a part of farm program costs, but also contribute to public welfare worldwide. These reserves, which sometimes reach excessive levels quite by accident (a good crop), protect importing countries from short supplies and high prices and help maintain U.S. interests in world markets when crops are poor. Expenditures for maintaining legitimate reserves, like those actually required to limit production, cannot be looked upon as production subsidies or as part of the "level of protection" provided by some elements of domestic farm programs. This fact needs to be learned and recognized both by U.S. negotiators and by the representatives of other countries.

Late in 1972, the president proposed to limit federal expenditures for all federal programs to $250 billion in the 1973 fiscal year. Indications are that this approach to budgetary planning will be continued in later years. Every program financed by the federal budget would carry a limitation more or less consistent with the priorities of the president, the Congress, and the overall budget limit. Late in 1972 and in the early months of 1973, it was announced that a number of programs administered by the Department of Agriculture would be ended or curtailed. Conservation and loan programs bore the brunt of the first reductions, but if major reductions in spending are to be made, the price support programs will not go untouched.

1. One alternative approach to establishing long-term limits on the farm programs would be to make a radical change in the method of financing them. Most of the price support and production control

243

programs have been financed through congressional authorizations, which enable the Department of Agriculture, acting through the Commodity Credit Corporation (CCC), to borrow up to $14.5 billion directly from the Treasury and to expend those funds at the discretion of the secretary, within the broad statutes governing the farm price support and production adjustment programs. No direct appropriations have governed the commitment of some $3 to $4 billion per year on payments to cotton, feed grain, and wheat farmers over the past eight years. Acquisition of surpluses to support prices is also done outside the appropriations process, by "back-door financing." It gives the USDA immense operational flexibility to pay producers, to reduce plantings, to add a degree of production or income subsidy to such payments, to establish export subsidies, or to acquire and store annual crop surpluses when the need arises. Such flexible financing for farm programs had its origin partly in the uncertainties associated with agricultural production; without it, some substitute would have to be found. But back-door financing arose also out of the desire of strong agricultural interests in Congress a generation ago to insure relatively unrestricted spending to help farmers. With the balance of political power now changed, the expenditure process may also be changed. This would almost surely lead to reduced levels of protection for farm products in the United States.

2. A second approach to limiting farm subsidies would be for Congress or the executive branch to establish ceilings by law or regulation beyond which annual expenditures for any single commodity program could not go. If crop conditions were to require larger expenditures in any year, the matter would have to be reviewed by Congress, and the increased amounts authorized in the same manner most other federal programs are handled. If Congress declined to allow spending beyond a fixed level, price and income support would either not be carried out as effectively as now or would achieve lesser results.

3. A third alternative would be for Congress to place in the law strict criteria for determining payment levels to farmers, with the objective of limiting the total level of expenditures. Payments would be geared strictly to the amounts required to achieve necessary production adjustment, or to a combination of production adjustment and overall farm income objectives. The cotton program, where payments have been $800 to $900 million per year for several years, at a time when no production adjustment by farmers was required or wanted, would come in for the closest scrutiny under this approach.

The wheat program, where existing statutory formulas yield payments substantially in excess of levels that would be required to avoid new wheat surpluses, would also require substantial payment reductions under such criteria. Payments to wheat farmers could probably be reduced by one-half or more over a three- to five-year period without risk of any serious interference with production adjustment requirements. Expenditures under the U.S. feed grain programs could not be reduced as sharply in percentage terms as for the other major programs, since payment levels have not been so far beyond the amounts needed to achieve an appropriate balance of production with demand. Feed grain program expenditures have sometimes approached $2 billion per year, however. Even a reduction of one-fourth from recent levels would be significant in budgetary terms. This would be easily possible in view of the sharp escalation of the subsidy element in feed grain payments in 1971-72 and 1972-73. Such a payment reduction would be in addition to reductions made in 1971 and 1973 because crop acreages could be expanded.

Finally, limiting the amount of payments the federal government makes to individual farmers under the various crop programs is another alternative method of budgetary restraint and an important potential source of farm program savings and reductions in levels of protection. Congress established a $55,000 per farm limitation in 1970, but left so many loopholes in the law that its administration has been ineffective. Savings have been negligible, according to studies by the General Accounting Office, and the distribution of benefits from farm programs and the overall level of protection are virtually unaffected. Grain farmers were hardly touched by such a high limit, since few of them receive government payments that large. Several thousand cotton farmers were affected, but were permitted under the law to divide large farms by various means, so that the payment limitation could be avoided.

A limit of $10,000 in federal payments per farmer, together with a requirement that farms could not be subdivided to circumvent the payment limitation, would affect only about 30,000 wheat, cotton, and feed grain producers in the 1970s if overall federal farm payment levels continue near recent levels. Applied to payment formulas in effect the past three to four years, this provision would reduce federal expenditures and basic protection via subsidies by about $500 million per year. If such a limit applied to the scaled-down levels of overall commodity program payments, as discussed above, savings would be smaller but still sizable.

The rationale for any of these approaches to limiting federal payments to farmers arises principally out of budgetary considerations, but also out of the strong U.S. competitive position for grains and oilseeds and the desirability of having other countries make suitable adjustments in their programs to aid farmers. Efficient utilization of limited public funds to provide the maximum benefits to farmers surely requires concentrating such funds on production adjustment and stabilization reserves as needed to support prices, not on outright subsidies.

Escalation in farmland values would also be allowed but not necessarily stopped by such limitations, depending upon their severity. The value of the present asset structure in U.S. agriculture would not be severely threatened, except possibly in cotton where subsidies could be reduced sharply. Such limitations, however administered, could be operated within the framework of the voluntary production adjustment programs that remain essential to stability in the U.S. feed grains and wheat sectors. In the case of individual farm subsidy limits, only a small percentage of aggregate grain production would be on farms affected by individual farm payment limitations, even down to the level of $10,000 or $20,000 per farm. Most farmers would still receive payment at levels that would provide just enough of an incentive to cause them to take part in the acreage diversion programs as in recent years. If demand were to increase faster than output per acre of grains, overall payment levels could be reduced to very low levels as the need to limit acreage declined, and the issue of payment limitations would no longer arise.

Continuation of present laws limits the ability of the United States to reduce her agricultural production subsidies in the 1970s either in furthering domestic priorities or trade negotiations. Production subsidies on key U.S. crops should be reduced and, if necessary, some type of compensation could be offered to persons who would be seriously and adversely affected by such a move. For example, if Congress or the president determined that payments to cotton producers had to be reduced by two-thirds from present levels over a three-year period, a formula might be established by which certain categories of producers would be compensated for declines in their incomes or in the market value of cotton-growing land when lower land values were clearly the result of reduced payments under the cotton program. Compensation of this kind would not be easy to administer, and it could be costly for a few years. It would surely be far less costly, however, than to continue existing farm payment levels in perpetuity.

Import Commodities

What to do with the federal programs for agricultural commodities that the United States either imports or would import in substantial volume except for the stringent import controls we apply is probably the most difficult trade-related agricultural policy problem facing the United States in the future. These are the commodities for which U.S. comparative advantage is low or at least in doubt, and where the U.S. stance is similar to that of Europe and Japan on the products the U.S. exports.

In the case of milk, the United States maintains a high level of protection—our prices for manufacturing milk now equal the average European price support level for all milk; our milk prices, in fact, are among the highest in the world.

The existence of two distinct milk markets in the United States provides a basis for changes in policies and price support procedures that would have only a very limited adverse effect on U.S. producers over time, but a positive impact on world trade. Such changes would represent a response to milk production adjustment trends long under way and would materially improve the U.S. negotiating stance on agricultural products.

Producers would continue to receive guaranteed price levels for milk, which is to be used for fluid or drinking purposes at levels required to assure an adequate supply, with a safe but not excessive reserve capacity. This policy would apply to all regions of the country, taking into account the ability of modern transport to move fresh milk, so that adequate fresh milk need not be produced in every area. The above policy would probably apply to slightly more than 75 percent of all the milk produced in the United States, but the rest of the milk produced would be priced at world levels. Fluid milk prices might well have to be higher in the late 1970s than now to insure adequate supplies, but lower prices would apply to manufacturing milk under a second policy.

The second milk price support policy would be applicable to "manufacturing milk." It would be designed to reduce the quantity of resources devoted to the production of milk for use in manufacturing at a slow but steady pace by lowering the price support from the level prevailing in 1973-74 if that were necessary to achieve trade objectives, or by not increasing the price support in future years. The latter approach would lower milk prices in real terms as production costs rose and might serve as an adequate disincentive to production. To achieve either change, the milk law would have to be amended.

Manufacturing milk production has been maintained at high levels in the United States in recent years only by virtue of substantial increases in price support levels designed to insure plentiful supplies so as to avoid a greater reliance on imports. Milk for manufacturing is now largely the overflow or surplus from drinking milk production in all parts of the United States, although some regions still produce a large part of their output specifically for manufacture of various products. The continuing trend toward fewer dairy farms and dairy cattle—especially major adjustments in the type of farming practices in the former specialized manufacturing milk-producing areas of Minnesota, Wisconsin, and Michigan—together with anticipated sharp increase in the demand for beef would allow the indicated changes in the U.S. milk sector to take place almost imperceptibly over a 10-year period. The question of compensation for producers seriously affected by the changes, as discussed above for export commodities, probably would not arise out of such a slow transition, but compensation procedures could also be applied to the dairy sector if necessary.

As U.S. supplies of manufacturing milk declined marginally from year to year because price supports no longer were designed to insure production of virtually all U.S. milk requirements on our own dairy farms, we would probably experience a perceptible shortage of manufactured dairy products. This would provide the occasion for increasing the quotas now applied to the importation of manufactured dairy products as has been done in 1973 on a temporary basis. This could be handled in much the same manner as the increase in Section 22 dairy product import quotas was arranged in 1966. That situation arose out of an unexpected decline in U.S. milk production and a shortage of manufacturing milk. Dairy product imports tripled in slightly more than one year on that occasion, partly by virtue of some evasion of import controls, and partly by liberalization. Increased imports were soon cut off, however, as milk production increased in response to higher farm price guarantees, so that greater imports could no longer be justified.

The objectives of policy and program changes of this type could be modest, and the timetable quite relaxed; yet they would provide some leverage for U.S. negotiators in agricultural forums of the GATT, because other nations would see tangible benefits to their producers. Perhaps it would be reasonable for the United States to move from the present level of 1.5 percent of its dairy products imported to 10 percent imported by 1980; some might think that too slow and others too fast. An increase of that magnitude in the volume of U.S. imports would be a very important addition to the exports of efficient milk-producing countries such as New Zealand, Australia, Denmark, and Ireland—all relatively small countries. Yet, spread over several years, it would have little adverse impact on U.S. farmers. United States dairymen would still be supplying 90 percent of U.S. milk requirements in 1980. The changes would be made slowly and would follow the well-established trend of declining milk production, while recent increases in U.S. price support guarantees have been working unsuccessfully against that trend.

Other commodities imported by the United States offer similar opportunities. Sugar is a special case, responding to somewhat different political forces than other commodities, and existing in a stormy international climate. The United States is clearly an inefficient sugar producer. With returns per ton roughly double recent world prices, the United States can produce only half her sugar needs and has a very limited capacity to increase output.

The Sugar Act will have to be reviewed by the Congress in 1974, or sugar import restrictions will lapse, so the opportunity to make constructive changes is not far ahead. No other program for farm products in the United States is more vulnerable to criticism in terms of its cost to consumers or its adverse impact upon friendly and efficient developing countries that produce sugar for export. The present U.S. sugar system probably cannot be changed unilaterally, nor should its benefits to some supplying nations be overlooked. It would be helpful if Japan and Europe also moved to reduce their trade-restrictive practices in regard to sugar. Asking other nations to accept from the United States a lower price than they have recently received in return for a larger share of the U.S. market would be one approach to constructive amendment of the Sugar Act.

Congress could also consider a limit to the degree that U.S. sugar prices are subsidized through escalation of the parity price formula, which fixes prices to growers. A small start could be made toward increasing sugar import quotas and limiting high-cost U.S. expansion as the market grew. By 1974 the debate on sugar should include consideration of a return to importation of the long-suspended Cuban quota, assuming a long-overdue political detente is achieved. Western hemisphere countries, to which the Cuban quota has been temporarily transferred, could be given a part of the quotas formerly held by U.S. producers.

Rice and peanuts fit rather easily into the same framework. All are produced in the South, in fairly limited areas, by a declining number of farmers and under rigid acreage and quantity controls. It has been possible to preserve U.S. prices above world levels since the 1940s for rice through use of direct export subsidies and for peanuts through a subsidized disposal system for oil and products. These practices need to be ended.

Wool is another example involving both high duties and high-cost subsidies. There is every reason for the United States to lower her wool duties in the next trade negotiations and to limit wool subsidies on a phased basis. The wool market in the United States is geared principally to imported wool despite the tariffs and subsidies. The sheep industry is declining annually. In such a situation, it makes eminent sense to recognize an existing situation and to move toward its logical conclusion.

For these commodities, price support formulas should be revised to permit slow, phased reductions over a decade. Where it is necessary to protect and compensate small family farmers who are important especially in the production of peanuts and tobacco, payment formulas could be written into the law which would provide compensation for a limited time to the small farmers who would otherwise be damaged financially by the change in policy. Large, efficient farms, long the beneficiaries of federal price support guarantees which have enabled them to progressively buy out the smaller and less efficient farmers, should not be protected through such federal compensatory programs, except where program changes cause tangible losses. They would be increasingly exposed to the discipline of world market value.

These do not exhaust the possibilities for trade-improving changes in U.S. policies. Beef and lamb import quotas and marketing procedures that limit the importation of some fruits and vegetables should also be reviewed as the trade negotiation begins. The 1972-74 period of high food prices provides an excellent occasion for such a review and for needed program amendments.

APPENDIX: COMMENTS

Martin E. Abel

In reference to the discussion of information about the implications of farm programs, as presented in the next to the last paragraph in the sub-section entitled "A Suitable Environment for Negotiations," it is terribly naive to think that information will bring about a rationalization of agricultural policies which, overall, will increase world agricultural trade. It needs to be supplemented by strong and determined political leadership willing to foster the necessary policy and resource adjustments. In the process of moving to agricultural policies that promote trade, some farmers will, of necessity, be required to relinquish favored positions and bear the cost of adjustment. Wise and humane governments can help facilitate these adjustments. But adjust they must, and it is doubtful that they will do it voluntarily. Without strong and sensible political commitments on the part of all governments, there is little hope for meaningful liberalization of agricultural trade.

In addition, I find the subsequent section ("Changing U.S. Agricultural Policies") disappointing on two counts. First, the discussion of limiting those government payments that have no significant impact on production levels is strictly a domestic issue which has no relevance to world trade. It does not take an international trade negotiation to resolve the payments question.

Second, and more important, the reader is expected to accept as an article of faith that trade liberalization is a good thing. But the case for expanded agricultural trade has not been adequately illustrated, let alone demonstrated. Is it not worth something if liberalized agricultural trade leads to lower real prices of food and fiber to consumers, contributes to overall price stability, and leads to more rapid economic growth? If, by miracle of miracles, the United States would expand imports of dairy products and the EC would expand grain imports, would this make it easier to achieve the social and economic objectives for the farm sectors in both the EC and the United States? In other words, can expanded agricultural trade solve more farm problems that it creates? If these and similar questions can be quantitatively answered in the affirmative, and I think they can, then one would have gone a big step forward in demonstrating the real value of altering domestic farm policies in the direction of expanding world agricultural trade. Unfortunately, this study does not clearly show the mutual advantages that large numbers of countries could reap from a multilateral liberalization of trade.

André Herlitska, Pierre Malvé, Asher Winegarten

Dealing first with the issue of trade relations between the United States and the EC, which should be developed on the basis of reciprocity, we cannot accept the view expressed at the beginning of Chapter 9 that the interests of U.S. agriculture in general and of grain farmers in particular were in fact prejudiced during the 1960s by the operation of the CAP. Taking the total movement of grain and feeding stuffs, including soya, the figures show a beneficial development of trade for U.S. farmers.

The misunderstanding could perhaps be attributable to the difficulty of distinguishing between the mechanisms of the CAP—which are neutral by definition—and the ways in which they are applied—which are governed in turn not only by the domestic price level but also by world market conditions.

At a time when new negotiations are due to begin, it is worth recalling that in the past the Community of six did, in fact, demonstrate its willingness to participate fully in finding new ways of reconciling the differing agricultural interests in the sphere of production and trade through the "montant de soutien" approach and commodity arrangements.

Next, we must categorically state our strong belief in the merits of the first alternative described in the section entitled "Organization of International Markets." This is because we believe that the most effective way of making progress in the direction of an orderly development of international trade in agricultural products is by reaching agreement on the essential conditions, criteria, and ground rules. Hence we cannot agree with the inference that expansion of trade would necessarily be less secure than if the approach were based upon commitments to liberalize specific aspects of national or regional farm programs.

251

The emphasis in the second alternative on liberalization seems to us to indicate a confusion between ends and means. While this may, perhaps, be a question of emphasis and while the social implications of the policy are indeed viewed with some sympathy and understanding, the impression left with the reader is that basically there is no reason why the treatment of agricultural products should differ in any way from that accorded to industrial products.

As pointed out in "Summary of Alternative Approaches to Negotiations," the two alternatives do have important common elements. But it would, nevertheless, be inadvisable for us to pretend that these will be enough to gloss over important differences. In our view, the emphasis must be on an orderly expansion of trade. This will occur more rapidly, and farm production will be organized on more rational lines if the nations of the world in the multilateral negotiations proceed along the road charted by the first alternative. We believe that events during the past year, in North America and in the EC, have abundantly justified the need to agree on a system of reference prices and on new arrangements for holding stocks in the interests of not only greater stability for producers but also in the interests of shielding the housewife from temporarily excessive increases in prices and of helping governments in their task of fighting inflation.

For the developing countries, we consider that the alternative course, which we propose, is more likely to result in an increase in their earnings and to abate their fears of loss of income from sharply fluctuating and depressed price levels for the commodities of major concern to them. Though for developing exporting countries, removal or reduction of trade barriers may in theory enhance their opportunities to sell their products in the markets of developed countries, as experience shows, the lowering of tariff barriers does not automatically lead to an increase in the volume of their exports. If, however, this were to happen, the greater volume of trade could well be accompanied by a decline in the total value of their exports, leaving them worse off. By underpinning the international market and by establishing coordinated arrangements for stocks, alternative one, if applied to such products as sugar, oilseeds, cocoa, and coffee, could augment existing assurances and extend new ones to developing countries, which would enable them to boost their overseas earnings and to plan ahead their development programs.

For importing developing countries, price stability is also of cardinal importance for their economic development. Moreover, for these countries food aid is of considerable relevance, provided it is regarded not as a means of disposing of occasional food surpluses by exporting countries but as an essential supplementary element to their own agricultural and general economic development plans.

The study, by showing that the family farm in the United States will continue to be the basic type of agricultural unit for many years to come, throws into relief the community of interest that exists among farmers in Europe, the United States, and other parts of the world. We believe that, like his European counterpart, the American farmer wishes to operate and to plan for the future in an environment free from the vicissitudes occasioned by the lack of coordination between the existing national agricultural support policies and systems. It is our firm belief that if the governments are prepared to negotiate criteria and rules relevant to the basic circumstances of agricultural production and trade, the world can, in future, look forward to a harmonious evolution of trade in this vital sector of the world economy. Through such worldwide organization and cooperation, conflicts, for example arising from the alleged transference of the costs of agricultural adjustment, will be minimized.

Asao Miyawaki

Without specifying the argument to a particular nation, I feel that agriculture should not be dealt with along the same line of thinking that is applicable to manufacturing industries. No nation can expect to maintain its economic well-being under conditions in which it has to rely on other countries to supply the basic food items of its people. It should be internationally recognized that each country should pursue a secure supply of basic food items from within its own lands.

Viewed from another angle, without waiting for the advocacy of the ecologist, the importance of maintaining adequate environmental conditions should be well recognized, especially for contemporary societies, which are urbanizing at such a rate and in such a way that the natural life cycle is threatened with collapse. It is a universal fact that no country will be able to preserve environmental health without maintaining an active agricultural sector which, much better than any other industry, can perform this function.

Viewed from the angle of the national economy, agriculture is, on the one hand, a supplier of food and raw materials and, on the other hand, an important market for other industries and thus a significant component of the national economy. It is our common, recent experience that when the balance between agricultural and nonagricultural sectors of the economy disequilibrates, that is, when the domestic balance is lost, it leads to a disequilibrating international economic balance since some nations will intensify their export drive, while others will suffer from an international payments deficit. Thus no nation can maintain the health of the national economy without agriculture.

Viewed socially, the emergence or indeed the development of an excessive concentration of population in urban areas and the excessive depopulation of rural communities at such a rate that makes community functions ineffective or causes them to cease functioning are nothing less than a reflection of a lack of social health, as well as the light consideration given to agriculture.

I believe that the above arguments go to show that agriculture is the basis of a nation's economy everywhere, and a sound relationship between nations cannot be ensured where this consideration is not given adequate recognition.

As a supplement to what has been described so far, let me draw your attention, although it is already widely recognized knowledge, to the recent violent jump in the prices of the major international agricultural commodities. It is needless to mention that the deficit of the wheat harvest in the Soviet Union, equivalent to almost 3/5 of the normal world trading volumes, has forced her to take emergency recourse to international markets which, for that reason, experienced 50 percent price rise from the beginning of the year and which had an immeasurable effect on the importing countries. This was accompanied by a similar or, in some cases, greater rate of price increase as exemplified by a 100-percent hike in the price of rice, 60 percent for sugar, and 30 percent for soybeans and coffee beans. Such a violent movement in the international prices of agricultural products has driven the consumers as well as the agricultural producers of importing countries into a critical situation. This experience has taught us most eloquently that unless a system to pursue a maximum degree of self-sufficiency in major commodities is pursued, stability of the nation's economy as a whole is jeopardized. Reflection of this is evident in Japan too, in the form of growing public opinion advocating further improvement of our self-sufficiency in agricultural products.

The above considerations lead us to a conclusion that agricultural trade should not be given the purpose of establishing a division of labor internationally based on the principle of comparative advantage as applied to manufactured products, but should rather be given a marginal place in the entire agricultural economy. It follows then that the responsibility of the people involved in agricultural questions in the United States should, in this committee, attempt to seek out the role of U.S. agriculture in the 1980s and consider the issue not in line with the principle of comparative advantage, that is, logics of power, but on the premise of seeking ways in which every nation can establish and maintain self-sufficiency in food and thereby be ensured of the stability of the national economy, wherein agriculture develops and agricultural producers prosper.

Let me also make a few comments about Japanese agriculture.

First of all, let us examine the price level of rice. The producer price or the government purchase price of (hulled) rice has been around $380 for the past few years; this is partly due to the governmental policy to freeze the level. On the other hand, the export price of Thai rice, which is the international reference price, was at the lowest point in recent years at some $140 per ton in 1970 (during which year the international price level was pulled down partly due to the spread of high-yielding varieties in the traditionally importing countries). Moreover, in comparing price levels of rice in the world market, these levels can by no means be taken as the normal prices because they are usually pulled down by export subsidization of a considerable amount.

Secondly, the theory that liberalization of agricultural imports would result in substantial increases in livestock production in Japan is a thinking contradictory to the reality. While producers have devoted much of their endeavor for over 10 years to livestock production, as this was offered by the government as one of the selective expansion sectors (a sector of this economy in which growth was desired), increased production has not been fully satisfying the need or demand. What I mean to say here is that the above has been, to a not inconsiderable extent, a result of imports of meat that have expanded as a trend over the years. Should livestock products from other countries flood the Japanese market, it would, without failure, have a serious adverse impact on our producers and nip the bud of livestock development in Japan, especially the production of beef for which there is a global shortage of supply over demand. This would destroy our domestic industry and thereby bring to the food life of the nation extreme instability.

Finally, let us consider the view that, for her level of income, Japanese meat consumption is very low and that this is due to a governmental policy of restricting the availability of livestock products. These are comparative statements based on a lack of understanding about our dietary lives. Our dietary pattern has for a long-established period centered on rice as a staple item, and all other items, including meat, have been considered subsidiary, despite the fact that the weight of rice in our diet has been declining as a tendency, while the rate of decreased per capita consumption of rice has been stagnant during the recent past. The Japanese dietary pattern is fundamentally different from that of Europe and America, and the thought that our dietary habits should become automatically occidental does not necessarily follow. Based on the study of food consumption trends of the Japanese people, the Ministry of Agriculture and Forestry envisages the formation of a unique Japanese diet pattern in the future. The growth of meat consumption will be a function of the basic pattern grounded on rice. As rice is also a source of protein and fat, substitution by animal protein will take place only within certain limitations.

Eugene Moos

The National Association of Wheat Growers supports the control or elimination of the U.S. wheat export subsidy program only if there is reciprocal action by the other major wheat-exporting countries. The National Association of Wheat Growers does not support the elimination of the U.S. wheat export subsidy program in return for greater access to international grain markets.

As long as other major wheat-exporting countries continue the use of such export aids as export subsidies, forward sales, special credit arrangements, government quality guarantees, internal and external transportation subsidies, and so on, then the National Association of Wheat Growers believes there is a need for the United States to continue export subsidies to remain competitive.

The National Association of Wheat Growers does not support the use of the U.S. wheat export subsidy program as a tool to depress world wheat prices below those levels reflecting normal world wheat supply-demand relationships. Using export subsidies for this purpose tends to confuse producers and processors alike by giving them signals that, in the long run, work to their disadvantage.

Kenneth D. Naden

The National Council of Farmer Cooperatives wishes to amplify its views on certain key issues covered in this study. The concept of organized international agricultural cooperation should have the flexibility to relate access to productive and marketing efficiency. Competitive forces should guide markets to the extent that they can be reconciled with fair income objectives for farmers. Finally, we would emphasize that changes in U.S. agricultural policies should be negotiable within a framework of overall reciprocity in a coordinated trade-monetary-political package of considerations.

Harald B. Malmgren

This is an important study. It has been an honor to participate in the development of it with such distinguished colleagues. I agree with the broad thrust of what it says, but in joining the other signatories I wish to warn that there are many specific points of assessment of

the present situation where I would put different emphasis or make
a different judgment. Moreover, I believe that some of the specific
recommendations interspersed in the study are not sound as they
are presented. Some of these recommendations touch issues that are
highly sensitive economically and politically. For example, the recommendations on U.S. dairy import protection treat this mainly as
a question of concessions by the United States in exchange for concessions by others, as if it were simply a matter of units of butterfat
in exchange for bushels of corn. The world negotiating problem is
more complex than that. None of our trading partners will offer to
change their trade or domestic policies in fundamental ways unless
we do. But if policies are changed, the need for import protection in
the United States would be changed automatically, in relation to the
degree to which export subsidies and artificial incentives to production are eliminated. It is in the context of more internationally harmonious policies that I visualize major trade-offs. That is why, in
the background paper I prepared for the group before my return to
government service, I emphasized the importance of developing an
internationally agreed policy framework within which particular negotiating strategies should be considered.

As for the long-term production, price, and trade outlook, I
think that depends on government policies more than the study sometimes suggests in its optimism about world market forces. But again,
that is a matter of emphasis or judgment, which only time can settle
one way or the other.

NOTES

1. Parity Returns Position of Farmers, report to the Congress
by the Department of Agriculture (Washington, D. C.: U.S. Government Printing Office, August 1967).

2. A Future for European Agriculture (Paris: The Atlantic
Institute, 1970), p. 37. The reference to these proposals is not intended
to imply that they have the support of our European colleagues, who
believe that the Atlantic Institute proposals are not administratively
feasible or politically acceptable.

MARTIN E. ABEL is Professor of Agricultural Economics and Director of the Economic Development Center at the University of Minnesota. He acted as Program Advisor in Economics with the Ford Foundation in New Delhi, India, and as Deputy Assistant Secretary of Agriculture for International Affairs. He has written extensively on U. S. agricultural policy and international agricultural trade and development issues.

HENRY H. FOWLER, Chairman of the Atlantic Council of the United States, is currently a partner with the investment banking firm of Goldman Sachs & Company. He served as the Secretary of the Treasury from 1965 to 1968, as well as Under Secretary of the Treasury from 1961 to 1964. An authority on international monetary matters, he played a leading role in the international negotiations which lead to the creation of Special Drawing Rights (SDRs) within the International Monetary Fund.

ANDRÉ HERLITSKA, a citizen of Belgium, is the Secretary General of the Committee of Agricultural Organizations of the European Economic Community (COPA), as well as Secretary General of the Committee for Agricultural Cooperatives (COGECA). A graduate of the University of Leuven (Belgium) he has held research positions at the Universities of Leuven, Kinshasa (Zaire) and the International African Institute in London.

D. GALE JOHNSON is the Eliakim Hastings Moore Distinguished Service Professor and Chairman of the Department of Economics at the University of Chicago. He served as a consultant to the President's Council on International Economic Policy and has written both books and scholarly articles on world agriculture, economics and trade, including World Agriculture in Disarray, and Farm Commodity Programs: An Opportunity for Change.

HARALD B. MALMGREN is currently the Deputy Special Representative for Trade Negotiations in the Executive Office of the President. Prior to his appointment to this post in 1972, Ambassador Malmgren was, respectively, President of Malmgren, Inc., an economic consulting firm in Washington, Senior Fellow at the Overseas Development Council, and Assistant Special Representative for Trade Negotiations. He is the author of many articles and monographs on economic policy and international political and economic problems, including International Economic Peacekeeping in Phase II, Assisting Developing Countries, and Pacific Basin Development: The American Interests.

PIERRE MALVÉ is presently the Deputy Chief of Cabinet to the President of the European Commission. A native of France, he served previously as the Counselor for Economic and Trade Affairs at the Washington Delegation of the European Communities. Specializing in agriculture, commercial policy and trade, Mr. Malvé represented the Commission of the Common Market in the "Kennedy Round" negotiations of GATT from 1964 to 1967.

ASAO MIYAWAKI, born in the Kagawa Prefecture of Japan, is the President of the Zenkoku Nogyokyodokumiai Choukai, or the Central Union of Agricultural Cooperatives of Japan. A prominent figure in the Japanese cooperative movement, Mr. Miyawaki was also the Director of the National Federation of Marketing Agricultural Cooperatives and the National Federation of Purchasing Agricultural Cooperatives.

EUGENE MOOS is an active wheat producer in Edwall, Washington. He is currently the International Trade Affairs Representative for the National Association of Wheat Growers, President of the East-West Trade Council, and a member of the Executive Commission of the Washington State Council for International Trade. He has served as President of the National Association of Wheat Growers, President of the Western Wheat Associates and Government Advisor to the International Wheat Negotiations.

KENNETH D. NADEN is the President of the National Council of Farmer Cooperatives. Long a leader in agricultural policy, Mr. Naden has served on many advisory committees including the Secretary of Agriculture's Cooperative Advisory Committee, the U.S. Delegation to Conferences of the UN Food and Agriculture Organization, Rome, the Executive Committee of the International Federation of Agricultural Producers, and the President's Commission on International Trade and Investment Policy, to mention but a few.

JOHN A. SCHNITTKER is the President of Schnittker Associates, an international economic consulting firm in Washington. He was Under Secretary of Agriculture from 1965 to 1969 and President of the Commodity Credit Corporation, U.S. Department of Agriculture. Prior to establishing his own consulting firm, he was Vice President of Robert Nathan Associates and has held the post of Professor of Economics at Kansas State University.

T. K. WARLEY is the Director of the School of Agricultural Economics and Extension Education at the University of Guelph, Ontario, Canada. A native of Great Britain, Professor Warley was a consultant to the Commission of the European Communities on U.K. agricultural policies and to the U.K. Ministry of Agriculture and Food on European farm programs. Since coming to North America, he has participated in study groups for the Council of Agricultural Science and Technology, the Brookings Institution, the Canada Grains Council, and the Ontario Economic Council. He has written extensively on problems of agricultural trade and marketing policies.

ASHER WINEGARTEN is Deputy Director General and Chief Economist of the National Farmers' Union (UK). He is Chairman of the Group of General Experts of COPA, Representative of the NFU to the conferences of the International Federation of Agricultural Producers and Advisor to the British delegation to the UN Food and Agriculture Organization Conference in Rome. In Great Britain, he serves on the Agricultural Wages Board, the Economic Development Committee for Agriculture, the Confederation of British Industry and the British National Committee of the International Chamber of Commerce.

THE ATLANTIC COUNCIL OF THE UNITED STATES is a private, nonpartisan, educational organization whose objective is to improve relations between North America, Western Europe, and Japan. Through its conferences, committees, monographs, and books, the Council and its distinguished Board of former government officials, business, labor, and academic leaders, seeks to increase public awareness of the issues and to stimulate informed debate on policy matters. The Council is associated with two international organizations: the Atlantic Treaty Association and the Atlantic Institute for International Affairs.

AGRICULTURAL DEVELOPMENT PLANNING:
Economic Concepts, Administrative Procedures,
and Political Process
> Willard W. Cochrane

SOVIET AGRICULTURAL POLICY:
> Stephen Osofsky

AGRICULTURAL MODERNIZATION THROUGH
PRODUCTION CONTRACTING: The Role of the
Fruit and Vegetable Processor in Mexico and
Central America
> J. David Morrissy

AGRIBUSINESS IN LATIN AMERICA
> James E. Austin

AFRICAN FARMERS: LABOR USE IN THE
DEVELOPMENT OF SMALLHOLDER AGRI-
CULTURE
> John H. Cleave

THE GREEN REVOLUTION IN WEST PAKI-
STAN: Implications of Technological Change
> Leslie Nulty

THE TECHNICAL TRANSFORMATION OF
AGRICULTURE IN COMMUNIST CHINA
> Leslie T. C. Kuo